SWISS ALPS

D1304825

Produced by AA Publishing

European Regional Guide

PASSPORT BOOKS
a division of *NTC Publishing Group*
Lincolnwood, Illinois USA

Published by Passport Books, a division of NTC Publishing Group, 4255 W. Touhy Avenue, Lincolnwood (Chicago), Illinois 60646-1975 U.S.A.

Written by David Allsop

Copy editor: Helen Douglas-Cooper

Edited, designed, and produced by AA Publishing. Maps © The Automobile Association 1993.

Library of Congress Catalog Card Number: 93-83187

ISBN 0-8442-9969-3

Published by Passport Books in conjunction with The Automobile Association.

Color separation: Daylight Colour Art Pte, Singapore

Printed by Printers Trento S.R.L., Italy

Cover picture: **Grindelwald**
Title page: **Appenzell building detail**
Opposite: **Lugano**
Pages 4–5: **The three peaks of the Jungfrau massif. From left to right: the Eiger, the Mönch and the Jungfrau**

·CONTENTS·

FEATURES

MAPS

The main entries in this book are cross-referenced to the regional map on pages 110–111. All heights on maps are in metres.

·INTRODUCTION·

This guide reveals the true character and flavour of the Swiss Alps, its people, legends and traditions, with detailed information and special features, illustrated throughout in full colour.

Specially drawn, easy-to-follow maps accompany over 25 walks and tours which take you out and about into the countryside as well as round the most popular towns and cities.

With practical information and a glossary of useful words and phrases, this is an invaluable guide to visiting this fascinating region of Switzerland.

•THE SWISS ALPS•

The small, landlocked country of Switzerland comprises three distinct natural regions: the Jura, a mountainous region occupying a 10 per cent strip of the total territory in the northwest; the Mittelland, or Swiss Plateau, a central belt of relatively low-lying land occupying a further 30 per cent of the country between the lakes of Geneva and Constance; and the Alps, the magnificent mountain chain covering the largest proportion of Swiss territory with an average altitude of 1,700m. For the purposes of this guide, some parts of the Mittelland that lie on the fringes of the Alps – often termed the pre-Alps – are included.

The formation of the Alpine range began about 300 million years ago. The subsequent geological evolution of the region has created arguably the most beautiful region in Europe – deep valleys, precipitous gorges and more than a hundred peaks over 4,000m high. The Alps comprise two distinct parallel mountain chains. The northern range is formed by the Bernese Alps (or Bernese Oberland), stretching north and eastwards into the Central and Glarus Alps. There are only two overland crossings of this 177km stretch: the Grimsel Pass and the narrow Reuss valley. Conversely, the southern range comprising the Pennine ('Valais'), Lepontine and Rhaetian (or Graubünden) Alps is traversed at frequent intervals by ancient mountain passes such as the Great St Bernard, the Simplon, and the St Gotthard. Equally important as a transportation route is the almost straight longitudinal trench between the two mountain chains formed by the valleys of the upper Rhône and Rhine.

The total area of the Alps is surprisingly small but the variety of the region's landscape and topography, languages and cultures, climate, flora and fauna,

makes it a place of endless diversity and contrast.

For centuries the mountains were perceived variously as a source of superstition and dread, and in practical terms they inevitably posed a formidable obstacle to communication. Since the mid-19th century, however, they have been increasingly harnessed to the demands of possibly the world's most sophisticated tourist industry.

The area that now constitutes Switzerland was formerly the dominion of each one of its present neighbours. In the 1st century BC the Romans dislodged the ruling Helvetii tribe in what is now western Switzerland, and overcame the Rhaetians in the east. The Romans, in turn, were driven out by the Alemanni and the Burgundians in the 5th century AD, who were themselves replaced by the Franks a century later. After the disintergration of Charlemagne's empire, the area was divided between the Franks, Burgundians and Lombardians. In the 11th century it regained unity of a sort under the auspices of the Holy Roman Empire. Various feudal dynasties ruled it thereafter, including the house of Hapsburg.

The history of the Swiss Confederation begins in 1291, when the regions (or 'cantons') of Uri, Schwyz and Unterwalden formed an alliance that, during the course of the next century, slowly forced the Hapsburgs back to the Austrian border. Inspired by their military successes, the Swiss cantons (now eight) embarked on a period of territorial expansion. In 1499, Swiss independence was finally recognised by the Holy Roman Empire, and after continuing bloody conflict with the Milanese and the French, the Confederation decided in 1515 to renounce once and for all further territorial expansion. This decision laid the foundations of Switzerland's future prosperity.

Not all was peace at home at this time. With the arrival of the Protestant Reformation in the 16th century, religious strife became severe. Yet Switzerland survived this new threat to its stability with a mixture of compromise and common sense, demonstrating not for the first time the admirable ability of the Swiss to extend tolerance to fellow citizens of different religion and race.

At the end of the 18th century, yet another threat emerged. In 1798, Napoleonic troops invaded under the pretext of helping to 'free' the Swiss. An 'Helvetian' republic was imposed on the country, based on France's own interpretation of government. Conceding that it was unworkable, Napoleon restored the Confederal constitution of equal cantons. Meanwhile, Switzerland had become a battleground between the French against the Austrians, Prussians and Russians. At the Congress of Vienna in 1815, Swiss independence was finally restored and neutrality guaranteed.

Thus it has remained; in a world frequently ravaged by war Switzerland has not ceased to maintain its neutrality. In that time it has used its privileged status to provide a safe haven for war refugees and to develop humanitarian functions that do it considerable credit. Perhaps the most celebrated of these is the International Red Cross founded by Henri Dunant in 1863.

Today, the Swiss citizen is primarily a member of a 'communite' (commune), of which there are over 3,000, active within the structure of the 23 cantons forming the Swiss Confederation. Both commune and canton are self-governing. The Federal Parliament consists of two legislative chambers, and executive power is shared by the seven ministers of the Federal Council. The office of President of the Confederation is rotated among these ministers annually, but ultimate power is vested in the people. Perversely, in a country that so fiercely upholds the virtues of democracy, women were denied the vote until 1971. In parts of the country they are still denied the right to vote on local issues.

But this puzzling contradiction in Switzerland's image of itself as an advanced, enlightened and thoroughly civilised society is of minor significance when set against its considerable achievements in other respects. A country with no natural resources beyond the tourist-pulling power of its landscape has Europe's highest per capita income and its highest standard of living.

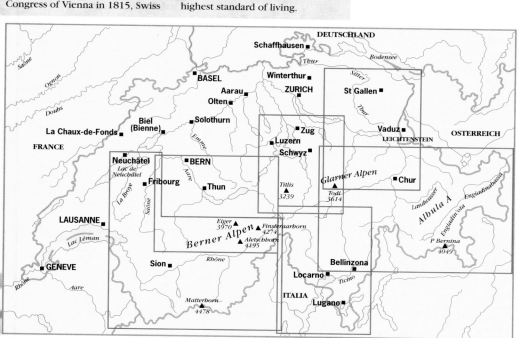

•THE PEOPLE•

The question, 'Which is the world's oldest democracy?', frequently has the most erudite of participants groping for their history books. To anyone with a reasonable grasp of general knowledge, the answer seems to be tantalisingly obvious - but all too frequently elusive. When it is revealed to be Switzerland, only the boldest of bluffers claim to have known but for a temporary lapse of memory. A useful follow-up question is to ask the name of any Swiss president within the last century; invariably the boldness vanishes like a thin wisp of smoke.

In truth, although Switzerland has more annual visitors per capita than any other country in Europe, very few of them ever leave with more than the faintest understanding of the country or the people they have visited. Even long-term foreign residents in Switzerland rarely develop more than the most rudimentary knowledge of their host country's system of government, its political creed, or even the 'national character' – if such a thing exists. It is this latter element in the complex Swiss equation that poses the most intriguing questions about the country and its citizens. How does the world's oldest democracy succeed, where countless others have failed, in holding together a union of three ancient and disparate European peoples? Divided by language, culture, ethnic background and natural mountain barriers, the Swiss have proved for over seven centuries that racial integration is not a fanciful ideal but a practical reality. Yet it would be wrong to imagine that there are distinct French, German, and Italian communities, each stubbornly hanging on to their mother country's apron-strings. In an admirable showcase for aspiring mixed-race sovereign nations, there is instead a system of symbiotic cultures with obvious links to their national origins, but whose respective members recognise the desirability of remaining defiantly 'Swiss'. And well they might. Throughout the world the word has become synonymous with civilisation, humanitarianism, enlightenment, efficiency, advanced technology and affluence.

All of these attributes are deserved, but at a cost – perceived by outsiders if not by the Swiss themselves. The old joke runs that, having created the most beautiful country in the world, God decided that He should appease the natural envy of other less fortunate countries by populating Switzerland with the most boring people. It would be a nigh impossible task to explain the underlying point of this schoolboy humour to a Swiss with any degree of diplomacy, or in the hope of an amused reaction. Famously sensible, the average Swiss citizen would doubtless shrug his or her shoulders uncomprehendingly and comment sadly on the destructive forces of jealousy and ignorance. Perhaps that is the most appropriate of responses, for it is difficult not to be jealous of the Swiss for their surroundings and their lifestyle, and it is difficult to be anything other than ignorant when it comes to identifying the Swiss character.

The concept of a national 'character' is notoriously difficult to analyse – more so, perhaps, in the case of the Swiss; a farm worker in the remote Ticino village of Bosco-Gurin probably has more in common with a crofter in the Hebrides than a Zürich banker. But generally, it is true to say of the Alpine and lowland peoples alike that they are hospitable (if lacking in gregariousness), industrious, law-abiding and fiercely proud of their country. Although they have a reputation for being an unflappable and impassive people, they are none the less quick to show their disapproval of any failure to meet their own high standards. In a national opinion poll that coincided with the country's 700th anniversary, nearly half of the electorate indicated that it believed that the country was in crisis and that the government did not deserve its people's confidence. The irony of this demonstration of discontent is illustrated by the fact that political stability is total, unemployment is negligible, industrial strife is virtually unknown and the Swiss have the highest per capita earnings in Europe. The majority of the 6.5 million population is concentrated in the predominantly German-speaking Mittelland, the vast central plateau north of the Alps stretching from the French to the Austrian border. Fifty-four per cent of the working population is employed in service industries such as banking and tourism, 39 per cent in industry, and just 7 per cent in agriculture – a percentage which is shrinking progressively.

A striking indication of the heterogenous population structure is the multi-lingual character of the country. For 74 per cent of Swiss the first language is German, 20 per cent speak French, 4 per cent Italian and the remaining 2 per cent Romansch (or Rhaeto-Romanic). The Romansch speakers, mainly inhabiting the mountainous canton of Graubünden are the descendants of early Celtic settlers, 'romanised' by the creation of the province of Rhaetia in 15BC by the Romans. Their language, divided into a number of tangled dialects, is either dead, dying or making a promising recovery depending on the sympathies of the commentator. All four Swiss

languages are officially recognised throughout the country, and although standard German is deemed to be the formal language of government, in fact the preferred alternative is 'Schwyzerdutsch' or 'Swiss-German'. This is derived from the old Alemannic language, and 'fragmented into a series of local and regional dialects.

It would be wrong to suppose that most Swiss have a reasonable grasp of each of their official languages. In just one example of the many contradictions underlying the intricate cultural and linguistic framework of the country, it is often the case in the Valais that travellers will find themselves in an exclusively German-speaking community a matter of minutes away from one where only French is spoken. It is also a myth that all Swiss speak English, although most people employed in service industries have at the very least a moderate grasp of the language.

As much in the banking houses of Zürich as in the remotest of mountain hamlets, the outlook of the Swiss people has been shaped largely by economic and political necessity. This has made them pragmatic, instinctively cautious, and prudent in adopting innovation.

It has also made them ingenious in the use of what few natural resources they have. Their lives demonstrate intelligence, industriousness, discipline, thrift, a noticeably Teutonic love of order (mixed with an equal amount of Latin flair), independence of mind, and a commitment to quality and craftmanship that makes their products highly valued throughout the world.

Traditional women's apparel worn in the mountainous canton of Graubünden

•VALAIS•

If there is one visual image that captures the essence of the Swiss Alps, it is the distinctive outline of the Matterhorn. Few mountains command the same instant recognition, or possess the same seductive mixture of stark beauty and intimidating scale. However, it is by no means the highest mountain of this western region of the Swiss Alps, which includes more than 50 peaks exceeding 4,000m .

configuration and relative solitariness. This splendid monolith is reason enough to visit the Valais, Switzerland's third largest and mostly French-speaking canton, but there are many other compelling reasons to explore this southwest part of the country. Not least of these is the spellbinding contrast between high Alpine terrain and the gentle, sunny slopes and ancient villages of the Rhône valley. Arctic and Mediterranean climates co-exist, almost impossibly, within a few kilometres of each other.

Within the space of an hour, travellers will find themselves juggling with the contrasting images of picturesque medieval towns surrounded by countless acres of sun-baked vineyards, and the awesome might of the highest peaks and longest glaciers in the country crowding in around mountain villages. This is the region of remote and wild valleys, mountain hamlets untouched by time, scorched-wood chalets over 500 years old, sun-bleached scree slopes, crystal-clear mountain lakes and stunningly beautiful Alpine scenery. Perhaps unsurprisingly it is also the region that offers the largest choice of mountain resorts, ranging from the most sophisticated in the world to the pleasingly unpretentious.

In places, particularly around the world-famous winter resort of Zermatt, the scenery is on a Himalayan scale. Here, the highest cablecar lift in Europe ascends to the Kleine Matterhorn at 3,820m.

On the north side of the Rhône valley, which traverses almost the entire length of the Valais, the

This distinction is earned by the 4,634m Dufourspitze, part of the Monte Rosa range on the frontier with Italy, or – the highest peak completely within Swiss territory – the 4,545m Dom, part of the massive Mischabel range between the resorts of Zermatt and Saas Fee.

The particular allure of the Matterhorn is therefore not simply a matter of size, but more the result of its uniquely jagged

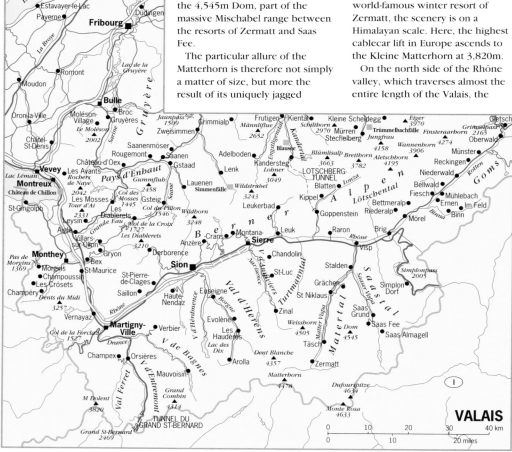

VALAIS

long and sunny shelf occupied by the sprawling resort of Crans-Montana offers a superb vantage point for views over the entire range. This is further enhanced by a trip by cablecar to the peak of Bella Lui beneath the ominously named Plaine Morte glacier. Near by to the west lies the small (but growing) modern resort of Anzère; to the east, the ancient spa town of Leukerbad is beautifully sited in an amphitheatre of towering peaks. Further east still, on the north side of that part of the Rhône valley known as the 'Goms', is a collection of charming little resorts beneath the huge Aletsch glacier, including Riederalp and the high-lying settlement of Belalp at 2,130m. South, up the Binn valley, are Im Feld and Binn – two of the loveliest (and most isolated) villages in the canton.

Those who prefer a blend of stunning Alpine scenery, wide-ranging leisure facilities and pulsating nightlife would be hard-pressed to find a better example than that offered by Verbier – a large, modern and lively resort linked by mountain lift to a vast skiing and rambling region.

The world's largest linked skiing region straddles the Franco-Swiss border, with the Swiss resorts of Champéry, Morgins, Champoussin and Les Crosets connected to the 11 French resorts that make up the 'Ski Sans Frontières' region of Les Portes du Soleil – a mind-boggling 650km of marked ski runs. At the opposite end of the scale, further south along the frontier, is the tiny 'jewel' of the Valais – Champex – a delightful little mountain resort set in pine forests in the Val Ferret.

In the Vaud Alps, the four leading Alpine holiday centres are the impressively sited Les Diablerets at the foot of the mountains of the same name; the old health resort of Leysin; the charming family resort of Château-d'Oex, capital of the Pays d'Enhaut; and the traditional British favourite of Villars, high above the Rhône basin. On the canton border with Berne is the picturesque village of Rougemont, part of the 'White Highlands' skiing region with the exclusive resort of Gstaad as its undisputed centre.

Aficionados of a different type of high life need look no further than the Vaud Riviera on the eastern shores of Lake Geneva. Enjoying a remarkably mild climate throughout the year, this is the location of one of the world's leading adult playgrounds and

international festival centres. Montreux, magnificently set on the lakefront with its dramatic Alpine backdrop, is surrounded by some of the lushest vegetation in western Switzerland. Here, fig, cypress, almond, mulberry and palm trees lend an exotic splash of colour to the sometimes severely angular hotel and apartment blocks.

Those who prefer peace and quiet to glitz and glamour will be rewarded by exploring the scores of narrow, winding valleys leading off the Rhône. These are among the most beautiful and unspoilt in the Alps, varying in character from the rugged gorges of the spectacular Lötschental to the lush and fertile pastures of the Val d'Hérens. Many of these valleys accommodate ancient communities that demonstrate a refreshing reluctance to embrace modern influences. Centuries-old traditions and festivals are very much alive and, contrary to some perceptions, do not form part of an elaborate pastoral cabaret for the amusement of tourists. These customs are deeply rooted and as much a part of the villagers' lives as their ancient chalets and *mazots* (small timber storehouses supported by mushroom-shaped stone piles).

In the villages of Evolène and Les Haudères in the Val d'Hérens, the local people are remarkably faithful to traditional dress and it is not unusual to see a herdswoman sitting side-saddle on muleback, dressed in a rough cotton frock and crocheted straw hat that are unlikely to have varied in style since the 17th century. On Sundays and feast days these are replaced by the colourful silk

aprons and lace bonnets of similar vintage.

In the Val d'Anniviers, even the cows are dressed up for the annual journey to the high Alpine pastures when the snows melt. With flowers entwined around their horns and ribbons trailing from their cowbells, this is one of the most colourful spectacles in the southern part of the Valais.

A different form of culture is found in the historic towns of the Rhône valley. In Sion, ancient capital of the Valais canton, the sense of history is almost tangible. Perhaps that is not so surprising in the light of its age – over 2,000 years old. Here, and in splendid medieval towns like St Maurice, Sierre and Saillon, there are marvellous examples of Savoy and Burgundy architecture. Encircled by the largest concentration of vineyards in the country, they are excellent places to relax and enjoy a glass of the local wine. East, beyond the strategic old trading centre of Brig at the foot of the Simplon Pass, the architecture and the language becomes noticeably more German-influenced. In the picturesque villages of the Binntal, for example, French is rarely spoken. But for the ultimate showcase of the two distinct cultures living side by side, there can be no better example than the charming medieval city of Fribourg on the fringe of the western Alps. Here the German- and French-speaking communities live in peaceful co-existence on opposite banks of the Sarine River, a far cry from the days of grudging obeisance to the Bernese overlords throughout the Middle Ages.

The Upper Valais

AIGLE

MAP REF: 110 A2

An attractive little town that takes its name from the Roman *Aquilea*, Aigle is situated on the banks of the turbulent Grand Eau in the Rhône valley. Formerly a feudal stronghold of some importance, it was ruled by the House of Savoy before being taken by Berne in the 15th century, and it remained under Bernese control until the French invasion of 1798. The French influence is still predominant. The town is known chiefly for its wine-making heritage and its imposing 13th-century château, surrounded by vineyards. Rebuilt by the Bernese in the 15th century, the château is one of the most important fortress sites in Switzerland. Comprising a square keep and three round towers, it now houses two museums, one devoted to wine, the other to salt. The former features a collection of bottles, casks and labels dating from the 17th century, and includes two massive winepresses. The salt museum has a surprisingly comprehensive collection of articles associated with the salt industry over the past four centuries. A huge 17th-century barn with a half-hipped roof adjoins this impressive old building. In Cloitre, the town's oldest quarter, the church of St Maurice founded in the 12th century is notable for its late-Gothic steeple. In the Fontaine quarter, the Rue de Jérusalem is a charming alley of old arcaded houses. Other attractions include the old market square, the pedestrianised Rue du Bourg, and the medieval church of St Jacques with a tower dating from 1642.

BRIG

MAP REF: 110 C2

This lively and historic town is a key road and rail junction in the Valais and, because of its position at the head of the Simplon Pass, it has traditionally provided a trade route with Italy. It also stands at the mouth of the famous Simplon rail tunnel, built between 1898 and 1904, which at 19.8km is still the world's longest. Perhaps because of this geographical location, Brig has earned an unhelpful reputation as a place to pass through. However, that does a considerable disservice to the town and its inherent attractions.

Foremost amongst places to visit is undoubtedly the celebrated Stockalperschloss (Stockalper's Castle), built between 1658 and 1678. This formidable structure is generally acknowledged to be the finest of Switzerland's baroque palaces, and its three striking, onion-domed gilded towers give the visitor an early impression of the rich architectural treasure in store.

Elsewhere in the town there are a number of other fine buildings, including an old Jesuit church (built in 1662), and a collection of elegant mansions built on the profits of cross-border trade with Italy. Another point of interest is the fountain in the Marktplatz commemorating one of aviation's unsung pioneers, Georges Chavez. A citizen of Peru, he was the first man to fly over the Alps - from Brig to the Italian town of Domodossola in 1910. He was killed on landing.

STOCKALPER

Kaspar Jodok von Stockalper was a great entrepreneur of his era. Born in 1609, he was a talented merchant who amassed considerable wealth by monopolising the salt trade over the Simplon Pass. Ensuring that it was well guarded by a private army of 70 men, he dominated the vital trade route for years and poured a sizeable proportion of the resulting profits into grandiose building schemes around his native Brig. These included the magnificent Stockalperschloss (above) and many of the churches dating from the same period. A popular figure in courts and palaces throughout Europe, he none the less aroused fierce resentment among the local people he sought to benefit and was forced to flee in disguise over the same mountain pass that had made him his fortune. He was permitted to return six years later to die in his castle.

BULLE

MAP REF: 110 A3

Lying in the heart of Gruyère, the small town of Bulle is best known for the famous cheeses named after the region. This delightful pastoral area in the northwest foothills of the Alps is justly celebrated as one of the prettiest parts of Switzerland and despite its proximity to the N12 autobahn, Bulle has managed to retain much of its rustic flavour, with numerous cheese shops lining its main street. Its unusual underground museum, the Musée Gruérien, has a cheese room faithfully reconstructed from part of a herdsman's mountain lodge. The rest of the collection includes other reconstructions of peasant dwellings, engravings and paintings (including works by Courbet), and some fine examples of intricately carved and painted furniture from the 17th century.

The town has an imposing 13th-century castle built by the Bishops of Lausanne in the style introduced by Peter II of Savoy, and showing interesting Burgundian influences. Its large round keep lies on the southwest side; the main section of the building is crowned by turrets. Near by is a 14th-century Capuchin chapel, formerly part of a long-vanished hospital. Rebuilt in 1454 after a fire, its splendid carved wooden doors and baroque high altar date from 1662.

CHAMPERY

MAP REF: 110 A2

A one-street village facing the jagged peaks of the Dents du Midi, Champéry is a sleepy Alpine winter sports resort in a spectacularly beautiful setting. Linked to the largest skiing region in the world – the 15 resorts of the Portes du Soleil (11 of them on the French side of the border) – it is popular with those skiers who prefer rather more Alpine charm than the neighbouring French ski-dromes provide. Most of the main street is closed to traffic and the best of the restaurants and shops are found on its gentle descent to the main cable-car station to Planachaux. One of the most attractive of its buildings is an early 18th-century church, with an intriguing old lantern capping its baroque bell tower.

The majority of the resort's recent development is concentrated around the valley road curving beneath the heart of the old village which, as a result, has managed to retain much of its traditional flavour. As befits an all-year resort attracting almost as many summer visitors as winter, Champéry offers a full range of facilities including an extensive sports centre with ice and curling rinks.

Nearby Of the three other Swiss resorts accessible by ski, mountain lift or road, Morgins is the furthest from Champéry on the map, but the closest in sophistication and appeal. Quiet and relaxed, it has strong British connections going back to the turn of the century.

Champoussin is a mini-resort that has made a commendable effort to cloak its modernity under a neo-Alpine skin. Les Crósets has been less successful in promoting itself, and is little more than a ski-station set in the middle of somewhat bleak surroundings high above the timber line.

MOTOR TOUR

This tour, through some of the best countryside in western Switzerland, is 170km long. *From Aigle drive northeast on Route 11, signed Leysin and Château-d'Oex, taking the steep road on the left bank of the Grande Eau to Les Planches. Continue up to the Col des Mosses and then make the gradual descent to Château-d'Oex, threading the rugged Gorges du Pissot. From the centre of this resort, take the road signed Rossinière and Gruyères.*

Rossinière
One of the most attractive villages in the Pays d'Enhaut, Rossinière is also home to one of the most notable timber buildings in the canton of Vaud – the mid-18th-century 'Grand-Chalet' in the

village square. The church of St Marie-Madeleine was founded in the 13th century and rebuilt in 1645, retaining its original frescos. *Cross the Vaud/Fribourg canton border into the village of Montbovon, a pretty part of the Sarine valley. 7km ahead is a right turn to Grandvillard, 1.5km off the main road.*

Grandvillard
This interesting old village has a number of fine old wooden chalets dating from the 17th

Medieval Chateau d'Aigle

century; note particularly the Maison Banneret, built in 1666. One of the most notable feaures of the village is the waterfall at the foot of the 2,389m Vanil Noir lying to the southeast. *Return to the main road and continue north to the medieval town of Gruyères, perched on a hill to the left of the road. Turn right immediately after the town, passing through Broc towards Charmey on the Jaun Pass road.*

Jaun Pass Road
The main pass road past Charmey climbs through the scenic Jogne Gorge to the small village of Jaun with its waterfall and ruined castle. Ahead, after passing through some dramatic corniche sections, lies the 1,509m Jaunpass, with a number of spectacular viewing points over the upper and lower Simmental valley. *A winding road descends steeply to Reidenbach in the Simmental valley. Regain Route 11 here, driving south up the Ober Simmental to Zweisimmen. Continue up the main road to Saanen, turning left and south here for Gstaad. From here take the road south to Gsteig, from there ascending to the Col du Pillon beneath the impressive peaks of Les Diablerets. At the resort of the same name, which lies 4km ahead, take the mountain road south over the Col de La Croix to Villars-sur-Ollon, passing through the resort and turning left for Gryon and Bex. This is an extremely steep descent to the main Route 9 which leads north back to Aigle.*

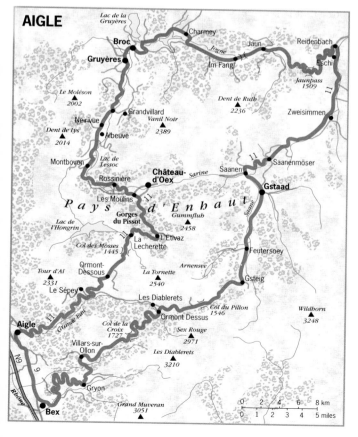

CHAMPEX
MAP REF: 110 A2

One of the most delightful spots in the Valais, Champex is a charming all-year resort attractively sited on the edge of a miniature lake. Close to the border with France, it stands at the mouth of the densely wooded Val Ferret sheltered by the Mont Blanc massif to the west and the Grand Combin to the east.

The Lac du Champex is so evenly contoured that one might be forgiven for assuming that it is man-made, and its glass-like surface lends further substance to that impression. During the summer it offers swimming and boating (with hire-vessels including some interesting art deco pedallos); in winter, it becomes a natural ice-rink.

On its northern shore the resort's only road curves around the water's edge, lined by elegant Victorian hotels and somewhat newer restaurants and cafés. Across the lake stands a tiny, 19th-century Protestant chapel, illuminated at night and reached by a pretty path through fir trees. From the western end of the village a 15-minute chair-lift rises to La Breya, which offers splendid views of the Grand Combin to the left and a collection of glittering glaciers streaking the mountains of Aiguille d'Argentière and Mont Dolent to the right. The $1^1/_2$ hour walk up to the d'Orny glacier from here is visually stunning.
Nearby A few kilometres down the valley to the east is the village of Orsières, through which travellers must pass on their way south to the Grand St Bernard Tunnel. The late 19th-century Church of St Nicholas retains a battered, 13th-century Romansque belfry.

CHATEAU-D'OEX
MAP REF: 110 B3

Midway between the Bernese Oberland and Lac Léman (Lake Geneva), Château-d'Oex is a small but increasingly popular resort with its own modest skiing area and a reputation for being something of a mecca for hot-air-balloon enthusiasts. The surrounding Vaud Alps, renowned for sunny and temperate weather, suit this latter pursuit admirably. The village stands at the gateway to the Pays d'Enhaut, the 'White Highlands', which separate it from Gstaad. They may be high, but by other Alpine standards they are low enough to be relatively friendly to balloonists. Moreover,

Summer golf at Crans-Montana

this is justly described as one of the most scenically rewarding areas of western Switzerland.

The castle that gave Château-d'Oex (pronounced 'day') its name no longer exists, but it is thought that parts of it are incorporated into the church that stands on its former site. The village also has its own folk museum, the Musée du Vieux Pays d'Enhaut, which has an extensive collection of exhibits recalling seven centuries of the region that was once part of Gruyère. Other facilities include an ice rink, an indoor riding

A frozen lake in a wintery Champex

school, and river-rafting.
Nearby The Col des Mosses, a 14.5km drive south, is a delightful open plateau with a striking panorama of the southern Alps. The little village of Les Mosses is a quiet, unpretentious resort with 50km of good intermediate skiing. A trip in the mountain lift up to Lac Lioson, and from there to the Pic Chaussy at 2,351m, with views stretching from Lake Geneva to the Jungfrau massif, is a highly recommended excursion.

CRANS-MONTANA
MAP REF: 110 B2

Before World War I the adjoining villages of Crans and Montana were two quite separate resorts. In some respects they still are, with Crans (sur-Sierre) strong on city chic and designer boutiques, and the lower village of Montana noticeably more parochial. The 'merger', which took place for the soundest of Swiss financial reasons, has made this one of the largest sports resorts in Switzerland.

Frequently described in pejorative terms as a 'suburban sprawl', the extraordinary beauty of Montana's 'balcony' setting makes any criticism seem almost churlish. Sir Arnold Lunn, the respected British skiing pioneer, rated the view across the Rhône valley as 'one of the seven finest' in the Alps. Admittedly, the architecture is at best undistinguished and the traffic-choked roads and rows of parking meters leave something to be desired, but this is an unashamed 'super-resort' geared to the comfort and convenience of its largely affluent clientele.

Because of its extensive range of facilities, which include two golf courses (one of which hosts the Swiss open), it has become a popular place to buy a second home for many Swiss who, doubtless sold on the beauty of the surrounding landscape, have few objections to living in soulless apartment blocks. There are many of those, but there are also a number of good hotels, night-clubs, restaurants, and a casino.

In the summer there is ample scope for swimming in the many small lakes that surround the Crans part of the resort, and the walking possibilities are extensive. There is also summer skiing on the sinister-sounding Plaine Morte glacier. In the winter 40 lifts serve 150km of piste and, although by comparison with other Valais resorts the skiing is fairly low, it is undeniably pretty, split evenly between open and wooded terrain. With over 60 per cent of the runs falling into the modest intermediate category, Crans-Montana is not a great favourite with advanced skiers, who are likely to tire quickly of its limited challenges. Two base stations operate, respectively, from Crans and Montana, and there are two more at Vermala and Aminona, giving rapid access to three well-linked, extensive areas. **Nearby** From either Crans or Montana base stations, the ascent by gondola and then cable-car to Bella Lui at 2,543m offers one of the great Alpine panoramas over the Rhône valley.

HOT AIR BALLOONS
A balloon flight is a unique adventure, but the experts claim that a flight over the Alps is the experience of a lifetime. Château-d'Oex provides fine conditions for flying, protected

from the strong Alpine winds by its sheltered position in the heart of the Vaud Alps. The International Alpine Hot Air Balloon Centre is based in the village, and holds its annual championships every January with about 80 balloons from 17 countries participating. In flight the balloon drifts with the wind and the pilot has to use the variations in wind speed and altitude to steer it. Flights are only made in good weather and the balloons must be in radio contact with a recovery vehicle at all times.

MOUNTAIN WALK

Allow 3 hours

From the western end of Champex take the chair-lift up to La Breya. The retrospective view of the diminishing Lac de Champex is spellbinding; so, too, is the tangle of bluish glaciers at the head of the Val d'Arpette on the right. Take the path directly ahead of the top station and climb at first steeply, then more gently on the narrow path signposted d'Orny and Trient. This is a precarious-looking but well-kept trail with the mountain wall to the right and a dizzy drop down through the Combe d'Orny to the left. From the beginning, the view ahead and to the left of the Grand Combin and the Valais Alps is most impressive. The path continues up to the fork where it meets the route up from Champex via the Combe d'Orny. For the moment, continue ahead for another 1km to where another path joins from the left for a fine view of the Glacier d'Orny, draped between the 3,269m Pointe d'Orny to the right,

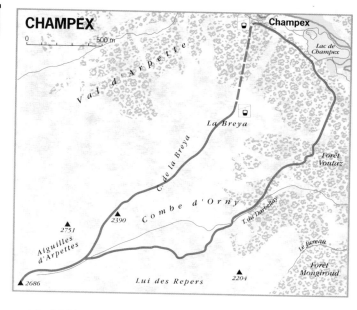

CHAMPEX

0   500 m

Champex

Lac de Champex

Val d'Arpette

La Breya

Forêt Voutaz

C. de la Breya

Combe d'Orny

T. du Darbellay

Le Jureau

2751

2390

Aiguilles d'Arpettes

Forêt Mongiroud

2686

Lui des Repers

2204

and the 3,344m Le Portalet to the left. Ahead lies the huge and icy Plateau du Trient beneath the 3,540m Aiguille du Tour. Good walkers can continue from here up to the Cabane du Trient, about 2.5km ahead, but be warned – it is a strenuous climb. Follow the path back to the first fork and turn right for the descent to Champex. The first third of this is above the tree line, but at the point where the path crosses the Darbellay stream, the path enters the dense Voutaz Forest where it remains virtually level until Champex. Continue along the wooded lakeside path around to the left, past the tiny chapel, and return to the starting point.

LES DIABLERETS
MAP REF: 110 B2

A relaxed, scattered sprawl of traditional richly decorated chalets, Les Diablerets is an all-year resort lying at the bottom of the broad Ormonts valley beneath the craggy peak of the mountain that gives it its name. The village is linked by mountain lift to the larger resort of Villars-sur-Ollon, but it is very much a ski resort in its own right with plenty of good glacier skiing and an efficient network of lifts. Its setting, in gently rolling maple-covered meadows is particularly impressive and summer visitors can take advantage of a broad range of activities, including riding, swimming and walking. As a base for excursions it has much to offer.

Nearby Four kilometres out of the village, the Col du Pillon offers a choice of excursions to Lake Retaud or the exotic-sounding Sex Rouge peak. The former, a tranquil little oasis in a glorious mountain setting, is reached via a narrow road north of the Pass. The 2,971m peak of Sex Rouge is reached by cable-car, either from the Pass or from the small village of Reusch on the road to Gsteig. This vantage point offers fabulous views of the Diablerets massif and the Tsanfleuron Glacier. In fine conditions the sprawling panorama includes the Matterhorn and Mont Blanc.

ERNEN
MAP REF: 110 C2

A small village midway up the Goms valley on the south bank of the Rhône, Ernen has a number of fine 15th- to 18th-century houses characteristic of this part of the Valais. The late 16th-century Tellenhaus in the main square has, as its name suggests, associations with the story of William Tell. Well-preserved wall paintings depict the legendary archer's feats in colourful detail. Other buildings with more contemporary frescos on their façades include the 16th-century school house, and the stone-built, mid-18th-century Rathaus, with paintings dating from the 1940s and 1950s respectively. The village's oldest building is the Catholic church of St George, built after 1510 on the site of a church founded in 1214. The interior is lavishly decorated with a mixture of Gothic, baroque and rococo features, and includes an impressive sculpture of St George and the Dragon. The nearby presbytery was built in

1733 and incorporates part of an earlier building in its structure.
Nearby Two kilometres east, past a hill on which are the remains of the former gallows, is the village of Mühlebach where Cardinal Schinner, Bishop of Sion, was born. His birthplace is said to be one of the oldest wooden buildings in Switzerland.

Nine kilometres south up the beautiful Binntal valley are some of the loveliest villages in the Valais. The largest, Binn, is a picturesque collection of ancient, blackened chalets, bedecked with flowers, set on both sides of a tumbling mountain brook. Four kilometres east is the equally picturesque hamlet of Im Feld. The chapel of St Martin dates from the late 1600s.

EVOLÈNE
MAP REF: 110 B2

Evolène is one of those Swiss mountain villages apparently untouched by time. A mountaineering centre of some repute, it lies halfway up the

The all-year-round resort of Les Diablerets, sitting below its snowy mountain peak

beautiful Val d'Hérens south of Sion, and is notable for its picturesque grouping of old, dark brown, larchwood-fronted chalets – many of them colourfully painted. The church of St John the Baptist was erected in 1852 on the foundations of an earlier structure, and retains a late medieval tower. The 19th-century addition of some small hotels to the village, and a limited number of other more contemporary structures, detracts little from its air of old-world charm. This is enhanced in delightful fashion by the locals insistence on wearing traditional costume on Sundays (and many of them more often than that). Evolène is also well known for its coarse, hardwearing knitting wool, but chief among its attractions must be the exquisite nature of its setting. In every direction a scenic wonderland overwhelms the senses. To the northeast rises the

Sasseneire, to the west the Mount de L'Etoile, and at the head of the valley the Dents de Veisivi. Soaring majestically above them all is the formidable Dent Blanche, 4357m high.

Nearby Other villages of the Val d'Hérens, notably Euseigne and Les Haudères, are worth investigation. The former is renowned for the 'Pyramides d'Euseigne', remarkable pillars of earth crowned by huge boulders. Further down the valley from Evolène, the lovely hamlet of Les Haudères also has some fine examples of three- and four-storey wooden chalets arranged in ordered chaos in an equally impressive setting. The valley divides here and a winding mountain road climbs through larches and pines to the tiny mountaineering resort of Arolla, another haphazard collection of chalets clinging tenaciously to the mountainside. It is one of the highest villages in the Valais at 1,998m.

FRIBOURG

MAP REF: 110 B3

Lying between the Alpine foothills and the lush pastures of the Swiss plateau stretching from Berne to Lake Geneva, Fribourg is an historic city of curious ambiguity and great charm. The first characteristic arises from its inability to decide whether it is ethnically and linguistically French or German; the second, in large part, from the resulting confusion. Over the centuries it has sought to resolve the matter by dividing itself into two distinct halves: the French-speaking community on the left bank of the River Sarine, and the German on the right side. It would be iniquitous to suggest that there is any ill-feeling between the two, but there are none the less intriguing cultural differences. These are reflected in the architecture, the names of the streets, and even the attitudes of the people. In this sense, Fribourg is a microcosm of the Swiss Confederation – and extensive exploration of the steep, narrow streets of this delightful old city is therefore a rewarding and educational experience.

Founded by Duke Berthold IV of Zähringen in 1157, its site on the crest of a rocky knoll, protected by the twisting curves of the Sarine, had obvious strategic advantages. The old town still shelters comfortably behind some of the original fortified walls built in the early medieval period. Ruled at various stages by the Habsburgs and the Dukes of Savoy, and, later inevitably absorbed by the Napoleonic regime, it stubbornly refused all entreaties to revoke its Catholicism, and to this day it remains the most Catholic of Swiss cities. The cathedral of St Nicholas, with its magnificent 15th-century Gothic tower dwarfing the ancient buildings of the old town, is the most impressive of the city's fine inheritance of churches. Dating from the 13th century, it has many fine features including a vivid depiction of the Last Judgement in the tympanum above its main doors, a late 15th-century carved stone font, and an organ that in the early 19th century was treated as one of the wonders of the world.

The church of the Cordeliers, rebuilt in the 18th century, is another fine example of ecclesiastical architecture and includes an extremely impressive high altarpiece painted in about 1480 by the Masters of the Carnation – two anonymous artists who habitually signed their works with a red and white carnation.

More medieval and religious treasures can be found in the Museum of Art and History, part-installed in an elegant hotel on the Rue de Morat and rated as having the finest collection of religious sculptures in Switzerland.

The town hall is also worth more than a passing glance. An early 16th-century building with an octagonal belfry, it has an unusual exterior double staircase, which was added a century later.

A town of two halves, Fribourg is part German-Swiss and part French-Swiss, with the River Sarine acting as an unofficial borderline. The resultant architecture is equally cosmopolitan

GLETSCH

MAP REF: 110 C3

The chief claim to fame of this meeting place of the Grimsel and Furka passes, located at the eastern end of the Goms valley, is its dramatic view of the Rhône Glacier, the birthplace of the Rhône river. Not surprisingly perhaps, it owes its name to the German word for that natural phenomenon. The town, the most easterly of the Valais, is also one of the highest large communities in the canton standing at an altitude of 1,759m and it is acknowledged to be a mandatory stop on any tour of the three passes. Without the 10km-long glacier, which hangs forbiddingly above it, it would be a conventional Swiss town with a busy main street and a huddle of unremarkable buildings. Instead it has been a popular destination for travellers for well over a century, and has recently developed something of a reputation for winter sports and summer hiking.

Nearby The famous Ice Grotto, a huge vault hewn out of the compacted turquoise-blue ice of the Rhône Glacier, has been attracting visitors since the late 19th century. Close by are a number of vantage points for magnificent mountain panoramas, arguably the best of which is from the splendidly sited if rather shabby old Victorian hotel above the grotto on the pass road.

Sixteenth-century, thickly wooden chalets in the small village of Münster, situated below a soaring, snow-dappled mountainscape

The gargantuan icy bulk of the Rhône Glacier near Gletsch

THE GOMS VALLEY

MAP REF: 110 C2

Also known as the Conches valley, or Upper Rhône valley, 'Goms' is the name given to this upper region of the Valais by its predominantly German-speaking inhabitants. The road along the valley floor climbs steadily along the north bank of the river for 48km from Brig to Gletsch. On a map the Rhône strongly resembles a spine, joined in perfect symmetry by slender blue ribs of water descending from their mountain lakes or glaciers. The cartographical equilibrium is further illustrated by the positioning of villages at regular intervals along the route, and even the mountains crowding in on either side appear to fit some cleverly contrived pattern of scale and balance.

The reality is, of course, a different matter, with scenery of ever-increasing grandeur unfolding at every stage of the upward climb from Brig, and each charming old village stubbornly resisting any notion of uniformity. At Mörel, 7.5km east of Brig, a cable-car

The village of Binn dwarfed into vulnerable insignificance

ascends to the small and beautifully sited resort of Riederalp at 2,230m. A short distance from the terminus is a chair-lift to the summit of Moosfluh at 2,335m, which provides a splendid view of the lower reaches of the Aletschgletscher (Aletsch Glacier), the largest in Switzerland, which starts its 27km descent from beneath the Jungfrau massif. There are more lifts from a roadside station a little further ahead, which ascend to the next village of Betten and from there to the

modern resort of Bettmeralp by a small lake.

Just before Fiesch, another 6.5km up the valley, there is a road leading south to the lovely old village of Ernen, and from there up the pastoral Binntal to the charming hamlets of Binn and Im Feld. From Fiesch itself, there is yet another cable-car climbing in two stages to the Eggishorn, which, at an altitude of 2,927m, affords one of the finest views in the Valais. The Aletsch curves down to the left, and to the right the Fiesch Glacier appears poised to sweep away the small hamlets beneath it. Immediately to the

north is the 3,906m Wannenhorn, to the northwest the 4,195m Aletschhorn and, between and behind them, the mighty Jungfrau.

The next village of significance is Bellwald, reached either by narrow road or cable-car 3km from Fiesch. An attractive huddle of typical larchwood chalets, it is surrounded to the north by a number of tiny hamlets each distinguished by 17th-century Alpine chapels. The view south from Bellwald, lying at an altitude of 1,563m, is worth the diversion. The village of Niederwald, notable for its baroque, mid-17th-century parish church, is approached next. Another picturesque collection of traditional timber houses and farm buildings, it also has some modest fame as the birthplace of César Ritz, the renowned hotelier. Reckingen, straddling the road some 5km ahead, is also notable for its handsome 18th-century baroque church (complete with glass-encased, robed skeletons) and fine blackened-wood buildings. The principal community of the Goms, Münster, lies just beyond, after which the valley becomes wilder and more mountainous and the road climbs through the high village of Oberwald, notable for its early 18th-century baroque church, whose avalanche deflector gives it an unusual appearance. The interior is lavishly decorated in baroque style. From this point the road twists tortuously past the Rhône Falls until it reaches the canton border town of Gletsch with its stunning view of the Rhônegletscher (Rhône Glacier).

VALLEY WALK

Allow approximately 2 hours for this walk from Münster to the Goms valley

From the east of Münster village centre, walk up any one of the little, narrow lanes on the north side of the main road, opposite the church of St Maria. After a short, fascinating walk past 16th-century, blackened-wood chalets, many of them raised on mushroom-shaped piles to protect them from rodents, these lanes emerge on to a rough track rutted by farm vehicles.

Continue walking in a northerly direction until a wide footbridge crosses the Minstiger stream on the left. At the end of this turn right and follow the bank of the stream for approximately 0.5km.

There are then a couple of kinks in the path, left then right, before it straightens out again. After a further 10 minutes a fork is reached. Take the lefthand path, which at this point becomes steeper. At the next fork, turn sharp left where the path almost doubles back on itself for the even steeper climb to Judestafel. This is a pretty, if at times strenuous, climb up a gladed path until a narrow gorge is reached. The stream here is generally little more than a trickle, and it can be traversed by hopping carefully over boulders.

The path continues upwards through woodland until it begins to level out at the righthand turning for the Galmihornhütte. You are then presented with a choice: whether to climb the additional 200m to that point, or continue ahead along a level path

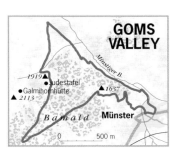

to an equally impressive and expansive vantage point beneath another mountain hut. The views of the Goms valley from both are splendid. Continue from the latter down a wider track through a dense forest. After approximately 10 minutes it curves sharply to the left. Follow it round for a further 1km and then immediately after another sharp righthand bend, take the steep forest path on the left back down to Münster village.

Time could have stood still in the medieval town of Gruyères – today the only threat to this once-impregnable fortress is the daily invasion of tourists

GRUYERES

MAP REF: 110 A3

This delightfully picturesque town, founded in the 13th century by Peter II of Savoy, occupies a hilltop site in possibly the most scenic part of the Sarine valley. Its fairy-tale appearance belies the fact that it was a feudal stronghold of the Counts of Gruyère from the 12th to the 16th centuries. It was an impregnable fortress never taken by force, but ultimately sold to meet the mounting debts of the Gruyère estates. Now its sturdy, fortified walls are breached daily by the hordes of visitors who throng its one main street and threaten at times to engulf it. One of Switzerland's 'must-sees'

Early evening bestows a festive patina upon the village of Gsteig. If Christmas could exist perpetually anywhere…

because of its reputation as one of the most beautiful medieval small towns in Europe, it is very definitely a 'must-see-out-of-season'.

As the town is closed to motor vehicles, a steep walk up a ramp from a large car park on the outskirts is necessary to reach the main cobble-stoned street. This is lined with fine 15th- to 17th-century Gothic and Renaissance houses, protected by statute as historical monuments. The street dips gently to a central fountain before rising again from the wide oval 'square' towards the castle. On the lefthand side stands the 14th-century Maison de Chalamala, notable for its elegant façade and formerly the home of the court jester to the Counts of Gruyère. The castle itself, built in stages between the 12th and 15th centuries, is a superbly preserved example from the period, and its

terrace offers tremendous views of Le Moléson peak to the south and the Dents de Broc to the east. In the courtyard is a 14th-century chapel dedicated to St John the Baptist; partially rebuilt in 1480 it has some fine 15th-century stained-glass windows. The château now houses a museum, and amongst its many splendid exhibits are robes once worn by the Knights of the Golden Fleece.

There also stunning views of much of the Alpine range, from Mont Blanc to the Jungfrau massif, from the town's ramparts.

Before leaving, a visit to the Wax Museum close to the top of the main street is recommended. If not quite on a par with Madame Tussauds, it none the less repays investigation of some interesting wax figures of famous Swiss people. The costumes are particularly noteworthy.

Nearby Six kilometres southeast of Gruyères is the relatively new resort of Moléson-Village. A two-stage cablecar ascends to the 2,002m peak of Le Moléson, where there is a rewarding and varied view across the meadows of the Gruyère region, with the Berner Alpen (Bernese Alps) as a backcloth. This excursion involves passing through Pringy, where there is a working cheese dairy with viewing platforms for visitors. Here the famous Gruyère cheese is produced. (Note that the cheese and the region drop the final 's', distinguishing them from the town in spelling, if not in pronunciation.)

GSTEIG

MAP REF: 110 B2

A pretty little village, high in the southern Sarine valley (known locally as 'Saane'), Gsteig is splendidly set in an amphitheatre formed by impressive peaks. To the northwest is the 2,050m Walighürli, to the southwest the 2,971m Sex Rouge, and to the east the spiky summit of the Spitzhorn at 2,807m. Set midway between Gstaad and Les Diablerets, Gsteig has managed to resist absorption by either. The Gothic church of St Theodul has a fine carved ceiling, a baroque early 18th-century pulpit, and an ancient timber steeple. The general appearance of the traditional old chalets, with their carved and painted friezes, and the delightful nature of their

setting make this a pleasant halting point particularly for those on their way to or from the Col du Pillon just over 6km south.

KIPPEL

MAP REF: 110 C2

The small hamlet of Kippel offers a fascinating insight into the way of life of the people of the Lötschental valley, south of the Jungfrau massif and north of the Rhône. Until the opening of the Lötschberg railway tunnel between Goppenstein and Kandersteg in 1912, the communities higher up the valley between Ferden and Gletschertafel were largely cut off from modern influences. The legacy of that period of isolation is manifested in some intriguing folk festivals quite unique in their esoteric variations of costume and displays – all well-documented in the village's small museum. Kippel is the largest village of the valley, standing at an altitude of over 1,400m. In the middle of some wonderful scenery, its picturesque, blackened-wood houses and barns are grouped around the parish church of St Martin, rebuilt in 1779 and retaining some interesting 16th-century features (including the adjoining ossuary). Inside is a fine 18th-century high altar and a Renaissance tabernacle. Worshippers come from considerable distances to Sunday services here, and the Corpus Christi procession (on the Sunday immediately following the holy day) is one of the great Swiss religious festivals. Local participants, known as 'God's Grenadiers', provide a charming and colourful spectacle.

A cable-car leaves from the outskirts of the village to a point just beneath the Kummenalp where there are fine summer walks.

Nearby Blatten and Kühmad, both tiny hamlets a few kilometres further up the Lötschental, provide excellent vantage points for scenic views of this wild and remote part of the Valais. In the latter, there is an interesting mid-17th-century chapel.

LEUK

MAP REF: 110 B3

This small market town, once the summer residence of the Bishops of Sion, lies in a bleak position high above the Rhône. It has two imposing episcopal castles, one of which is now the town hall. Founded in the 13th century and rebuilt in 1541, this is arguably the more impressive of the two with its unusual, stepped gables and four jutting corner turrets. The other, also founded in the 13th century, has a single square tower, built 1541, which is the most conspicuous architectural feature of the town. The late 15th-century church of St Stephen has a fine 12th-century Romanesque belfry and contains some interesting examples of 17th-century woodcarving skills. A remarkable wrought-iron swordsman stands guard outside the church.

Nearby Fourteen kilometres north is the ancient old spa town of Leukerbad, set in a dramatic mountain landscape. The extraordinary healing properties of its hot spring waters have been well known for centuries, and Mark Twain described the resort and its elderly patrons in some satirical detail in *A Tramp Abroad*. As a spa and climatic health resort it has expanded significantly in recent years and its facilities include a remarkable range of indoor and outdoor pools, an attractive skiing area, a sports centre, skating-rink, and a number of curling-rinks. There is a cablecar to the famous Gemmi Pass where, from an altitude of 2,346m, there are superb views of the southern Alps. There are also excellent altitude walks around the summit.

LEYSIN

MAP REF: 110 A2

This is a rambling old health resort on a sunny balcony site in the heart of the Vaud Alps. Although it has a strong institutional flavour, with its splendid old Grand Hotel now the home of an American college, it has none the less retained much of its 19th-century charm, complemented by a wide range of modern facilities. These include a major convention centre, two sports centres, a fitness complex, and a magnificent revolving panoramic restaurant on the 2,048m Berneuse peak. From it there are sweeping views of the Mont Blanc massif and the Bernese Alps.

In summer there is a well-developed network of hiking paths, and the Leysin Mountaineering School is something of a mecca for serious climbers attracted by the great Dolomitic towers of Tour d'Ai, 2,331m, and Tour de Mayen, 2,326m, which dominate the resort. In winter, it provides a pretty and relatively gentle skiing area, and has become popular with school parties from many different countries.

Kippel in the Lötschental valley

•GLACIERS•

Of the great natural phenomena that characterise the Swiss landscape, its glaciers must rank among the most impressive. Their attendant neighbours – mountains – have a quite different effect on the beholder: they may impress, they may inspire, they may often instil fear – but they do not move.

Glaciers are slowly rolling rivers of ice that advance or retreat in response to varying climatic conditions. Their impact on the mountainscape is often dramatic, particularly when they take on the image of a mass of water petrified in wave formation. The sensation of standing on or beneath one, aware of its imperceptible movement, is at once unnerving and strangely bewitching. Those who have heard the thunderous sound of a glacier 'crack' say that it awakens some hidden primeval instinct that warns of impending destruction. Perhaps that it is not surprising. Glaciers are essentially destructive forces that move forward under their own weight, pulverising everything in their path. Fortunately, their progress is slow – generally no more than a few centimetres a day – and their pattern of movement is usually predictable. In some parts of the world, however, particularly in Alaska and Iceland, glaciers can move very rapidly – as much as 8kph.

Any large mass of permanent, shifting ice that forms on land through the recrystallisation of snow may be characterised as a glacier. Occupying about 11 per cent of the earth's total land surface, but comprising about 75 per cent of its fresh water, the vast majority of this perennial ice is concentrated in Antarctica and Greenland. The remainder is widely spread throughout the world's continents (with the exception of Australia). It is estimated that as many as 200,000 glaciers exist in various parts of the world – and about 600 of them are in the Swiss Alps, covering an area of approximately 2,000 sq km.

About 10,000 years ago the entire Mittelland, the great plateau between the Alps and the Jura, was covered in a sea of ice and many of the Alpine valleys were filled to heights of over 2,000m. The legacy of that period remains in the form of today's glaciers – many of them still 'growing', others progressively retreating. The two largest in the Alps are both in the Valais – the Aletsch,

Creeping and scouring imperceivably down the mountainside, the ice-blue bulk of the Rhône Glacier

rolling down from beneath the Jungfrau to the upper flanks of the Goms valley for 23.5km, and the 14.5km-long Gorner at Zermatt. However, by polar standards these are small. The 'continental' glaciers that cover most of Antarctica are thick enough to bury entire mountain ranges; most of Greenland is similarly submerged by an ice sheet that has a maximum depth of about 3,350m (or two and a half times the height of Ben Nevis, the highest mountain in the British Isles.) Any appreciable variation in the amount of this glacier ice would have critical consequences for man. If, for example, all the world's existing glacier ice were to melt, the resulting rise in sea level of about 60m would swamp practically every coastal city in the world, including London, New York and Sydney.

A glacier is formed when snow accumulates above the 'snow line', defined as the lower limit of perpetual snow. In polar regions the snow line starts at sea level, progressively rising towards the Equator. In the Swiss Alps it lies between 2,500 to 3,200m. Continually fed by fresh snowfalls, the snow is gradually compacted into ice by pressure. The layers of this new snow on the surface of the glacier are known as firn or neve, and build up, layer on layer, until the weight of the accumulation exceeds the strength of the ice. At this point the ice-mass at the base of the glacier begins to move slowly, its speed dependent on the gradient of the slope and the temperature of the ice. The movement of the Alps' valley glaciers is similar to that of the flow of a river, with velocity greater in the centre than at the sides. The upper layers of hard, brittle ice are carried by the mobile ice-pack below, which, as it moves, causes the surface to fracture into wide fissures known as crevasses. Often concealed by flimsy 'snow bridges', these open and close according to the pulling action of the ice. They represent unquestionably the most dangerous area of the glacier for those seeking to traverse them. Many thousands of climbers and skiers have discovered to their cost that – should they survive a fall of anything up to 60m into the heart of a glacier – any hope of rescue is generally a forlorn one. Bodies of victims are sometimes found many years later, in remarkable states of preservation, as the glacier disgorges them at its side or terminus. In some instances, 19th-century climbers (where identification is possible from their possessions) have been interred over a century after their death by their own distant descendants. The 5,000-year-old 'Iceman', found by hikers on the perimeter of a glacier on the Austrian-Italian border, is the most dramatic example of how this macabre process of freezing entombment works.

The irony of the treacherous nature of crevasses is that they also provide the most pleasing of spectacles for observers (from a safe distance). Frequently, they take the form of jagged pinnacles and towers as the upper surface of the glacier is broken up into a chaos of ice sculptures. Known as seracs, they are caused by fractures in the ice created by abrupt changes of gradient. At the sides and at the end of glaciers are lateral and terminal moraines, accumulations of stone and debris and other loose material carried by the ice during its inexorable progress down the mountainside. It is these involuntary passengers of the glacier that provide its erosive power.

At the melting tip or snout, of the glacier, amid piles of rocky detritus, water is discharged in a distinctive milky-coloured flow, a feature caused by the fine stone-

The Grialetsch Glacier seen from the Fluellapass

dust created by the abrasive grinding action of the glacier and its contents. Often the flow takes the form of a spectacular and turbulent torrent – as in the case of the Glacier Gorge in Grindelwald – in other cases it is little more than a turbid trickle. But the real glory of a glacier lies not so much at its end as in the extraordinary depth and range of colours in the ice formations of its body. Inexpressibly beautiful shades of blue and green combine to create one of the most spectacular features of the Swiss landscape.

MARTIGNY-VILLE
MAP REF: 110 A2

Formerly the site of a Roman camp called *Octodorum*, and a Celtic settlement even earlier than that, Martigny is a small industrial town of modest charm but important geographical location. It is at this point that the Rhône takes a sharp right turn up towards Lake Geneva. However, of more commercial significance for the town, it is also the place where the routes from the Grand St-Bernard, Forclaz and Simplon passes converge. Traditionally, the highest accolade paid to the modern town, of slight interest in itself, is that it is an excellent starting point for excursions. The French and Italian borders are both well within an hour's drive, and major international skiing resorts such as Verbier, Crans-Montana and Champéry are similarly accessible. However, in recent years Martigny has experienced something of a Roman renaissance, which has given it new pride in its cultural inheritance. In 1976 a 1st-century Roman temple was excavated near the Rue du Forum, and two years later the Gallo-Roman Museum of Octodorum was constructed over the foundations. This impressive building has a range of galleries overlooking the site of the temple (thought to have been dedicated to Mercury) and it contains a comprehensive collection of Roman artefacts, including statues, jewellery and bronzes. It also includes a veteran car collection of

Montreux extends fingers of land into the waters of Lake Geneva

more than 40 vehicles dating from 1897. A short distance away, across the Route du Levant, is a late 1st-century Roman amphitheatre which once held up to 6,000 spectators.

The town has other, later historical treasures as well. Prominent among these is the Château de la Bâtiaz, an imposing, ruined medieval castle built in 1259 by the Bishops of Sion and a short while later occupied by Peter II of Savoy. It stands high over the town on a rocky bluff, and offers delightful views of the Martigny basin and its vineyards. Other buildings of interest include the 17th-century Nôtre-Dame de Compassion church, just below La Bâtiaz, and the Nôtre Dame des-Champs – another 17th-century church with a tall Gothic belfry. Any tour of the town should also include the 19th-century town hall in the delightful Place Centrale, an ambitious architectural enterprise in its time that is justly celebrated for its remarkable 54.8 sq m stained-glass window illustrating the Rhône and Dranse rivers.
Nearby Seven kilometres northwest, high in the remote Trient valley, is the old summer resort of Salvan from where an impressively engineered road leads by way of the small resort of Les Granges to the artifical lake of Salanfe. A road southwest of Salvan leads to the all-year resort of Les Marecottes, beautifully sited amidst pinewoods, and offering outstanding summer walking. Among its facilities is the 'Reno Ranch' Alpine zoo and a fine natural swimming pool. A chair-lift leads to La Creusaz, at an altitude of 1,780m .

MONTREUX
MAP REF: 110 A3

Calling itself 'The Pearl of the Swiss Riviera', Montreux, perhaps more than any other resort in Switzerland, provokes sharply differing reactions from its visitors. Once described dismissively as 'a pleasure resort with all the deserts of ennui and fatuity which that phrase must evoke', the town has an enviable geographical position stretching for 6km along the eastern bank of Lake Geneva. The town's critics say it has vandalised this lovely site with some violently ugly modern building projects. Not even its most stalwart champions could deny that, but there are compensations in the shape of some elegant 19th-century hotels along the quayside, and in nearby Territet, the famous Grand Hotel, built by Maillard in 1887, can fairly claim to be one of the great hotels of its era.

The town has, in the process of its undisciplined growth, developed a formidable reputation for its international festivals and as a conference centre. Perhaps the best known of its annual events is the television competition, held every spring, where the premier award is the coveted Golden Rose of Montreux. Montreux also hosts a series of international music festivals every year, and has become renowned as a centre for jazz *aficionados*. Among the many other facilities it offers visitors are a comprehensive range of water-related sports, delightful strolls along lakeside paths, and a world-famous casino.

Diligent explorers will find an attractive old quarter, tucked well

away from the tower blocks, at the end of the Rue du Marche. Here can be found the Museum of Old Montreux, housed in a former convent, and the church of St Vincent, which dates from 1509 with a slightly earlier tower. The terrace of the church offers fine views of the lake and the former village of Clarens (now a suburb) which gave Rousseau the inspiration to write *La Nouvelle Héloïse*. Worthwhile excursions from Montreux include the trip by rack railway to Les Rochers de Naye at 2,042m, offering stunning views of the whole of Lake Geneva, the Swiss Alps and the Jura. The small resort of Les Avants at 968m can be reached by a pretty, if at times punishingly steep, path through the wooded Chauderon Gorge. Other interesting resorts within a short drive of Montreux include Glion and Caux, both on the mountain-railway route to Les Rochers de Naye. There is limited skiing here in winter.

Nearby Three kilometres southeast of Montreux is the 13th-century

Beneath slopes of green pine trees and smooth white snow nestles the Goms valley village of Münster

Château de Chillon, often described as the most beautiful castle of its era in Europe. Erected on the foundations of a Roman fortress by those indefatigable builders, the Bishops of Sion, it then became the chief residence of the Dukes of Savoy, who had a habit of expropriating episcopal property. Strategically sited on a rocky islet on Lake Geneva and connected to the shore by a short bridge, it was immortalised in the famous poem *The Prisoner of Chillon* by Lord Byron. This was based on the six-year confinement of Francoise de Bonivard, four of them in chains – for imprudently attempting to introduce Protestantism to an exclusively Catholic region.

MÜNSTER
MAP REF: 110 C3

This is the principal village of the Goms valley, attractively located at

the foot of the rugged Minstigertal valley plunging steeply from the high Aargrat ridge on the Valais/Bernese Oberland border. The centre is split by the main valley road, which runs alongside the north bank of the Rhône. Münster is particularly notable for its fine 15th- and 16th-century blackwood chalets and traditional storehouses raised on stone mushroom-shaped staddle stones.

The parish church of St Mary, set just to the south of the main road, was founded in the 13th century and retains a Romanesque belfry from the same period. The chancel dates from 1491, and the main body of the church from the mid-17th century. The interior contains a number of interesting features, including an ornate, Gothic high altar of 1509, several more finely carved baroque altars, and a 17th-century font. The church presbytery is an early 16th-century building, substantially altered in 1745.

Above the village, on the western side of the Minstigertal, is the small chapel of St Anthony of Padua, built in 1680 and altered a century later. Just outside Münster, on the road east, is the chapel of St Peter dating from the same period as the main church, and altered in the 17th century.

Nearby Three kilometres west of Münster is the hamlet of Reckingen, also notable for its fine old farm buildings. For the ghoulish, there are some grim-looking skeletons in glass cases, garishly dressed in gem-encrusted robes, by the altar of the 18th-century baroque church of La Naissance de la Vierge.

CYCLE TOUR

Distance 36km: total climb 800m

From the church in the old quarter of Montreux, ride south through Territet on the lakeside road, past the Château de Chillon on the right towards the old town of Villeneuve. About a 0.5km before the centre there is a church on the left. Take the first left after this landmark, left again, then right and pass over the autoroute, following the signs for Col de Chaude. Take the second left, over La Tiniere River and begin a series of increasingly steep switchbacks, which continue for about 3km. Take the first road on the left, signposted Sonchaux and Caux. This continues to climb until the tiny hamlet of Sonchaux is

reached, after which it levels out and then descends into the village

of Caux. This is the halfway point and is an excellent place to rest awhile. Continue steeply down into Glion, where cyclists wishing to return to Montreux can take the shorter route straight through the village.

For those completing the tour, turn right at the village church following the signs for Les Avants. Continue through this beautifully sited resort, taking the mountain road left to the Sonloup Pass. This lies about 1km ahead, after a short climb, and offers marvellous views of the lake and the Savoy Alps. Just after the top station of the railway from Les Avants, turn left for Saumont and then continue down to Chamby. Cross the railway tracks here, and keep them to the left for the ride down to Chernex. Turn left in the village centre for the return to Montreux.

ROUGEMONT

MAP REF: 110 B3

On the site of a pre-Reformation Cluniac priory on the north bank of the Sarine River, this delightful little village lies just within the border of French-speaking Vaud. Characterised by an appealing cluster of old wooden chalets and barns, its fine 12th-century Romanesque church is the outstanding feature in an attractive village centre. The main aisle and transept lie beneath a vast sloping roof, and the stained-glass windows above the altar recall the 400 years (the 12th to 16th centuries) during which the entire Sarine valley was ruled by the Counts of Gruyères. Adjoining the church is a 16th-century château; it was badly damaged by fire in the 1970s, but has since been faithfully reconstructed. Rougemont has lately become popular with a small number of winter sports enthusiasts who prefer its quiet charm to the more raffish appeal of nearby Gstaad.
Nearby Just over the river is the station for the gondola lift to the summit of the 2,156m Videmanette, where skiers and walkers can descend to Gstaad or enjoy an attractive mountain panorama from the terrace of the restaurant. Close by to the east is the higher peak of Le Rubli, and it is also possible to see Les

Suuny conditions and fine slopes await the skier above Saas Fee

Diablerets to the south and the Jungfrau massif to the east. La Pierreuse Nature Reserve, accessible by foot in summer, lies to the southwest in the lee of the north face of the 2,458m Gummfluh.

SAAS FEE

MAP REF: 110 C2

Saas Fee vies with Zermatt for the most dramatic of mountain locations in the Valais. History, skiing terrain, facilities and the sheer visual power of their settings, has given them much in common. However, Saas-Fee does not care for comparisons, maintaining that it has a unique and distinctive identity of its own, and pointing to its growing international reputation as a year-round resort of more tranquil appeal. It calls itself the 'Pearl of the Alps' and, in topographical terms at least, that description is justified. It lies at the narrow end of a pear-shaped ring of mountains dominated by the 1,545m Dom – a peak even higher than the Matterhorn and the highest mountain completely within Swiss borders. The village is car-free and electric carts whirr past the lovely old log-cabins that line the sometimes steeply inclined streets.

Saas Fee has long had a celebrated reputation as a mountaineering centre and is the terminus of the famous 'Haute Route' for ski tourers, or hikers, travelling south from Verbier. These days it is also widely known as a sophisticated ski resort, offering excellent snow conditions and summer skiing on the huge Fee Glacier draped impressively down from the Mischabelhörner group. An extensive network of chair-lifts and cable-cars reach high into the mountains together with, since 1984, an underground funicular railway to the 3,500m Mittelallin, which Saas Fee claims to be the highest in the world. The village has a museum dedicated to its Alpine history and traditions, and a host of facilities geared to the requirements of an increasing number of visitors. These include an indoor swimming pool, ice rinks, toboggan runs, tennis courts, miniature golf and bowling alley.
Nearby Saas Fee has two satellite villages lower down the valley, Saas Almagell and Saas Grund. The latter might justly claim to be more than a satellite because of its self-contained, if substantially smaller, skiing area. However, it has little of its larger neighbour's charm and is often plagued by traffic. Back towards the town of Visp, and off the road up to Zermatt, is another small resort, the old town of Grächen. Set on a high, sunny shelf at the end of a precarious serpentine road, it enjoys a spectacular position. Much of the building is new and of little appeal, but submerged somewhere in its heart is the discernible legacy of a once-beautiful mountain village.

SAILLON

MAP REF: 110 B2

Built on a high rocky outcrop north of the Rhône, the old fortified town of Saillon preserves the medieval ruins of a castle once occupied by Peter II of Savoy. At that time, and until the late 15th century, the town had considerable strategic value and was one of the most important military strongholds in the Valais. The castle was destroyed in the late 15th century, but the 13th-century town walls and their great towers survive to this day, making an impressive silhouette against the snow-clad Grand Muveran behind. A huddle of buildings in the old town still shelter behind their rampart walls, with the mid-18th-century church of St Laurence and its Romanesque belltower standing out. Next to it is a 13th-century presbytery.

Nearby In the village of St-Pierre-de-Clages, 5km to the east, stands the splendid 12th-century Romanesque church of a former priory. Distinguished by its unusual octagonal tower, it is generally held to be one of the finest buildings of its style and period in the Valais.

ST-MAURICE

MAP REF: 110 A2

According to legend St-Maurice, commander of the Theban Legion, chose to die here with his troops rather than fight against fellow Christians in Gaul. A little more than a century later, in AD515, King Sigismund of Burgundy founded an abbey at the place of the warrior saint's martyrdom. The little town is now thought to be Switzerland's oldest Christian site, and it retains much of its religious heritage.

The predominantly baroque abbey church is a hybrid of architectural influences, with its fine belfry dating from the 11th century and stone spire from the 13th. Near by, excavations have revealed the foundations of the original abbey, and a network of labyrinthine catacombs lead to what is believed to be the tomb of the town's illustrious patron saint. Much restoration work has been carried out to the church over the years, not all of it entirely successful, but it remains none the less enormously significant in the Christian world. This is due in no small part to its Treasury, an extraordinarily comprehensive collection of early ecclesiastical artefacts, including a golden, 9th-

century jug of Byzantine origin once owned by Charlemagne, and the skull-reliquary of St Candidus. The abbey's stained-glass windows are a superb, but savage, rendering of martyrdom in impressively strong colours.

Dominated by Les Dents du Midi, the town of St-Maurice itself is picturesquely laid out with narrow old streets winding beneath sheer cliffs at its northern end. A 16th-century château houses the Valais Military Museum. Also of interest is the triple-aisled, 18th-century

A quiet autumnal moment for a square in St-Maurice

church of St Sigismund with its splendid baroque side altars, the 18th-century two-storey town hall, and the Haus de la Pierre with its three-storeyed arcade.

Nearby Just to the north of the town, via a footpath from the bridge over the Rhône, are the stalactitic caves of the Grotte aux Fees. Adjoining them is a restaurant with a fine view of the town.

MOUNTAIN WALK

Allow 3 hours

From the southern end of Saas Fee's main street, follow the path up to the Felskinn lift station and ascend by cable-car to the summit. Take the path leading left from the Felskinn top station, following the signs to Britanniahütte. Stay on the wide track traversing the Chessjen Glacier, passing beneath the Hint Allalin to the right and the great red, flat-topped pyramid of the 3,366m Egginer to the left. The track then climbs the saddle of the Egginerjoch, narrowing to a path and curving slightly right to the Britanniahütte. This was built in 1912 by British members of the Swiss Alpine Club, and it flies the

Union Jack next to the Swiss flag. It provides a superb vantage point for views of the Allalinhorn and Rimpfischhorn to the southwest and across the Mischabel range. From here take the path signed Plattjen down through the steep, broad expanses of the glacier past a small lake on the left. The descent becomes more gentle beneath the rock wall of the Egginer and Mittaghorn to the left, where the view right of the Saastal is quite stunning. At Plattjen there is a choice of descent by gondola lift, or following the easy zigzag path back down into Saas Fee. The latter (taking about an hour) starts behind the lift station, passes under the the top of the chair-lift and gondola, and doubles back at the bottom of the chair-lift for the start of the short switchbacks

down to Chalbermatten and the outskirts of the village.

SIERRE

MAP REF: 110 B2

Perched on a hill overlooking the Rhône valley, Sierre claims to be the sunniest town in the Valais. Foremost among its attractions is the ancient main street, the Rue du Bourg, with several fine 16th- and 17th-century buildings. Close to the station is the 17th-century town hall, sumptuously decorated with frescos, painted ceilings and stained glass. It was formerly an hotel and once the home of Rainer Maria Rilke, the Austrian poet who died in 1926. His former living quarters are now a museum, and in the cellar of the same building is another museum displaying tin and pewter artefacts dating from the 17th to 19th centuries. Further down the street is the imposing 16th-century Château des Vidomnes, distinguished by its huge tower and four corner turrets. Other notable buildings include the Maison de Chastonay, built in 1636 and notable for its elegant arched façade and projecting upper window, and the Château de Villa in the Rue de Manoir, built in the 16th century. On the southeast of the town, surrounded by vineyards, is the fine old 13th-century watchtower of Goubin. The catholic church of St Catherine in the Rue du Bourg dates from the mid-17th century, and is notable for its baroque chancel and lofted organ-housing. The town's other church, Our Lady of the Fens, dates from 1422, and has some well-preserved 16th-century frescos on its façade.
Nearby Sierre stands at the foot of the lovely Alpine valley of Anniviers, where there are several charming old villages. Offering splendid views of the Valais Alps from a height of 1,936m, Chandolin is one of the highest communities in the canton. Vissoie, further south, also occupies an attractive site. The village has a fine country church, founded in the 12th century and rebuilt in 1808 retaining a late 18th-century belfry.

SION

MAP REF: 110 B2

There was a settlement on the site of Sion, the capital of Valais, over 2,000 years ago. The town therefore has a strong sense of history, which grips visitors from their first glimpse of its distinctive twin crags, each crowned by a spectacular castle. On the more northern of the two are the ruins of Tourbillon, a 13th-century episcopal residence built for the

Bishop of Sion. On the lower hill, on the site of a Roman fort, stands the 12th- to 13th-century fortified church of Our Lady of Valeria, which claims to have the oldest working organ in the world dating from the 14th century. The church interior is a distinctive blend of Gothic and Romanesque, notable for its rich collection of Byzantine tapestries, a fine 15th-century marble statue of the Madonna on the high altar, and the intricately carved mid-17th-century choir stalls. The 12th-century carved capitals in the choir and the 15th-century frescos in the semi-circular apse are particularly splendid.

The fortified twin crags of Sion tower over the settlement that has grown beneath their protective vigil

Vineyards frame the small town of Sierre, basking in the late summer sunshine

There is a cantonal museum next door with various religious artefacts and some interesting examples of medieval furniture.

Below, in the town itself, the Gothic cathedral of Our Lady dates from the 15th century, although its Romanesque bell-tower is some three centuries older. Adjoining this is the elegant 16th-century church of St Théodule, built on the site of at least two earlier churches – the remains of which have been excavated and are now exhibited beneath the nave. On the Rue du Grand-Pont (so called because of the River Sionne which flows underneath it) stands the

town hall, dating from the mid-17th century, and notable for its elaborately carved doors and unusual astronomical clock. To its left the Rue des Châteaux leads up to the former episcopal residence, La Majorie, built in 1536 and now the Museum of Fine Arts. Opposite it to the right is the Archaeological Museum with a fine collection of Roman, Greek and Etruscan artefacts including glassware, jewelry, ceramics and statuettes.

In the lower town, on the south side of the Rue de Conthey and entered via an arcade, is the formidably ostentatious mansion of the Supersaxo family, built in 1505. The Renaissance ceiling in its main hall is another superb example of medieval woodcarving skill. There are two fine 18th-century mansions in the Rue de

height of 2,362m. In winter, this is a pleasant ski area best suited to intermediate standard. Other excursions include the steep 30km road north to the Col du Sanetsch at 2,243m with stunning views west towards the Tsanfleuron Glacier beneath the peaks of Les Diablerets; and an equally rewarding mountain drive north leading up the Triquent valley to the Forest of Derborence, now a nature reserve of considerable attraction.

VERBIER

MAP REF: 110 B2

Verbier is one of Switzerland's few purpose-built ski resorts, not that there appears to have been much method about its planning when it was conceived in 1950.

homes. The village is famous among ski-tourers as the start of the Haute Route, a high traverse across the Alps to Zermatt and, ultimately, Saas Fee.

VILLARS-SUR-OLLON

MAP REF: 110 A2

Situated in the heart of the Vaud Alps, Villars-sur-Ollon is a long-established, all-year resort. Attractively set at an altitude of 1,300m above the Rhône valley, it sprawls over a densely wooded basin at the foot of a crescent of peaks including the Croix de Chaux, Les Diablerets and the Grand Chamossaire. The latter is reached by mountain railway to Bretaye, and thence by chair-lift to a height of 2,120m. This is a marvellous vantage point for views

Shallow roofed with wide projecting eaves, the wooden chalet is designed to withstand the onslaughts of winter snows

Savièse, and a notable early 16th-century residence in the Avenue Ritz. The Rue du Collège preserves a number of elegant 16th- to 18th-century buildings as well.

Very little remains of the town's original fortified walls, but one notable survivor is the 12th-century, conical Tour des Sorcières at the foot of terraced vineyards on the northwest of the town in the Avenue Ritz.
Nearby Sixteen kilometres north of Sion via a winding mountain road is the modern sports resort of Anzère with magnificent views across the Rhône valley. A gondola lift ascends from the western perimeter of the village for an even more dramatic view from a

Magnificently sited on a broad, high, sunny plateau above the original village of the same name, the resort is a jumble of chalets of differing ages and no particular appeal. What it lacks in architectural merit, however, it makes up for in the unquestioned excellence of its skiing and walking terrain. The views of the Grand Combin and the Mont Blanc massif are an added compensation and are worth the visit alone. It is linked by mountain lifts to nine other villages, including Haute-Nendaz situated high on the steep southern wall of the Rhône valley, and the ancient and charming hamlet of Isérables. Verbier's central square is the hub of a complicated maze of one-way streets, heavily congested at the weekends when large numbers of the international community from Geneva flock here to their second

of the Bernese Alps, the Weisshorn, the Muverans, Mont Blanc and the glittering peaks of Les Dents du Midi. Lake Geneva is also visible in fine conditions.

The town is an agreeable mix of the old and new, with some delightful old chalets on its fringes. In summer the range of activities is extensive and includes a nine-hole golf course; in winter Villars is well known as a thriving ski resort.
Nearby The larger resort area includes the unremarkable satellite villages of Chesières and Arveyes. The road down to Bex (pronounced 'Bey') passes through the more attractive old village of Gryon perched on a terrace above the Avançon valley. Bex itself, about 6km down the valley, is an ancient spa town dating from 1544. Victor Hugo and Tolstoy were once regular visitors at the height of its fame.

VISP

MAP REF: 110 C2

An ancient settlement west of Brig, much abused by military aggressors during its turbulent history, Visp is today a busy road and rail junction serving the resorts of Zermatt and Saas-Fee from its position on the southern side of the lower Rhône valley. Parts of the medieval town survive in reasonably good order, and there are some fine examples of 16th- and 17th-century mansions once occupied by merchants enriched by the trade over the nearby Simplonpass. The remains of the town's former ramparts are still conspicuous. The older of the town's two Catholic churches, the Church of the Three Kings, is an imposing, white, baroque building dating back to the 11th century. It underwent major rebuilding in the early 18th century, but retains its fine Romanesque belfry. Adjacent to it is a well-preserved, 16th-century mercantile mansion.

Nearby Seven kilometres west is the equally ancient village of Raron on the northern bank of the Rhône, dominated from a rocky hill to the east by the austere, early 16th-century church of St Romanus. It is surrounded by the rampart walls of the former 13th-century seat of the Lords of Raron. Ten kilometres south, up a steep, narrow road through the highest vineyards in Europe, is the small village of Visperterminen. An unusual succession of 18th-century chapels line the 'Way of the Cross' from the village up to the 17th-century pilgrimage chapel of the Visitation in the heart of a forest.

ZERMATT

MAP REF: 110 B2

Zermatt is arguably the quintessence of all things Swiss. It has matchless scenery, beautiful Alpine architecture, a dramatic history, and a local economy by which all tourist centres might be measured. Perhaps best known as one of the world's most fashionable ski resorts, this reputation does a disservice to the varied activities that this most cosmopolitan of Alpine villages offers the traveller during the summer and autumn months. It is not cheap, but the very best of Switzerland rarely is; and as captivating mountain retreats go, Zermatt is hard to beat.

The town takes its name from the meadows (*matten* in German) that surround it. Until 1855 it had little significance other than as a predominantly agricultural

Hardy mountain goats are herded through the streets of Zermatt

community set in the shadow of one of the world's most spectacular mountains. The awe-inspiring pyramid of the Matterhorn (4,478m) dominates the village and is largely responsible for wrenching Zermatt out of its quiet pastoral seclusion and putting it close to the top of the superleague of international winter-sports resorts.

The mountain, known doggedly as Il Cervino by the Italians on its southern side, has acted as a lure to climbers the world over since the mid-19th century. With modern climbing techniques, the ascent is no longer considered to be particularly difficult and is made by more than 3,000 climbers every summer.

The focus of life in this car-free resort (cars must be left at the railway station in Tasch) is primarily centred on the main street – the Bahnhofstrasse – which runs from the station to the market square. This has earned a reputation as one of the most exclusive shopping streets in the Alps, and its elegant boutiques are attractively interspersed with flower-decked old chalets and 19th-century hotels. Just a few steps off this busy, colourful thoroughfare the visitor enters a different world of narrow alleys with typically blackened, Valais timber chalets, many raised on *mazots* (stone mushroom-shaped piles). It is up one of these alleys, by the Mont Cervin Hotel, to the west of the Bahnhofstrasse, that the famous English church is found. Built by the Alpine Club in 1871, this delightful old Victorian

A cloud-shrouded, but no less distinctive, Matterhorn

building is both a monument to the contribution of the English in the development of Zermatt as a resort – and a graveyard for many of the early English climbers who lost their lives on the surrounding mountains. Near by is undoubtedly the finest Alpine museum in the country, containing a fascinating collection of 19th-century mountaineering paraphernalia. This often macabre collection includes the actual rope that broke on the side of the Matterhorn, sending four members of the British-led team to their deaths in 1865. Other items of their personal effects are also exhibited.

Near to the top of the main street is the Monte Rosa Hotel, built by the celebrated hotelier, Alexander Seiler, in 1852, and the base 'camp' for thousands of 19th-century climbers. A bronze plaque commemorates Edward Whymper, who led the afore-mentioned ill-fated but successful ascent of the Matterhorn.

Arranged around the village square are a number of charming old village houses, including the home of the Taugwalders – the father and son who accompanied Whymper as mountain guides. Here also is the imposing Gemeindehaus (council house), and the delightful Marmot Fountain erected in 1902.

Most visitors to Zermatt come either to walk, climb or ski, and of the wide choice of uphill transport available the three most favoured

Monte Rosa, Europe's highest peak

routes are: the journey by rack railway to the 3,131m Gornergrat; the ascent by cable-car to the 3,820m Klein Matterhorn; and the funicular and cable-car to Sunegga and Unterrothorn. The views from all three vantage points are breath-taking (literally in the case of the Klein Matterhorn, the highest ski station in Europe, where the air is thin). For those who prefer to keep their feet on the ground, the two-hour stroll (including return) to the Gorner Gorges is a fine excursion. These impressive gorges, overlooked from a path cut into the rock, are reached from the south end of the village.

ZINAL
MAP REF: 110 B2

A tiny mountaineering and skiing resort at the head of the beautiful

valley of the same name, Zinal is 30km south of Sierre. The village is divided into three parts: a commercial section with shops, bars and restaurants; the main accommodation centre – a collection of largely unremarkable chalets; and the carefully preserved original mountain village at the end. The latter is an authentic gem. Jealously protected by Les Amis du Vieux Zinal, it comprises some marvellous old wooden chalets, raised several feet off the ground on stilts in the typically Valaisanne style. On several of the buildings are carvings of the traditional Valais sport, 'combat de reines', otherwise known as cow fighting (cow against cow).

There are many delightful walks around the village, the most popular of the easy ascents being the 2,581m Roc de la Vache, the 3,124m Frilihorn and – simpler still – the 2,896m Corne de Sorebois, which can be done by gondola for all but the last 450m. From the summit it is a gentle and pretty descent back to the edge of the village.

Nearby Nine kilometres north down the Zinal valley is the charming village of Grimentz. Superbly preserved, the little resort stretches along a narrow street bordered by timber and stone chalets and typically Valaisanne cowsheds and storehouses. The oldest building dates from 1550.

ZINAL

33

MOUNTAIN WALK

Allow 3 hours

Take the funicular, east of Zermatt's main steet, to the station at Riffelalp. From here take the cliff path east towards the Findelgletscher, signposted Grüensee (the 'green lake'). This is a pleasant, level walk through woods of larch and pine trees. After about 1km there is a fork. Continue to the right along the upper path which begins to climb gradually towards the lake. Pass the restaurant and skirt the northern bank of the lake (which is popular with swimmers). The trail carries on, over a couple of streams, to a point where it merges with a lower path which leads over another stream by the side of a tiny lake on the right. Continue ahead to the delightful and relatively unfrequented Grindjisee, concealed in a fold between the mountain side and the glacial moraine. There is a

waterfall above the lake, feeding a sparkling mountain brook which flows gently into it. This is a fine picnic spot, with impressive views of the Matterhorn to the southwest and the Findelgletscher rolling down the flank of the Stockhorn to the east. The path continues around the lake, then after about 1km past the milky-coloured lake of Mosjesee on the left. It then descends to Findeln, a pretty hamlet of old wooden barns

and houses. From here, follow the signs for Winkelmatten descending on broad switchbacks through woods until the tracks of the cog railway. Cross these, and follow the path round to the left through the centre of Winkelmatten where there is a tiny white church and a small square. The path then descends to the bottom of the Furri gondola where it joins the road back into Zermatt.

·TICINO·

rustici – rural dwellings characterised by stone blocks laid without mortar. Their distinctive exterior stairways and stone-slab roofs determine the character of many mountain villages and outlying chalets in the north of the canton. Elsewhere the domestic architecture is more diverse and elaborate, comprising a mixture of styles. In the wooden block houses, found mainly in the Bedretto and Blenio valleys, the influence is demonstrably that of northern Switzerland. However, Italian influences predominate in the Lower Ticino where the houses are stuccoed and white-washed, with roofs of rounded terracotta tiles.

In botanical terms, the Ticino is arguably the most interesting region of the Swiss Alps, not only for the variety of its exotic flora, but also for the unique co-existence of Alpine and Mediterranean species. Borne south by rivers and mountain streams, many Alpine plants have found their way to the foothills bordering the lakes, and give rise to the curious sight of Alpine columbines and dwarf willows growing side by side with camellias and azaleas. On the sweeping terraces of the Ticino foothills stretching from the

Shaped like an inverted triangle, with its base abutting the broad spine of the main Alpine chain, this 'Italian' corner of Switzerland represents 7 per cent of the country's territory and accommodates just over 4 per cent of its population. Administratively, politically and geographically it is part of the Swiss Confederation, but even the most chauvinistic of Swiss nationals would concede that, culturally, it is defiantly Italian.

The predominantly mountainous canton, stretching from the southern flanks of the St Gotthard massif in the north to the Lombardy plain in the south, offers an extraordinary variety of scenery. From the imposing massifs of the Alpi Lepontine (Lepontine Alps) in the Upper Ticino, great valleys spread southwards like the fingers of an outstretched hand, their rivers discharging an icy flow into the clear blue waters of Lake Maggiore. In the south of the canton, lower mountains are furrowed by shallower valleys dipping down into Lake Lugano, and further south still in the Mendrisiotto, low mountains and rolling hills form the last creases of a verdant landscape before flattening out into the vast plains of Lombardy. The canton is therefore divided into a high Alpine region, the central section of the lakes, and the southern end of the triangle which is often referred to as the 'Tuscany' of Switzerland because of its undulating green hills and picturesque farmhouses.

Lying amid glaciers and eternal snow, the Upper Ticino is a land of granite and gneiss, indestructible building materials used by local craftsmen for centuries in the construction of

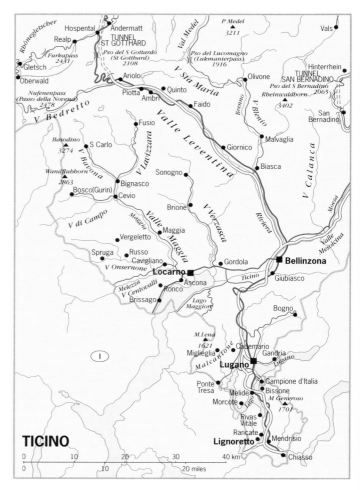

Mendrisiotto to the Leventina, the vine, the sweet chestnut and the walnut flourish in large numbers. In the higher valleys marmots and mountain hares proliferate; occasionally stone-martens can be spotted and, even more occasionally, an eagle circling high among the peaks. Colourful insects are also a feature of life in the canton, and include the resilient small tortoiseshell - one of the few species of butterfly that seems to thrive in the cold.

Climatically, the Ticino is also unique. Lying in the lee of the Alpine chain, it is seldom swept by strong winds. The temperature is remarkably constant, with an average of 12°C, rarely dipping below 0˙C or rising above 30˙C. However, it is the hours of sunshine that most distinguishes the canton from other regions within the Swiss Alps. The city of Locarno, the sunniest in Switzerland, has nearly 60 per cent of the possible maximum number of hours enjoying sunshine.

The history of the Ticino is interwoven with that of Lombardy, of which it was a part until the 14th century. At that time the early Swiss Confederation resolved to consolidate possession of the St Gotthard Pass, thereby signalling the start of a period of bloody conflict with their southern neighbours who were understandably reluctant to relinquish ownership of the south-lying approaches to the vital trade route. By 1512 the Swiss had won the entire region from the famous old Pass to the present Italian frontier. Thereafter the Ticino became a dominion of the Swiss cantons until the Napoleonic campaign, after which it became a free canton in its own right. It was not until 1882 however, with the opening of the St Gotthard railway tunnel, that the new canton was able to take full economic advantage of membership of the Confederation. Until then it had been completely cut off from its northern neighbours during the winter months.

The canton has achieved economic growth with mixed success, relying largely on the explosive increase in tourism in recent years and a solid industrial and manufacturing base, but with income from agriculture dwindling to just over 2 per cent.

However, it is less for its manufactured products, and more for its exquisite scenery, spectacular natural environments and beautiful cities that the majority of visitors to the Ticino are drawn. Chief among its

attractions is the lakeside city of Lugano. The old quarter with its ancient Lombardian buildings, narrow alleyways and cobbled streets is traditional in style, yet the city offers the widest range of cultural and entertainment facilities in southern Switzerland - as well as being one of the most important financial centres in the country. In the nearby suburbs of Monte Brè and Castagnola, the views of the city and its lake are splendid, but the wider environs yield even more seductive attractions, ranging from the picturesque and ancient old fishing villages of Gandria and Morcote to the sprawling mountain village network of the Malcantone district in the hinterland. To the south lies the town of Mendrisio, home of the celebrated Easter processions dating from the late 16th century. The Mendrisiotto countryside, on the threshold of the great Lombard plain, offers a distinct change of architecture and landscape and it is from this district that many of Europe's most accomplished stonemasons, stucco-workers and builders came.

On the banks of Lake Maggiore lies the charming old city of Locarno, a worthy rival to Lugano. While the spring camellias are blossoming on the lakefront promenades, skiers are plunging down the slopes of Cardada immediately above the town. The road on the lake's west shore leads to Ascona, a beautifully preserved ancient fishing village that has become the cultural corner of the Ticino. Beyond is the small resort of Brissago, close to the Italian frontier, with its two sub-tropical garden islands, which are an essential stop on any cruise of the

Castello di Montebello, Bellinzona

lake. On the opposite shore lie the villages and hamlets of the Gambarogno district perched on their mountain slopes, and between it and Locarno is the rich farmland around Magadino flanking the north bank of the Maggiore. The estuary of the River Ticino at this point, known as the *Bolle*, forms a protected and unspoilt wilderness.

The other major city of the Ticino is the canton capital, Bellinzona. This ancient fortified city lies at the southern end of the Riviera, the main Ticino valley, and together with the Valle Leventina (ending near the St Gotthard Pass) and the Valle Blenio (reaching up towards the Lukmanier Pass) - both of which meet at the old town of Biasca - this is the kernel of the ethnic and historical territory of this southern part of Switzerland.

Markedly different in character are the Valle Verzasca and Valle Maggia leading down to Locarno. Wilder and more remote, these divide into several higher and smaller valleys which are among the most dramatic in the Swiss Alps. The Onsernone and Centovalli (literally, 'a hundred valleys') complete this Alpine picture, and any exploration of these valleys will reveal isolated mountain hamlets, practically untouched by time. Ancient bridges, medieval churches, mountain grottos and *rustici*, set in a precipitous and wonderful landscape of snow-clad peaks, shimmering mountain lakes, thundering waterfalls and Alpine pastures, combine to make the Ticino one of the most beautiful regions in the world.

AIROLO

MAP REF: 111 D3

Still an all year resort of some importance, the town suffered almost total destruction by fire in 1877. Shortly after rebuilding, it was almost destroyed again by a massive landslip from the Sasso Rosso – a perpetual menace at the time, now largely obviated by a series of solid embankments. Its most distinctive building is an old church, with a Romanesque belfry, that survived the natural disasters of the last century. In the Gotthardbahn station is a moving memorial to the 277 men who died in the construction of the railway tunnel between 1872 and 1882. Today Airolo is a modest, unremarkable little town elevated from the ordinary by the beauty of its scenery and its convenience as a base for excursions. It also lies at the meeting point of the dramatic Nufenen and St Gotthard passes. Just south of the town a cable-car mounts to the 2,065m Sasso della Boggia with fine views northwest.

ASCONA

MAP REF: 111 D2

Separated from Locarno by the tributary of the Maggia, the enchanting little town of Ascona has managed to preserve its own distinctive identity, notwithstanding the proximity of its larger neighbour – only 4km to the east. The labyrinthine network of shaded alleys in the heart of the old village repays extensive exploration.

High on the list of attractions is the splendid Collegio Pontificio Papio on the street of the same name, founded in the 16th century and arranged around an elegant cloistered courtyard. The church of St Mary of Mercy, built in the late 14th century, forms part of the same building and is renowned for its ancient frescos. The church of St Peter and Paul, built 1530, is another fine old church located nearer the waterfront. For an example of a marvellous 17th-century baroque façade visitors need look no further than the tourist office in the Casa Serodine leading down to the lake. Close by, actually on the waterfront, the cerise-coloured, arcaded town hall has an equally impressive Renaissance façade. Cafés and shops line the palm-fringed lakeside where the clear blue waters of Lake Maggiore offer a variety of watersports, including windsurfing, sailing, waterskiing and, for the less energetic, gentle peddling on some ancient and

colourful pedallos (complete with chrome 'headlights'). Other facilities include riding, golf, ice skating and a generous selection of delightful walks.

BELLINZONA

MAP REF: 111 D2

In the middle of a fertile plain, surrounded by verdant hills and spectacular snowy peaks, and standing at the meeting place of major trade routes, Bellinzona had enormous strategic importance throughout the Middle Ages. The capital of the canton of Ticino, it is now a modern industrial city with an impressive cultural heritage. Chief among its inheritance of architectural riches is the triumvirate of medieval castles dominating the old town. Of these the centrally positioned Castello Grande, memorably illuminated at night, is the most imposing. Built in 1445 by the Duke of Milan on a rocky mound, its massive fortified walls are visible from any point in the city.

The Castello di Montebello, built

about 1300, is typical of the great fortress citadels built by the Lombardians. Extensively restored in 1903, it now houses the Museum of History and Archaeology, and is reached via a stepped alleyway that climbs up beside the great church of St Peter and St Stephen founded 1517.

The Castello di Sasso Corbaro is charmingly located among chestnut groves a short distance southeast of the old town.

Reached via the tortuously winding Via Sasso, it offers impressive views and – among other interesting features – contains the Museum of Folk Art.

Any tour of the city should also include a stroll along the Piazza Collegiata with its delightful baroque façades, and through the old quarter to the traditionally arcaded Piazza Nosetto.

BIASCA

MAP REF: 111 D2

A pleasant little town, much like nearby Bellinzona in its physical setting, Biasca stands in a narrow basin at the fork of the Valle Leventina and Val Blenio. Mountains rise spectacularly on all sides and the 12th-century church of St Peter and St Paul, cut into the southwestern flank of the 2,329m Pizzo Bagno, is one of the most impressively sited churches in the Ticino. Built in the Romanesque style, it has a tall campanile and contains fascinating frescos dating from the 13th century. The town

Castel Grande; one of three castles protecting Bellinzona

itself is the hub of the region's quarrying industry, well-known for its coarse-grained granite (from which the church is constructed). Biasca is an industrially orientated town, and although much of its building is modern, it none the less retains a special appeal, helped in part by a good selection of excellent Ticinese restaurants.

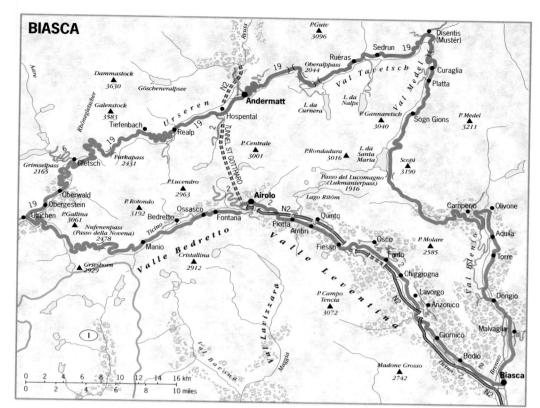

MOTOR TOUR

The tour, approximately 208km, includes the four mountain passes of Lukmanier, Oberalp, Furka and Nufenen. Passing through the cantons of Ticino, Graubunden, Uri, and Valais, it also includes the spectacular Ticino valleys of Blenio, Bedretto and Leventina.

From Biasca take the valley road north up the beautiful Val Blenio and the rocky Valle Santa Maria to the Passo del Lucomagno (Lukmanier Pass). This is a delightful drive of 42km through a series of villages, including the main valley centre of Olivone.

Lukmanier Pass
This is the lowest of the Swiss trans-Alpine passes. Flanked to the west by the 3,016m Piz Rondadura, and to the east by the 3,190m dark face of the Scopi, the Pass was one of the busiest through routes during the medieval period. Otto I is recorded as having made the the crossing in 965, and Barbarossa crossed it twice in 1164 and 1186.

The road now skirts the eastern side of the Santa Maria reservoir, formed by the construction of a dam in 1967, and follows a desolate Alpine valley until it crosses the clear waters of the Cristallina descending from the wild valley of the same name

leading down from the right. Here the steeply descending road enters the central basin of the Val Medel with its gently sloping pastures.

Val Medel and the Medelserschluct
Two churches are worth noting in the Medel villages of Platta and Curaglia. In the former the baroque church of St Martin, built in 1774, incorporates part of an earlier building including some ancient paintings. The pretty little resort of Curaglia has a church dating from 1672 which incorporates a late Gothic altar and a domed belfry. Also worth noting is an old farmhouse with a painted façade dating from 1510. Beneath the village the road enters the Medel Gorges, a romantic wooded defile with a series of impressive waterfalls.

At the monastic town of Disentis/Muster turn left on Route 19 towards the Oberalppass. After 8.5km the small resort of Sedrun is reached.

Sedrun
The chief village of the fertile Val Tavetsch, Sedrun is a winter sports resort of limited size lying at the foot of the Val Strem. Behind it to the north rises the 3,328m Oberalpstock. The church of St Vigilius is a baroque building of 1691 with a Romanesque belfry, and in the south chapel is a late Gothic winged altar dating from 1515.

The road now climbs in a series of zigzags to the Oberalppass. Descending into Andermatt, the road enters another series of wide curves before straightening out and rising again through Realp to the Furkapass. Descending steeply once more, past the spectacular Rhône Glacier on the right, it reaches the high-lying town of Gletsch. Continue west on Route 19 to Oberwald, passing the Rhônefälle on the left, and enter the Goms valley. At the village of Ulrichen, 5km beyond Oberwalden, turn left for the Nufenenpass.

Nufenenpass (Passo della Novena)
One of the highest of Swiss mountain passes at 2,478m, the Nufenenpass is also the newest – opened to traffic as recently as 1969. Lying between the 3,061m Piz Gallina to the north and the 2,929m Grieshorn to the south, it commands fine views of the Bernese and Valais Alps. To the west of the Grieshorn is the famous old Griespass, a former 'wine' route between Switzerland and Italy which lies immediately south.

The road now descends down the attractively wooded Valle Bedretto to the Ticino town of Airolo. Turn south following the old road through the scenic Valle Leventina, threading a series of old villages, including Quinto, Faido and Giornico before regaining Biasca.

LOCARNO
MAP REF: 111 D2

Even its most ardent admirers would be hard-pressed to find a sufficient range of superlatives to describe this beautiful city. Its tranquil lakeside setting, ringed by snow-capped mountains, is as delightful as any in the Alps. However, what really sets Locarno apart is its air of lazy charm, complemented by the soft pastel colours of the splendid Lombardian façades of its ancient buildings. This is close to where Switzerland meets Italy, and the influences of both cultures add up to an agreeable blend of Swiss refinement and Italian flair. Arguably the most romantic of the country's cities, it enjoys a subtropical climate and more hours of sunshine than anywhere else in Switzerland. This explains its rich variety of plants and the prodigious growth-rate of the twisting vines set in orderly terraces on the slopes of Cardada that form its backdrop. Tracing its history from the late 12th century, the city gained international prominence in 1925 when the Locarno Pact was signed by world statesmen in a vain attempt to prevent a second world war. Today it is the venue for a famous international film festival held every August, and it has become a popular rendezvous for music lovers, who flock to its music festival held from May to July.

BRISSAGO
MAP REF: 111 D2

The lakeside resort of Brissago, a stone's throw from the southwestern frontier with Italy, is unremarkable in itself with austere modern blocks contrasting unhappily with some fine old Lombardian villas. The village is the lowest spot in Switzerland at 196m above sea level, and the impressive pre-Alpine background goes some way to compensate for the less than imaginative use of a beautiful location. There is, however, a fine old 16th-century church, protected from the worst excesses of modern architecture by some tall cypresses. The best of the residential villas, situated high above the busy main road cutting through the resort, overlook the two tiny, subtropical Islands of Brissago a few hundred metres offshore. These make a fascinating excursion, and boats from Locarno and Ascona call regularly to visit their botanical gardens, home of over 1,000 exotic species.
Nearby The fine village of Ronco, high above the little port of the same name, has a charming Romanesque church. Erich Maria Remarque, author of *All Quiet on the Western Front*, is buried here.

GANDRIA
MAP REF: 111 D2

The unusual little village of Gandria is a few minutes drive from the eastern border with Italy, on the northern shore of the dark waters of Lago di Lugano (Lake Lugano). Barely signposted, it is easy to miss it and find oneself doing a conspicuous U-turn at the Dogana (customs post). Like many of the best-preserved lakeside villages in the Ticino, the centre is closed to motor vehicles and the car park is situated some way up a narrow lane below the main road. Motorists might be forgiven, therefore, for supposing that

visitors are not welcome to this quaint old smuggling haunt. In fact the reverse is true. It is just that most of them, like the 19th-century smugglers before them, prefer to come by boat, 30 minutes from Lugano. From the wharf the village rises in uneven tiers of colourful, arcaded houses and cafés, with Mount Brè brooding in the background. In the centre of its narrow, flower-decked streets is a charming baroque church, which, in the context of its surroundings, is much-favoured as a subject for paintings and photographs.
Nearby Across the lake, on the southern shore at Cantine di Gandria, is a fascinating smuggling museum that contains various devices relating to the once-flourishing, illicit cross-border trade between Switzerland and Italy. The museum is housed in a former customs office.

Gandria on Lake Lugano

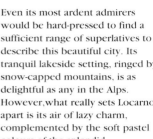

TOWN WALK

Allow 2 hours

*Start from the arcaded Piazza
Grande with its fine Lombardian
houses painted in various shades
of pistachio, mustard and
Wedgwood blue, and walk down
the palm-fringed Via della Pace
to Piazza Giovanni. Here there is
a splendid fountain surrounded
by sculpted mermen blowing
conches, and smiling mermaids
prising open the jaws of sea-
serpents. Continue south and
walk diagonally through the
shady avenue of trees in the
Bosco Isolino. Emerging on the
shores of Lago Maggiore, cross
the road and turn left up the
lakeside promenade.*

**Piazza Grande, Locarno; a meeting
point for townsfolk**

1 Lago Maggiore (Lake Maggiore)
Only about one fifth of this
enchanting lake is within Swiss
borders, but it is fed largely by the
Maggia, Verzasca and Ticino rivers
flowing down the Ticino valleys of
southern Switzerland. Its placid
surface is ideal for a variety of
watersports and leisurely cruises
by steamer, but chief among its
numerous attractions are the
scenic walks along its flower-lined
promenades. This northwestern
shore of Locarno's pretty bay
offers a pleasant gladed walk
through hanging willows and
lakeside gardens containing a
riotous profusion of magnolias,
camellias and hydrangeas.

*Continue northwards past the
Debarcadero landing-stage to the
funicular station for Madonna
del Sasso. Trains leave every 15*

minutes on the quarter-hour. The
journey through the dense foliage
of the gorge to the church takes
about 6 minutes. At the terminus,
walkers have a choice of
extending their journey by cable-
car to the Alpe di Cardada, and
thence by chair-lift to the Cimetta
at an altitude of 1,672m. This
diversion is strongly
recommended if time permits; the
panoramas from both view
points are magnificent, and it is
possible to walk back down
marked paths from Cardada to
Madonna del Sasso in about an
hour.*

2 Madonna Del Sasso
This famous 17th-century pilgrim
church, precariously perched on a
rocky spur above Locarno, offers
marvellous views of the city and
the mountains behind Lake
Maggiore from its terrace. Inside
are some fine examples of Gothic
carvings, the 1520 painting by
Bramantino, *Flight to Egypt* and an
intriguing full-scale figurative
depiction of the Last Supper by
Francesco Silva (*c.*1650).

*Continue walking down the
gorge, on to a brick road that
leads to the Contrada Cappuccini.
Turn right along Contrada
Borghese until a small cobbled
square is reached. Turn left in
front of the 17th-century church
of St Anthony down the narrow
Via San Antonio and then sharp
right into Via San Francesco. At
the 14th-century Church of St
Francis (which hosts the city's
music festival) turn left into Via
Ripacanova to Castello Visconti.*

Madonna del Sasso, Locarno

3 Castello Visconti
This 15th-century castle is the
major historical landmark of the
city. Built by the Visconti family,
and later occupied by the military
governors of the region, it is a
fortress-palace in the grand style.
There is a charming inner
courtyard, and its ancient halls
now house the Archaeological
Museum, which has a fine
collection of Roman artefacts.

*Continue up the Via Rusca back
into the Piazza Grande.*

Nearby A side trip for walkers
might include the historic church
of St Victor, in Muralto, about a 20-
minute walk from the Piazza
Grande, past the funicular station
and then east along the Via San
Gotthardo. This 12th-century
church, in the Romanesque style,
is the most impressive in Locarno.
On its tower is a 15th-century
relief of the eponymous saint by
the sculptor, Benzoni.

·LUGANO·

Although not the capital of the Ticino canton, Lugano (map ref: 111 D2) is the largest of its cities and unquestionably the most famous. It is also arguably the most beautiful, striking a happy balance between old and new and providing every conceivable amenity for the visitor at limited cost to its ancient fabric. Because of its enviable geographical configuration, curving gracefully around the shimmering waters of Lake Lugano and surrounded by snow-capped mountains on all sides, it has been called the 'Rio de Janeiro of the Old Continent'. Any qualitative comparison of that nature is unnecessary.

This is a city of rare qualities, although if comparisons have to be made then a likening to its more northern Swiss counterpart of Lucerne might be nearer the mark. In common with that equally delightful lakeside town, Lugano has a rich medieval inheritance, a sophisticated tourism infrastructure, marvellous lake and mountain viewss, two great rocky pyramids on either side, and a seemingly infinite choice of activities. More than that – it has an agreeable subtropical climate which accounts for the profusion of palm trees and exotic plants throughout its twisting streets and lakeside promenades.

Not surprisingly, the local tourist authority has taken to calling it the 'Garden City'. Its parks and gardens are among the finest in Switzerland, and any exploration of the old quarter might well start from the Parco Civico, which abuts the Cassarate, flowing gently into the lake. Within its extensive and shady confines, the park has a museum, library and Congress Palace, and during the summer it holds daily open-air concerts.

From this point, it is a short walk west along the lakeside and then north through the Piazza A

Manzoni into the heart of the old town, the Piazza Riforma – a popular meeting place for Lugano's café-society. Behind this typically arcaded square is a maze of narrow, cobbled streets that lead westwards to a funicular which takes pedestrians up to the railway station.

Beyond the funicular, and reached via the steps of the Via Cattedrale, is the Cathedral of St Lawrence. The baroque interior includes some well-preserved murals dating from the 13th century.The building's impressive façade, erected in 1517, has an unusual arrangement of three elaborately decorated Renaissance

doorways. By way of contrast, the church of St Mary of the Angels at the far end of Via Nassa has an unusually plain exterior. It is all the more surprising, therefore, that lying behind it are two of the finest frescos of the Lombardy Renaissance period. Painted by Bernardino Luini in the early 16th century, they depict the Virgin Mary and child with St John and – perhaps more memorably – his most famous work, the enormous *Passion and the Crucifixion*, which faces visitors as they enter.

Beyond the church, on the lakeside road to Paradiso, is the Belvedere Garden, much smaller than the Parco Civico, but a jewel of its type with a magnificent view and hundreds of palms, olive trees, lilac bushes, camellias, roses and oleander arranged around 12 modern sculptures commissioned by the city.

On the other side of the Parco Civico, a 20-minute walk or short tramride east along the road to Castagnola, is part of one of the world's great private art collections housed in the Villa Favorita.

Nearby At 912m, the tree-shrouded Monte San Salvatore rises majestically to the south of the city. It offers a magnificent panorama of the city, the lake and surrounding mountains. To the north, in the far distance, the Bernese Alps can also be seen. The summit is reached via funicular from the suburb of Paradiso, and there is a restaurant and café for those who want to linger and enjoy the view. For walkers there are marked paths back to Lugano.
For Children In the village of Melide, 5km south of Lugano, there is a fascinating 1:25 scale model of the different areas and features of Switzerland. Called 'Swissminiatur' and spread over 1 hectare of landscaped gardens, it accurately represents the great buildings and landscapes of the country.

Lugano and its lake from Monte Bré

MOTOR TOUR

Approximately 240km long, this tour requires an early start, although it can be shortened by an hour or so by heading immediately north from Lugano on the N2 autostrada to Bellinzona. Climbing the impressive mountain passes of San Bernardino and Splügen, it threads through some charming valleys in the Graubunden, Ticino and in neighbouring Italy, and skirts the great lakes of Como and Lugano. Do not forget passports.

From the centre of Lugano follow the lakefront road south through the suburb of Paradiso.

San Salvatore
A cable-car leads in 10 minutes from Paradiso to the 912m peak of Monte San Salvatore, which lies ahead to the right of the road. The summit offers one of the finest mountain panoramas in the southern Swiss Alps.

Continue south, under the N2 autostrada, turning off the main road just before the causeway into Melide. Follow the peninsula road round to Morcote, and from there turn north through Figino, joining the old Varese-Bellinzona road at Agno. Take the north road to Bellinzona, winding back and forth over the autostrada up to the scenic Passo Monte Ceneri. Continue to Bellinzona 13km ahead, pass through the centre and join the N13 autostrada, signed Passo del San Bernardino, at Arbedo-Castione just north of the city. From here it is a 54km drive north through the Mesolcina valley to San Bernardino. Leave the autostrada here and take the twisting road up to the San Bernardino Pass.

San Bernardino Pass
Lying at a height of 2,065m the pass was probably used as early as the Bronze Age. It owes its name to San Bernardino of Siena, who is said to have preached in the vicinity in the 15th century. Immediately to the east is the sharp peak of Pizzo Uccello (the 'Bird' mountain at an altitude of 2,724m). To the west there are stunning views of the Adula range.

Continue down from the pass, rejoining the N13 autostrada east to Splugen through the Hinterrhein valley. Exit after 10km for the village

Splugen
An ancient village, Splügen is a popular all-year resort with a

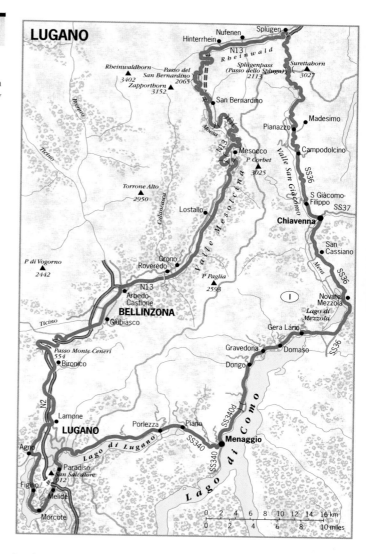

handsome collection of houses set on south-facing terraces. The tall 'Schorsch-Albertini' houses are particularly striking with their white façades and upper port-hole windows. The baroque church was built in 1687.

Take the mountain road south to the Splugenpass , climbing in a series of zig-zags to the summit of the pass at 2,113m . This point marks the Italian-Swiss border. Drive south for a further 30km down the rugged Valle San Giacomo to Chiavenna,

Chiavenna
Once part of the canton of Graubunden, the town became part of Italy in 1797. Known by the Romans as *Clavenna* (*clavis* means 'key'), because of its strategic location at the junction of the Splugen and Maloja passes, it is delightfully situated in the Mera valley.

Continue south on the S36, skirting the eastern bank of the Lago di Mezzola until you reach the S340D on the right signed Sorico and Gravedona.

Gravedona
An attractive town on the north bank of Lake Como, Gravedona has two ancient churches, St Vincent and the 12th-century St Mary. On the north side of the main street is the late 16th-century Palazzo Gallio with its distinctive corner turrets. The small town of Dongo, 3.5km ahead, was the scene of Benito Mussolini's capture by partisans, shortly before his execution in April 1945.

Follow the west bank of the lake, through Menaggio. Turn right here for Porlezza, ahead of which lies the Swiss frontier. After a further 9km, drive along Lake Lugano's northern bank.

Lake Lugano
Lying mainly within Swiss territory, the lake (also known as the Ceresio) has an area of 49 sq km with a maximum depth of 270m. It is one of the finest of the Swiss lakes, distinguished by its dark placid waters.

From the border it is a 7km drive back into Lugano.

MALCANTONE

MAP REF: 111 D2

This is a rugged, beautiful and heavily wooded district with chestnut and other deciduous trees intermingling with ubiquitous conifers. Northwest of Lugano, it is famed for its pretty, unspoiled villages – many of which are set in ascending terraces on the southern flanks of Monte Lema. Connected by a labyrinth of winding country lanes each has its own attractions, but Cademario is as good a starting point as any. From Cademario there are excellent views of the lake and the Ticino Alps, and the added bonus of the charming 12th-century church of San Ambrogio. Inside the church are some interesting murals painted between the 13th and 15th centuries.

There is another fine church in the village of Miglieglia, a few miles further west. Built in the 15th century, Santo Stefano Al Colle contains some equally impressive late Gothic frescos. Miglieglia is also the station for the chair-lift up to the summit of Monte Lema at 1,621m. From the restaurant at the top station it is a 10-minute climb up a steep path to the highest viewing point. From here there is a marvellous view of the surrounding countryside and the distant Alps. Monte Lema is also a popular, if limited, skiing area during the winter season.

MENDRÍSIO

MAP REF: 111 D1

The town lies at the hub of a network of attractive little villages in the southernmost part of the Ticino. The district, known as the

A distinct Italian influence pervades Morcote's architecture

Mendrísiotto, feels more Italian than Swiss, with a strong Lombardian inheritance and a reputation for producing some of the finest wines in the country. This is, therefore, a predominantly rural area, although Mendrisio-Borgo, to give it its full title, is hardly the sleepy backwater one might expect.

Just over 5.5km north of the heavily industrialised frontier town of Chiasso, it is a charming, lively place celebrated for its festivals and processions. Over the Easter period the streets are richly decorated with flowers and banners, and a series of colourful depictions of the main events leading up to the Crucifixion take place – complete with the main protagonists in full historical costume. The torchlight procession on Good Friday is a particularly arresting sight. The main church of St Cosima and St Damian is one of the town's most imposing buildings, but there are several earlier structures including the stately, 16th-century Palazzo Torriani-Fontana and the Palazzo Pollini (1720) which both repay investigation.

Nearby Of the many intriguing villages in the area that deserve exploration, Rancate and Lignoretto stand out. Both within a few minutes drive west, the former has a prized collection of 17th- to 19th-century paintings by Ticino artists. Lignoretto has the Vincenzo Vela Museum in the former home of this renowned sculptor, whose work enhances

Terracotta pantiled roofs hint at Mendrísio's proximity to Italy

many major European cities. Another rewarding excursion is up the Valle di Muggio to the tiny village that gives it its name.

Four kilometres north of Mendrísio is the unique village of Riva San Vitale. It owes its distinction to two interesting historical factors. First, it has the oldest surviving ecclesiastical building in the Ticino, the 5th-century baptistery south of the main square. Second, it made a unilateral declaration of independence in 1798. Its unusual status, prompted by objections over newly drawn boundaries, lasted just two weeks before the authorities sent in the army to teach the locals a salutary lesson in political reality.

MONTE GENEROSO

MAP REF: 111 D1

Reached from Lugano via the pleasant village of Bissone, on the southern shore of Lake Lugano, Monte Generoso offers one of the great Alpine panoramas. A perfect vantage point for views over the Lombardy plain, the Italian and Swiss lakes, and the distant Bernese and Valais Alps, it is reached after a 40-minute journey by cogwheel railway from the small village of Capolago opposite Riva San Vitale. At 1,701m, it is the highest mountain in the region, and it is famed for its rich variety of flora. Beneath the crest, on its southwestern flank, is a beautiful Alpine garden in the small hamlet of Bella Vista – also reached by road 7.5km northeast of Mendrísio. There are magnificent views from

Morcote on the shore of Lugano

here as well.

Nearby Bissone is worth lingering in, not least for the attractions of its gracefully arcaded centre. It is also the birthplace of Giovanni Tencalla, the 17th-century architect who spent most of his adult life in Vienna before returning to Bissone to die. The Tencalla mansion, a private house but open to the public in the afternoon, is one of the finest examples of late Renaissance building in the region.

Campione d'Italia, a small village located across the lake from Lugano and beneath Monte Genoroso, is an unusual anachronism in the intricate matrix of the Swiss Confederation. Territorially a part of Italy from the 8th to the 19th centuries, no one is quite sure to which country it now belongs. Although the

The summit of Monte Generoso

currency and administration are Swiss, the people pay Italian taxes and the village is still technically a part of Italy. Its famous casino takes full advantage of the blurred borderline, by attracting gamblers who prefer the more relaxed Italian attitude to gambling laws.

MORCOTE

MAP REF: 111 D1

Attractively sited on the tip of the Lugano peninsula, this is unquestionably the most picturesque of the many lakeside villages in the area known as the Ceresio. Palms, promenades, cypresses, ornate streetlamps and gloriously arcaded private villas create a colourful mosaic in this former fishing village – now an exclusive artists' colony. The predominant flavour of the splendidly preserved buildings is terracotta, both in colour and decoration. A short climb up narrow cobbled alleys leads to Morcote's principal landmark, the 14th-century church of the Madonna of the Rock with its tall, distinctive campanile. Inside, there are some fine 16th-century frescos and an impressive 17th-century organ.

Nearby Parco Scherrer is another delightful example of the many beautiful landscaped gardens in and around Lugano. Located just outside Morcote, it contains a rich variety of subtropical trees and plants, and some splendid classical buildings. Four kilometres north of the village is the small and equally exclusive resort of Figino, notable for its extravagant villas overlooking the left arm of Lake Lugano into Italy.

•TICINO VALLEYS•

The Ticino is renowned for its many beautiful valleys, ranking in scenic attraction with the most rewarding elements of the Swiss landscape. The following are among the most notable.

VAL BLENIO
MAP REF: 111 D2

Plunging dramatically from the Valle Santa Maria beneath the Lukmanierpass to the town of Biasca at its foot, Val Blenio is one of the most scenically rewarding of all Swiss valleys. At regular intervals along its twisting path are some of the most enchanting mountain villages in Switzerland. Too numerous to describe in any detail, it suffices to observe that they are characterised by their sunny, open setting and their diminutive size. Few seem to comprise more than 30 or 40 buildings. The exception is Malvaglia with a population of over 1,000, situated in the lower reaches of the valley. In the middle of a number of ancient houses is a Romanesque church with a tall, 12th-century belltower. Halfway up the Val Blenio is a collection of tiny villages on a terrace west of the main valley road. The church of St Ambrose in Prugiasco is worth noting, and left of it up a 2km-long mountain path is the 11th-century Romanesque chapel of St Charles of Negrentino, containing wall paintings from the 12th century. Back on the valley floor, Lottigna has a museum devoted to the area's history and contains a particularly fine collection of armaments dating from the 14th century. The other village of note is Olivone, right at the head of the valley and famous for its views of the nearby Sosto peak, beneath which it shelters.

The tiny village of Rossura

VALLE LEVENTINA
MAP REF: 111 D2

Running southeast from the Ticino end of the St Gotthard Pass to Biasca, the Valle Leventina has the largest 'vertical drop' of any traversible valley in Europe – a total of some 974m. It is surprisingly unaffected by the N2 *autobahn*, which follows its path. Far from blighting the surrounding area, the fast road has proved to be something of a boon in relieving the old valley highway of its former congestion. The result is that many of the towns and villages along the valley floor have been able to recapture something of their erstwhile tranquillity. The most appealing stretch of the valley lies between the villages of Quinto and Giornico. Three-and-a-half kilometres south of the former, the old road weaves through the Stalvedro Gorge – the site of a brave defence in 1799 by a retreating French force against a much larger Russian army. There are ruined fortifications near the road, some of Lombardian origin dating from the 8th century. The next village is Rodi, after which there is a considerable drop in the valley floor before the charming old town of Faido. This is the major resort of the Valle Leventina, a delightful spot characterised by some well-preserved, 16th-century wooden houses and a view of three spectacular waterfalls cascading into the Ticino River. Here the scenery softens, helped in part by the presence of chestnut forests and vineyards. Eleven kilometres further south is the village of Giornico, bisected by the river and linked by a quaint old arched bridge. The 12th-century Romanesque church of St Nicholas on the western bank is generally held to be one of the finest of its type in the Ticino. Higher up the hill, above the railway, is the small 12th-century chapel of St Mary of the Castle. Both churches contain fine 15th-century frescos.

VALLE MAGGIA
MAP REF: 111 D2

Climbing northwards from Locarno, the Valle Maggia is famous for its *rusticis* – former peasant dwellings two or three centuries old, now let to visitors who seek a taste of the simple life. However, there was nothing simple about the lives of the original occupants – constantly at risk from the unpredictable, swollen torrents crashing down the mountainsides above them.

Today these are contained and regulated by hydro-electric plants installed actually within the mountains. The abundant waterfalls streaking the precipices of the lower reaches remain, but they no longer pose the danger they once did.

The first village of any size is Maggia, halfway up the valley, and distinguished by the ancient church of Santa Maria della Grazie (St Mary of Grace) which preserves some fine 16th-century frescos. Cevio – historically the administrative centre of the valley and the seat of the former Milanese governors – is 6.5km further north. Among its elegant collection of old buildings is the chapel of the Madonna of the Bridges, built in 1615, and some surprisingly grand patrician residences. Cevio is also the point of access to a network of enchanting valleys fanning out in all directions. The road west leads up the spectacular Valle di Campo, and north of that the Valle di Bosco/Gurin, 2,863m. Wandfluhhorn Pizzo Biela is the highest in the Ticino at 1,505m. An added distinction is the fact that its inhabitants speak the Germanic dialect of their ancestors who migrated from the eastern Valais in the 14th century.

Immediately to the north of Cevio is the delightful Bignasco, and here the Maggia splits into another two valleys – the Val Bavona and the Val Lavizzara. The former is a densely wooded gorge of considerable beauty leading to the remote hamlet of San Carlo lying beneath the 3,274m peak of Basódino and its impressive glacier. A chair-lift leads up to a cluster of jewel-like mountain lakes. The Val Lavizzara has two

The small Ticino village of Vogorno, just north of Locarno

subsidiary valleys of its own, the wild and rugged Val di Prato leading east, and the Val di Peccia with its succession of pretty little villages leading west.

VALLE ONSERNONE
MAP REF: 111 D2

Running north and west of the Valle Centovalli (the 'hundred valleys'), itself an area of considerable beauty, the Valle Onsernone is entered from the village of Cavigliano 7km out of Locarno. Smaller than many of the neighbouring Ticino valleys, it follows a serpentine course up through the charming villages of Loco, Russo and Crana. It ends at Spruga, where a bridlepath leads over the mountainous frontier into Italy. The valley is one of the most fascinating in the canton, characterised by overhanging precipices and plunging ravines. It is still the centre of a traditional

straw-weaving industry. The side valley of Val di Vergeletto, another winding climb north of Russo up to the small resort of Vergeletto, is equally spectacular.

VAL VERZASCA
MAP REF: 111 D2

This is the most remote of the larger Ticino valleys – a veritable wilderness of dramatic defiles, river gorges and breathtaking Alpine scenery. It runs 25km north of Gordola on Locarno's eastern perimeter, and ends after a steep and beautiful climb to the mountain village of Sonogno. Two-thirds of the way up, at the river fork, is the principal village of the valley – Brione. Here there is a delightful little church, dating from the 13th century and containing some rather unusual 14th-century frescos. In the village square is a small fortress that has undergone conversion to house a restaurant.

Vogorno, in the Val Verzasca

·GRAUBÜNDEN·

Graubünden (also known by its French name of 'Grisons') is the largest of Switzerland's cantons, and shares over two-thirds of its borders with Austria to the east, Italy to the south and Liechtenstein to the north. It is also the most sparsely populated, with only 24 inhabitants per square kilometre, compared to a Swiss average of 150. Almost exclusively Alpine in character, the canton is the only one in the country that completely straddles the Alps.

The Grisons Alps extend from the Oberalppass on the canton border with Uri in central Switzerland, to the Rätikon range in the northeast, down to the Alpi Bernina (Bernina Massif) in the south, which forms a natural border with Italy. This latter range includes the highest peak in the region – the 4,049m Piz Bernina. Lying within Graubünden's borders are the Adula, Silvretta and Albula ranges, but all the mountains of the region tend to be collectively known as the Graubünden Alps, or the Grisons. Crisscrossed by 150 valleys, they fit no easily definable pattern and are described thus for simplicity's sake.

The intricate network of valleys is a welcome feature of the Graubünden scenery. The longest and most beautiful is the Engadine, which stretches for over 100km from the source of the River En (or 'Inn') near the Maloja Pass, via St Moritz, to Martina on the Austrian border. It is divided both administratively and geographically at the Zernez gorge into the Upper and Lower Engadine. The former, the highest valley in central Europe with a mean elevation of about 1,800m, is starkly impressive – bordered by the Bernina massif and its glaciers to the south – with sweeping forests of pine and larch, a rich variety of Alpine flora, and a chain of some of the loveliest lakes in the country. Along the Lower Engadine is a string of unspoilt villages cluttered with ancient houses decorated with distinctive exterior motifs known as *sgraffito*, a form of plaster-etching. Guarda, Zuoz, Sent and the intriguingly named S-chanf are among the pearls of this lower section of the valley. Bordered on its northern side by the Silvretta group of mountains, the valley also marks the northern perimeter of the huge Swiss National Park, justly famous for its rugged scenery. Other spectacular valleys include the Mesolcina, the Poschiavo, the Plessur, the Bregaglia and the lovely Müstair.

Whereas the name 'Graubünden' may be unfamiliar to those who have never visited this southeastern part of the Swiss Alps, the leading international resorts of St Moritz, Davos, Klosters, Arosa and Flims may be more familiar. These are the great showpieces of the canton's thriving winter sports industry. St

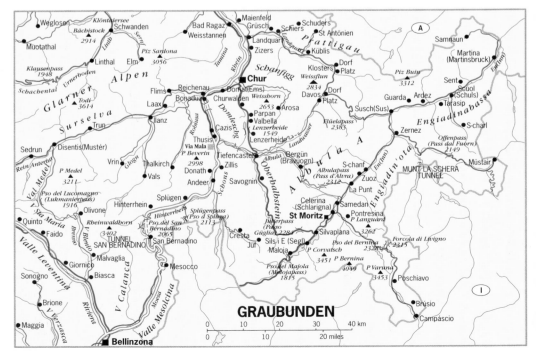

GRAUBUNDEN

Moritz is one of the most fashionable (and expensive) resorts in the world, set above a delightful lake in stunning scenery. Its range of summer and winter sporting facilities are second to none. Unpretentious Davos is the natural mecca for serious skiers who seek challenge on the famous Parsenn snow fields. Its linked resort of Klosters, smaller and more exclusive, is famous for its appeal to reclusive royals and their wealthy retainers. The isolated Arosa, almost completely cut off at the end of the dramatic Plessur valley by a circle of high mountains, best suits relaxed skiers and those who prefer not to ski at all. Flims and nearby Laax is a long-established resort with a vast interconnected ski area which appeals to the rich and not so rich, expert and novice alike.

pastures, vineyards and – particularly in the south – chestnut groves. Six-hundred-and-fifty mountain lakes reflect glittering images of silver-flecked glaciers, snow-capped peaks rising to over 4,000m, and sprawling forests of beech and pine reaching a higher timber line than anywhere else in the Alps. For every sophisticated winter resort there are 100 charming rustic villages, and for every sumptuous 5 star hotel there are countless more simple gasthofs, farmhouses or high altitude mountain cabins in which to put up for the night. And for those who seek more tangible reminders of the region's illustrious past, the lovely medieval city of Chur – the oldest recorded settlement in Switzerland – offers not only a splendid collection of 14th- to 18th-century

mythology records that when God was busy delivering languages around the world, his angel-couriers overlooked the early inhabitants of present-day Graubünden. When the mistake was discovered it was thought best to rectify it by dropping a selection of leftovers on the hapless mountain dwellers who responded to the resulting confusion by communicating mostly in eloquent silence. This perhaps explains the characteristic taciturnity of the people of Graubünden.

The earliest signs of civilisation in the region can be traced back to about 600BC when it was settled by people thought to be of Celtic origin, called the Rhaeti. In 15BC the Romans created the province of Rhaeti, of which the present canton formed the southern part. This was subsequently granted to the bishops of Chur, who faced mounting opposition from their disaffected subjects. The first sign of rebellion came with the founding of the *Gotteshausbund* (the League of the House of God) in 1367. This was followed in 1395 by the creation of the *Grauerbund* (Grey League), so-called because of the homespun grey cloth worn by the men of the region, and which subsequently gave its name to the canton. In 1436 a third league was formed: the *Zehngerichtbund* (the League of the Ten Jurisdictions). With one common goal – the removal of episcopal authority – the three leagues united in 1471 and their objective was partly achieved in 1496 when they allied with the newly born Swiss Confederation. By 1526 the last traces of the bishops' power had dissolved, but it was not until 1803 that the region formally entered the Swiss Confederation as its 18th canton.

History of a different kind was made in 1889 when the Rhaetian railway was inaugurated. Over its 375km of track the railway crosses 485 bridges and passes through 116 tunnels, an incidence of such structures unequalled anywhere else in the world.

For travellers who prefer to explore this mountainous region by car, the choice of motoring tours is considerable. With three of the country's great Alpine passes – the Julier, the Splügen and the Bernina – and with other lower but no less dramatic mountain routes, the motorist will be hard-pressed to cover them all. If the prospect of some of the highest roads in Europe fails to appeal, a drive down the Engadine valley will prove magical.

In a part of Switzerland where over half of the inhabitants earn their livings from the tourism industry, the Graubünden has made determined efforts to encourage visitors to think of it as a summer as well as a winter destination. These have worked with conspicuous success throughout the region, which attracts an ever-increasing number of summer tourists happy to take advantage of its summer skiing, windsurfing, sailing, tennis, riding, golf, skating, hiking, bike-riding and white-water rafting.

However, the region is by no means overrun by its international playgrounds. In fact, of all the Swiss regions, it is probably true to say that the southeast is the place where travellers can most easily find peace and seclusion. Against strong opposition, the Graubünden offers some of the most beautiful countryside in the country, rich in mountain

Summer sunshine in Davos

architectural masterpieces, but also three excellent museums devoted to fine arts, natural history, and Rhaetian culture and ethnology.

The outstanding feature of the Graubünden, however, may arguably have less to do with its magnificent scenery and wide range of facilities, than with its extraordinary mix of tongues. This is a modern Babel where the 168,000 strong population have three different languages – one of which is fragmented into five impenetrable dialects. Sixty per cent of the 'Bundner' speak German, 22 per cent Romansch divided into the five dialects of Sursilvan, Sutsilvan, Surmiran, Puter and Vallader), 14 per cent Italian, and the remaining 4 per cent probably a mixture of all three with some French thrown in for good measure. Local

AROSA

MAP REF: 111 E3

Situated at the end of a winding 30km cul-de-sac, and magnificently set in pine forests at the head of the Plessur valley, Arosa is one of the most remote of Swiss high-altitude all-year resorts. There was a monastic settlement here as early as 1220, but it was not until the late 19th century that the town first attracted international attention as one of Switzerland's leading health resorts. In Inner-Arosa, the older and higher part of the village, many of the traditional wooden chalets still retain their delicate fretwork and elaborate inscriptions, and there is an interesting example of a late Gothic mountain church. The lower village section of Obersee is a cluster of undistinguished grey buildings by the lakeside. The ski area, nearly all above the tree line, is divided into two sections – below the peaks of Weisshorn and Hörnli. The former is reached by a two-stage cablecar via the sunny plateau of Tschuggen, and a splendid panorama opens up from the summit at nearly 2,650m. This is the location for Arosa's most testing skiing. The gentle runs are found at Hörnli.

The resort is also famous as a ski-tourer's mecca. It was here that Sir Arthur Conan Doyle first arrived in 1894, after what for a novice skier must have been a gruelling journey over the mountains from Davos – about 10km east as the crow flies.

Arosa is also a paradise for walkers and cross-country skiers. There are three outdoor skating rinks, tennis and squash courts, horseback riding, a nine-hole winter golf course, a bowling alley and – unusually for such a secluded spot, a casino. The town's Schanflugg museum has a collection devoted to iron mining and winter sports.

CHUR

MAP REF: 111 E3

The capital of the canton of Graubünden, Chur is a small city of considerable historical and cultural significance. Claiming to be Switzerland's oldest population centre, it traces its history to the earliest signs of human habitation between 3000 and 2500BC. However, it was during the Roman period that the settlement of what was then known as Curia Rhaetorum laid the foundations for the medieval town that has survived.

The town is clustered around the Martinplatz, just north of the River Plessur, with the 15th-century church of St Martin on its eastern perimeter. Behind this is the ancient Kirchgasse, which leads to the Rätisches Museum, a fine 17th-century mansion containing a fascinating collection of prehistoric artefacts and later

The health resort of Arosa

cantonal antiquities. Above this is the Bischöflicher Hof, a complex of fortified buildings and episcopal residences surrounding a courtyard and reached via the Torturm, an old gate tower. On the northern side of this group is the Bishop's Palace, an early 18th-century, baroque reconstruction of a much earlier palace – parts of which are incorporated in the present structure.

The whole is dominated by the cathedral, a 12th-century, late-Romanesque building with some Gothic features and a domed tower added in about 1600. Built on the site of an older church, it is thought also to cover the remains of a Roman temple. The interior has a late 15th-century, carved high altar and four notable, early 13th-century statues of apostles at the entrance to the crypt. The treasury contains Carolingian reliquaries and charters dating from the 8th century. Behind the cathedral is the part 12th-century church of St Luzius, preserving an 8th-century Carolingian crypt.

The old town has many other interesting buildings, narrow cobble-stoned alleys, squares and courtyards, and richly rewards closer investigation. Of particular interest are the 15th-century Rathaus in the Postgrasse, just north of Martinplatz, and the 16th- to 17th-century patrician residences in the Reichsgasse which runs parallel. On the northeast corner of the Postplatz is

Chur Cathedral

the Kunstmuseum, housed in a late 19th-century villa and containing works by 18th- to 20th-century artists.

A short distance west of the Martinplatz are two interesting relics of the city's original fortifications, the Obertor and the Pulverturm (powder tower).

DAVOS

MAP REF: 111 E3

Comprising the two villages of Davos Dorf and Davos Platz, and with no discernible centre, the town sprawls for more than 4km along a flat valley basin flanked by impressive peaks. Settled by German immigrants from the Valais in the 13th century, Davos remained a quiet agricultural community until the mid-19th century, when it began to gain world renown as a health resort. To this day, it still has some of the most exclusive sanatoria in Switzerland. But it is best known as one of the world's leading ski resorts, providing access to the famous snowfields of Parsenn between it and the linked resort of Klosters.

Like so many of the traditional Swiss ski resorts, Davos was first patronised by the indefatigable British ski pioneers of the late 19th and early 20th centuries. It was quick to capitalise on the interest in recreational skiing by indulging its new visitors with the world's first skilift, a primitive arrangement of rope and a few spare motorcycle parts. Things have advanced somewhat since then. The skiing is divided into five areas, offering more than 320km of pistes. The focal point is the Parsenn area reached from the 2,693m Weissfluh via funicular from Davos Dorf. This is linked to Schatzalp/Strela above Davos Platz. On the other side of the valley, the Rinerhorn and the gloriously sunny Pischa all offer marvellous skiing.

The town of Davos is not an architectural gem, but some of the old hotels, many of them former sanatoria, are in the grand Victorian style. In Davos Dorf there is an early 16th-century Gothic church, and in Platz an earlier church with a fine tower dating from 1481. The Rathaus was built in 1564 but has since been much altered.

With Switzerland's largest natural ice-rink, plus a vast sports centre, Davos is a popular destination for fitness enthusiasts. There are also three museums: one illustrating the history of mining in the region, another tracing the development of winter sports, and the third containing the largest collection of original works by Ernst Ludwig Kirchner, the German Expressionist.

DAVOS WALK

Allow 3 hours

Take the two-stage funicular from Davos Dorf to the Weissfluhjoch, and exit from the rear of the top station. Make a short, steep descent to the foot of the Weissfluh. Turn right, following the signs to the Parsennhütte and keeping the Schifer gondola overhead to the right hand side. After a short distance there are a couple of paths dropping down to the tiny lake under the Totalphorn on the right. Ignore these and continue ahead for about another 15 minutes. Just past the Schwarzhorn there is a fork in the path, signposted Schifer to the left and Parsennhütte to the right. Take the latter and make the brief ascent under the gondola to the

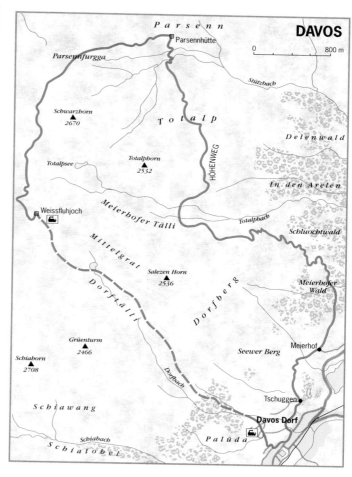

top of a short draglift on the Parsennfurgga. Here there is a steep but scenic descent to the Parsennhütte and the adjacent lift station. This is a pleasant place to stop for refreshments, with its large south-facing terrace offering sweeping views of the Jakobshorn and Rinerhorn on the other side of the valley.

The famous Parsenn snowfields are a short stroll behind the restaurant, but the route back to Davos is via the panoramic Höhenweg which involves going through the small tunnel directly in front of the Parsennhütte, and taking the left path. This winds briefly past a drag lift on the right, and then climbs gently beneath the Totalphorn. The views down into Davos are dramatic. The path then crosses another draglift and offers a choice of routes, either to the Höhenweg station or down a steep and very pretty descent through woods into Meierhof above the lake. From there it is about a 15-minute walk back to the starting point.

DISENTIS/MUSTER

MAP REF: 111 D3

The capital of the Surselva region on the western fringes of the Graubünden, Disentis preserves its Romansch translation 'Mustér' as a suffix. The town looks down from its mountain terrace on the meeting point of the two rivers flowing down from the Lukmanier and Oberalp passes. Because this is also where the two great historic routes converge, over the centuries Disentis has played unwilling host to a succession of retreating and advancing armies – and not always to its advantage. The town grew up beneath a Benedictine abbey, founded in the 8th century but repeatedly destroyed by foreign aggressors. The present abbey buildings, on the original site, date from the 17th century and the intrinsic church of St Martin is a robust and imposing baroque structure (1695–1712) which resisted the best French efforts to level it in 1799. Flanked by two distinctive onion-domed towers, it contains a 15th-century altar and some fine period details. In the late 19th century, Disentis enjoyed a considerable reputation as a health resort, famed for its 'radioactive' waters. Today it is a small ski resort, not widely known as such outside Switzerland.

Nearby The handsome village of Trun, 11km to the east, is famous for being the place where the canton of Graubünden was founded in 1424. Members of the 'Grey League' (Graues Brund) swore their oaths here, and the occasion is commemorated by a series of paintings in the early 18th-century baroque chapel of St Anna opposite the railway station. The village church of St Martin was built in the mid-17th century.

THE ENGADINE VALLEY

MAP REF: 111 F3

One of Switzerland's most

The Engadine valley

beautiful and unspoilt valleys, the Engadine stretches for nearly 100km from the Malojapass to the eastern border with Austria. It takes its name from the River En (or 'Inn'), which flows ultimately into the Danube. The Engadine valley is the main tourist region of this part of Switzerland and is arguably better known to visitors than the canton of Graubünden, which it traverses. Certainly, many of its inhabitants think of themselves as people of the Engadine in preference to any other generic description, and much of the architecture, cuisine and culture is similarly distinguished. In the majority of the small and ancient villages along its course, the principal language is Romansch.

It is divided into the Upper and

Lower Engadine, with the boundary marked by a point just west of the village of Zernez. The valley floor of the Upper Engadine rarely drops below 1,500m above sea level, and because much of it is almost level, a chain of delightful lakes have been formed by the En and other mountain brooks between Zuoz and Maloja. The highest part of the valley, west of St Moritz, is perhaps the most beautiful. The mountains on each side are all well over 3,000m , with the Piz Bernina rising to over 4,049m. The treeline is higher in the Engadine than anywhere else in the Alps, with the result that the larch and stone-pine forests climb high up the mountainsides, providing a fascinating contrast with the silver-streaked glaciers descending them in frozen motion.

The Lower Engadine may be the poorer for lakes, but it suffers no lack of dramatic mountain scenery. Moreover, it has a rich catalogue of marvellous old villages along its route, each preserving some fine examples of typically Engadine architecture. Between the charming Susch, at the bottom of the Flüelapass, and the frontier village of Martina are some of the most attractive little hamlets in eastern Switzerland. Guarda is particularly appealing, with an enchanting collection of

The village of Maloja at the Austrian end of the Engadine valley

peasant dwellings elaborately decorated with 'sgraffiti' – a form of wall etching. Many of the houses also have colourful coats of arms hanging above their front doorways. Ardez is another perfectly preserved village, with the unusual distinction of imported Venetian ironwork gracing some of its fine, 16th-century buildings. All these settlements are set back from the main valley road, against a magnificent Alpine backdrop.

FLIMS

MAP REF: 111 E3

Flims' history goes back much further than its development as a leading all-year resort. It was first mentioned in a document scripted by the Bishop of Chur in the 8th century, when he formally conveyed it to the abbey at Disentis. In the Middle Ages, the people of Flims regained self-government, and thereafter the village grew in importance and played a vital part in the violent struggles of the Graubünden.

The ruins of the medieval castle of Belmont are still visible on the rocky heights above the little hamlet of Fidaz, about 1.5km east of Flims Dorf. Later, Napoleon's soldiers recuperated in Flims' meadows after the bloody Battle of Reichenau.

One of Switzerland's most popular and fashionable ski resorts, Flims is part of the extensive 'White Arena' skiing region linked to the two attractive old farming villages of Laax and Falera. The people still speak the local Romansch dialect, apparently indifferent to the colourful mix of tongues brought by the international skiing set. Situated on a wooded sun terrace high above the Rhine valley, Flims is a sprawling village divided into two distinct sections about 1km apart – Flims Dorf and Flims Waldhaus. Dorf is the older of the two, but strangely the less appealing as its busy main road detracts from the undoubted merit of some of its traditional buildings. Waldhaus, on the other hand, is a handsome cluster of elegant hotels attractively set in conifer trees, close to three pretty lakes.

The resort enjoyed modest fame in the late 19th century as a spa, attracting a number of illustrious guests including members of the Dutch royal family. It really took off, however, after World War II, when Europe's first chair-lift was

Flims Dorf, the old residential half of the world famous ski resort

installed between the village and Foppa, about 320m above it. Because of the scarcity of iron it was constructed entirely from wood. In 1956 the 2,675m peak of Cassons Grat was connected by cablecar from Naraus, and Flims' reputation as one of the country's leading ski resorts was assured.

Today it offers excellent, varied

The Benedictine abbey founded by St Sigisbert, in Disentis/Muster

skiing, including some gentle runs on the Vorab Glacier above the Crap Masegn. It is also a popular summer resort, with mountain-lake swimming in the Caumasee, forest footpaths and horesback riding in splendid scenery.

KLOSTERS

MAP REF: 111 F3

The small town of Klosters owes its exclusive image largely to the patronage of some of the younger members of the British royal family. In common with so many old-established Swiss resorts, it is divided into two distinct parts, Dorf and Platz, the latter (also known as Zentrum) being where the rich and famous congregate. At first glance, it is difficult to see why the resort has become quite so voguish. Straggling along a narrow wooded valley under the dark and brooding Gotschna, it is no prettier than many similar-sized Alpine ski villages, and in mid-winter it receives very little sunshine. Added to that, it has a hazardous main street, which tends to impoverish its cluster of quaint old chalets.

However, what Klosters has that other resorts do not, is access to some of the best skiing in the world on the wide, white snow-fields of Parsenn above it reached by two-stage cable-car from the railway station to the 2,283m Gotschnagrat. The infamous and awesomely steep 'Wang' ski run leads back to the mid station at Gotschnaboden. It was on this slope in 1988 that an avalanche killed one skier and seriously injured another in the company of Prince Charles.

The neighbouring super-resort of Davos shares Klosters' fine skiing,

Lenzerheide

Exclusive Klosters

but it has little of Klosters' intimacy and undoubted charm. There is a second ski area, Madrisa, reached by gondola from Dorf.

The village takes its name from the cloisters of a 13th-century monastery, which has long since disappeared. Its 16th-century church in the centre of Platz is one of the few buildings of any historical significance, retaining some fine wall paintings dating from the same period. There is a museum in another fine old 16th-century structure on the northern side of the Monbielstrasse. Although best known as a ski resort, Klosters has many

advantages as a summer destination. Not least of these is its delightful Alpine walks through woods, meadows and alongside sparkling mountain brooks. Among many other sporting facilities, it also has a large, heated, outdoor swimming pool on the Doggilochstrasse.

LENZERHEIDE

MAP REF: 111 E3

Lenzerheide is a middle-ranking winter and summer resort on the high mountain road between Chur and St Moritz. It shares a linked skiing region with the adjoining resort of Valbella, surrounded by some stunning scenery but providing little in the way of

variety or challenge for keen skiers. The two villages are connected by the busy main highway skirting the charming little lake of Igl Lai, surrounded by woods and a marvellous mountain panorama. This latter feature is Lenzerheide's principal attraction and a trip by the two-stage chair-lift up to the 2,322m peak of Piz Scalottas is a recommended excursion. There is a pleasant refuge on the summit, which offers dramatic views of the Aroser Rothorn standing at 2,865m to the east. The lower peak of Rothorn is also accessible, by cable-car, and there are equally impressive views from the top station.

The village centre is busy and colourful, but generally featureless and lacking much in the way of architectural merit. Valbella is quieter, but little more than a collection of luxurious hotels and apartments.

Nearby The old village of Churwalden lies 7km to the north. Its 15th-century church stands on the site of a 9th-century monastery, and contains an impressive carved altarpiece dating from 1477. The village has its own small ski area.

PONTRESINA

MAP REF: 111 F2

A sedate and charming resort, close to St Moritz but far enough removed in style and character to

keep the traditionalists happy, Pontresina is attractively positioned off the main road up to the Bernina Pass amidst stone pines and larches. It is an important mountaineering centre in its own right, but it tends to attract skiers as well as climbers who prefer its tranquil appeal to the buzz and glitter of its famous neighbour.

It has many excellent examples of Engadine architecture along its narrow streets, and some of the elegant Edwardian hotels would not look out of place in the most prestigious of the world's resorts. The church of St Mary is its most distinctive building. Next to a curious 12th-century tower, called

for no easily discernible reason 'La Spaniola', it has a 12th-century tower of its own. The building dates mostly from the 15th century, although some of the murals pre-date that period. On the west wall are paintings of the Epiphany, Baptism of Christ and the Last Supper which date from 1230. The life of Christ is depicted from the south wall to the north.

Nearby Close to the main road beneath the village at Punt Muragl is a funicular station leading to the 2,450m peak of Muottas Muragl. The summit provides a superb view of the Engadine valley and the Bernina massif, and there is an excellent restaurant and small skiing area.

CYCLE TOUR

Distance: 18km – bikes are rentable in the village of Klosters Platz.

From the centre of Klosters Platz ride north on the main road to the centre of Klosters Dorf. At the crossroads turn left, over the railway tracks, taking the narrow lane to Bad Serneus. In a short while, the lane becomes a path running along the left bank of a stream. Ignore the first bridge on the right, and cross instead the wider Landquart river at the next bridge, still following the path to Serneus.

After another kilometre the Landquart is recrossed and the small hamlet of Walki lies directly ahead. Turn left here, following the road into the larger village of Serneus. Continue through the centre, following the signs to Schifer and remaining on the paved track. This is a winding, attractive, albeit increasingly steep

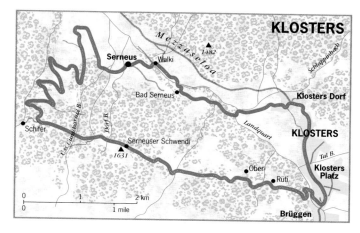

route through trees on a good surface.

After about a 5km climb of 500m, a turning off to the left leads to the Schifer gondola station and restaurant. There is, however, another restaurant just over a kilometre ahead, crossing a succession of mountain brooks, and through a slight dip in the terrain. This is in Serneuser Schwendi, the highest point of the

ride at 1,631m, and affording splendid views of the Gotschnagrat and Casanna immediately south and the Madrisa range to the north. From here take the main path which is all downhill to Klosters Platz. Turn left at the railway tracks, down through Ruti, left at the paved track at the bottom, then right over the Lanquart back into the centre of Platz.

POSCHIAVO

MAP REF: 111 F2

The most southerly town of any significance in the Graubünden, Poschiavo lies 13km below the Bernina Pass. In view of its proximity to the Italian border (virtually surrounding it) it is perhaps hardly surprising that the town is predominantly Italian in character. It has little in common with any of the communities in the Engadine on the other side of the mountain pass but there are many buildings of merit, albeit in a sharply contrasting architectural style. The late Gothic church of St Victor in the main square dates from 1497, although the tower is much older. The building is distinctly Lombardian in style with a fine main portal. On the southern perimeter of the town is an intriguing Spanish Quarter, built in the early 19th century by local people returning from voluntary exile in Spain. The houses have colourful and attractive façades. Poschiavo is attractively sited among wooded slopes, and dominated from the west by the mountain chain between the 3,453m Pizzo Varuna and the 3,323m Pizzo Scalino. Its industry is mainly wine and flower orientated.

Nearby Seven kilometres south there is a fine retrospective view over Lake Poschiavo from Miralago (literally, 'look at the lake'). At the village of Brúsio, a further 3km south, past a series of waterfalls, is an early 17th-century Protestant church. Amidst the surrounding environs are tobacco fields, and walnut and chestnut plantations.

ST MORITZ

MAP REF: 111 E3

A measure of how fashionable St Moritz is perceived to be throughout the world is the fact that in 1986 it took the unusual step of copyrighting its name – the first town ever to do so. One of the world's most exclusive resorts, it could be said to have almost every diversion and sporting facility ever devised. These include, for devotees of unusual pastimes, both cricket and polo – on snow. It was not always so. In the mid-19th century St Moritz was a sleepy Alpine village with a reputation for its healing mineral springs and beautiful scenery, but little else. However, as with so many other Swiss resorts, the British took a hand in elevating it from relative obscurity to international renown. In the summer of 1864 Johannes Badrutt,

the owner of a small inn, remarked to four departing English guests that they were about to miss the best time of year in the Graubünden. Emboldened by their obvious interest in this revelation, he suggested that they return at Christmas – offering to pay their expenses if they were disappointed. They returned, and were not disappointed, and the moment marked the genesis of the world's first super-resort – and, incidentally, the beginning of the winter sports industry.

Today, the town still has few rivals. Divided into two parts, St Moritz Bad and St Moritz Dorf, the latter is the focus of social and sporting activity. A collection of unremarkable buildings, tightly grouped on a steep hillside, it is surprisingly small. Apart from a late 16th-century leaning campanile, little remains of the original village. In St Moritz Bad there is an English church, built in the late 19th century in neo-Romanesque style. The town made an early decision to take a firm grip on the future – evinced by the introduction of electricity in 1878 (the first community in Switzerland to do so). The Engadiner Museum on the Via del Bagn, between Dorf and Platz, makes a valiant effort to show what the area must have been like. A short way beyond this building is the town's other museum, commemorating the painter Giovanni Segantini.

However, the resort is less of a cultural centre than a massive playground, with a seemingly infinite range of facilities and an

Fashionable St Moritz

impressive list of credits to its name. It was the location for two Winter Olympic Games, in 1928 and 1948, it held Europe's first ice-skating championships in 1882, and since the building of the Cresta Run in 1884 it has been indisputably the world centre of tobogganing and bob-sleighing.

The skiing area is impressive, divided into five main sections and holding one of the best snow records in the Alps. The main area of Corviglia lies immediately above the town, reached by funicular, and from there a cablecar ascends to the splendid viewpoint of Piz Nair at 3,057m . Most of the Upper Engadine valley is visible from the terrace, with the River En filling a succession of beautiful lakes against a background of massive, glacier-draped peaks. On the other side of the valley the Corvatsch offers the highest skiing in the region at 3,304m and a marvellous view south to the Piz Bernina Glaciers. A two-stage cable-car leaves from above the little ski-village of Surlej. Past Pontresina, the sun-terrace at Diavolezza is similarly set among spectacular glacier scenery at 2,978m.

St Moritz's other great natural resource is its lake, dazzlingly set beneath St MoritzDorf and fringed on its southern bank by a dense stone-pine forest. Any number of activities take place on its frozen surface in winter, including horse racing on snow, ice polo, winter golf, skating and ice-hockey. In summer the range of water-related activities is equally extensive.

MOTOR TOUR

This fascinating tour of approximately 180km involves driving through the upper part of one of Switzerland's most beautiful valleys, the Engadine, crossing briefly into northern Italy and traversing two great mountain passes, the Splügen and the Albula, via a number of scenic gorges before returning to St Moritz. Do not forget passports.

Driving southwest from St Moritz, bypass Silvaplana and remain on the lakeside road towards Maloja. There are delightful views of the lakes of Silvaplana and Segl on the left, with the great peaks of Piz Bernina and Piz Roseg streaked by glaciers behind them to the south. From the Maloja Pass make the steep descent through the fertile Val Bregaglia, leaving the main road just before the border post, and driving through chestnut woods for the village of Soglio.

Soglio

This tightly packed village lies high above the valley floor with splendid views of the Bondasca Glacier to the south. This was once the seat of the Salis-Soglio family, whose legacy remains in the form of a number of elegant palaces. On the north edge of the village is the Casa Battista, dating from the early 17th century and now the Hotel Willy. The oldest building is the Casa Alta, built in 1524 (rebuilt in 1680).

Return to the main road and cross the frontier at the Swiss

Silvaplannersee, between Maloja and St Moritz

village of Castasegna. Just over 10km ahead turn right at Chiavenna following the signs to Slügenpass (Passo dello Spluga). After a steep 30km climb up the barren Valle San Giàcomo, passing an impressive waterfall between Campodolcino and Pianazzo, re-enter Switzerland at the southern end of the historic Splügenpass.

Splugenplass (Passo Dello Spluga)

Lying at an altitude of 2,113m, the pass is cut into a narrow ridge between the 3,279m Piz Tambo to to the west and the 3,027m Surettahorn to the east. The pass was used by the Romans and is first mentioned in a document dating from the 3rd century. In the winter of 1800 it was crossed in appalling weather conditions by Napoleonic troops with the loss of 200 men and horses.

The pass road descends in a series of hairpin bends for 9km to Splügen on the north side of the N13. Drive through the village centre, staying on the old

road and follow signs to Sufers and Andeer. This route involves passing through the gorge of Rofflaschlucht by the side of the Rhine.

Rofflaschlucht

The gorge is cut by the Rhine which crashes through in an impressive waterfall. The viewing galleries (entrance fee payable in the Rofflashlucht Inn) were hewn into the rock between 1907 and 1914.

Remaining on the old road, drive through the pleasant spa town of Andeer, passing beneath some pretty, high-lying villages, until reaching Zillis, with its famous old church. From here take the N13 autobahn following the signs to Chur and Zürich up through the celebrated Via Mala.

Via Mala

Another dramatic gorge through limestone cliffs bordering the Hinterrhein, the Via Mala is an ancient route now largely superceded by the expressway which passes through a series of tunnels. The cliffs rise to a height of 500m – in some places little more than 10m apart.

Exit at Thusis following the signposts to Tiefencastel, and pass through the wild and picturesque Schinschlucht (Schyn Gorge) of the Albula river. From Tiefencastel take the minor road signposted to Albulapass and St Moritz (ignore signs to the Julierpass). After about 17km the small village of Bergün is reached.

Bergun

Lying in the shadow of the 3,339m Piz Ela, this is a typically Engadine village with a 12th-century church with an ornate ceiling and 15th-century murals. The conspicuous 17th-century baroque dome of the Platzturm dominates the cluster of prettily painted buildings.

A steep and winding road leads up to the Albulapass (used since the 13th century) lying at an altitude of 2,312m, after which the descent is made to La Punt. Turn right here following directions to Samedan and St Moritz. Pass the airstrip on the lefthand side, and take the exit to Samedan. Pass straight through the town on the road to Celerina from where there is a winding uphill road back to St Moritz. This is the route of the famous Cresta Run, visible through the trees on the left.

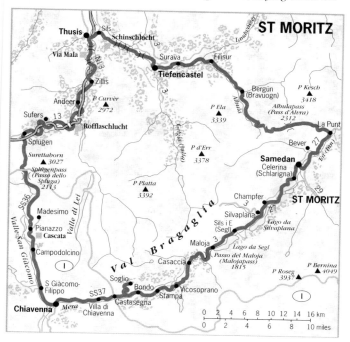

SAMEDAN

MAP REF: 111 E3

A charming, typically Engadine village, Samedan found international fame as a haven for golfers in the early part of the 20th century. Its 18-hole golf course is still one of the most enduring attractions in the game. Set back off the north side of the new road between Zuoz and St Moritz, the resort occupies a delightful site at the foot of the Bernina valley facing the Bernina massif. The church in the centre is 18th-century, and on the western side of the village is another, late Gothic church containing the family vault of the Plantas. This was an influential Engadine family whose imposing former residence is now a centre of Romansch culture. Situated on the road east out of the village towards the small hamlet of Bever, the Chesa Planta is one of the finest examples of Engadine architecture in the region.

Nearby Three kilometres west of Samedan is the pretty village of Celerina. A small resort in its own right, it offers easy access to the skiing above St Moritz. It is the finishing point of the Cresta Run.

SCUOL

MAP REF: 111 F3

The cultural centre of the Lower Engadine and the last town of any size before the Austro-Swiss border, Scuol is a major spa complex comprising the two smaller villages of Tarasp and Vulpera. Sandwiched between the valley road and the north bank of the En River, Scuol (also known as Bad-Scuol or Schuls) is divided into two distinct halves with the lower part comprising the core of the old village. There are some charming examples of Engadine houses dating from the 17th century, built around two paved squares. In the most imposing of these buildings, the 'Chagronda', opposite the 16th-century church, is housed a museum devoted to the history of the Lower Engadine. The two bridges crossing to Vulpera are of some interest in themselves, the lower one being of the roofed wooden type not characteristic of the region. Scuol is also increasing in popularity as a ski resort. Its sunny, south-facing slopes of Motta Naluns provide a number of gentle runs for predominantly Swiss and German skiers.

Nearby West of Vulpera, occupying a dominant site high above the village, is Tarasp Castle,

The Engadine village of Samedan

an impressive white-painted structure with a main tower dating from the 11th century. Austrian-owned until 1803, it fell into disrepair and was extensively restored earlier this century.

SILS

MAP REF: 111 E2

An attractive old resort scenically located in the Upper Engadine valley between the lakes of Silvaplana and Segl, Sils is in fact two different villages – Sils-Maria and Sils-Baselgia. The former is beautifully positioned among larch-covered slopes beneath the 3,451m Piz Corvatsch, one of the main skiing areas of nearby St Moritz. Like many of the small villages within commuting distance of its glamorous neighbour, Sils-Maria attracts visitors who prefer a less frenetic lifestyle. It would be difficult to imagine somewhere more suited to restful contemplation than this lovely spot at the foot of the Fex valley. In summer there are horse-drawn carriage excursions up to Crasta and Curtins about half way up the valley, which is generally accepted to be the most beautiful in the Bernina group. At its head is the Fex Glacier rolling inexorably down from the left shoulder of the 3,441m Piz Tremoggia. In winter, ski runs from Furtschellas drop down the side of the valley to the base station on the eastern side of the village.

Between the years 1881 and 1888 Friedrich Nietzsche regularly visited the resort, and his former house is now a small museum

dedicated to his work. He wrote *Thus Spake Zarathustra* here. Sils-Baselgia, the more northern of the two villages, has a small medieval church.

THUSIS

MAP REF: 111 E3

A busy market town at the foot of the Heinzenberg, Thusis is a major junction in the Domleschg valley midway between Splügen and Chur. Formerly a health resort of some repute, it now attracts more climbers than convalescents, drawn largely by the rocky pyramid of Piz Beverin to the southwest. To the southeast, set in a beautiful landscape, is the 2,972m snowy peak of Piz Curvèr. The town's late Gothic church dates from 1506 and the only other building of significance is the ruined 11th-century castle of Hohen-Rhaetian on a rocky outcrop south of the town. On the northern face of the same rock are the ruins of the church of St John, destroyed in the 15th century. Thusis is surrounded by thickly wooded hills and tiny pastoral communities set among lovely orchards high upon the eastern wall of the Domleschg valley. Many of these are close to more ruins of ancient feudal fortresses, the most notable being at Rothenbrunnen, Paspels and Rodels – all visible on the right of the road north to Chur.

Nearby Three-and-a-half kilometres north of the town, on the old road, is the small village of Cazis, notable for the venerable church of St Martin . There is also a Dominican convent with a fine, early 16th-century chapel.

MOTOR TOUR

Approximately 162km in length, this delightful tour of some of the most beautiful parts of the Graubünden includes the two mountain passes of the Julier and the Flüela, and passes through much of the scenic Upper Engadine valley and its major towns of Zuoz and Zernez. It also includes one of the Swiss Alps' most famous resorts – Davos.

From Samedan (or nearby St Moritz) follow Route 27 northeast along the Upper Engadine valley, leaving the main road to enter the small and picturesque town of Zuoz. Stay on the old road and drive through the equally pretty, narrow streets of S-chanf. From here rejoin the main road which descends gently along the left bank of the En River to the old town of Zernez. This marks the point where the valley becomes the Lower Engadine. Continue ahead to the traditionally rebuilt Engadine village of Susch, turning left here up the winding mountain road to the Flüelapass, threading through the rocky Val Susasca with several marvellous views west – particularly from Chantsura at the entrance to the Val Grialetsch.

Flüelapass

The highest mountain pass in the Graubünden, the Flüelapass lies at an altitude of 2,383m between the 3,085m Flüela-Weisshorn to the north, and the 3,146m Schwarzhorn to the south. The road was opened in 1867. It is likely to become obsolete for all but tourists by the digging of a motor-rail tunnel from Klosters to Susch which began in 1988.

The road descends through the barren landscape of the Flüelatal to the bustling health and sports resort of Davos. Drive southwest through its long main street, following the signs for Tiefencastel. Pass through the ancient hamlet of Frauenkirch, notable for its 15th-century church, which has an avalanche deflector. First threading a series of tunnels in the Zügen defile, the road then enters the lovely Landwasser Gorge, with several splendid views left, before meeting the Albulapass road just before Tiefencastel.

Tiefencastel

The little village is attractively

The high-altitude Flüelapass

situated on the floor of the Albula valley at the confluence of the Julia and Albula rivers. It is notable for the imposing baroque church of St Stefan, built in 1650, and surprisingly grand in the context of the surroundings. Its white-Italianate façade was painted in the 1930s.

Follow Route 3 for the Julierpass and St Moritz. This is the beginning of a fine mountain road, passing through a series of small Romansch-speaking villages in the Oberhalbstein valley. At Cunter, after about 7km, a road leads off to the right to the two ancient villages of Salouf and Riom.

Salouf and Riom

On the same minor road which runs parallel to the main valley road, these two villages – only 2km apart – are worth the slight detour. Salouf has a 15th-century, late Gothic church with stellar vaulting and late 14th-century murals; high above it to the west is the pilgrimage church of Ziteil where the Madonna is said to have

appeared to a shepherd in 1580. Riom is notable for a baroque church of 1677, and the impressive ruins of a 13th-century castle, restored in 1936.

Return to the main road at Cunter and continue south again to Savognin.

Savognin

The main town of the Oberhalbstein valley, Savognin has three fine 17th-century baroque churches – all Catholic. St Martin is the most imposing, with an original Romanesque tower from an earlier building, and some fine paintings dating from 1681. The town is also a popular winter sports resort with an extensive network of ski lifts.

From Savognin the road continues through the small village of Tinizong and climbs south through Rona and Bivio through a bleak, unforgiving landscape to the spectacular Julierpass.

Julierpass

Completed in 1826 and still showing weathered stumps of Roman columns by the side of the road, the pass lies at an altitude of 2,284m between the peaks of the 3,380m Piz Julier to the northeast and the 3,165m Piz Lagrev to the south.

The road now descends sharply to the old resort of Silvaplana, where it joins Route 27 northeast along the north bank of Lake Silvaplana to St Moritz, and from there skirting the lake of St Moritz back to Samedan.

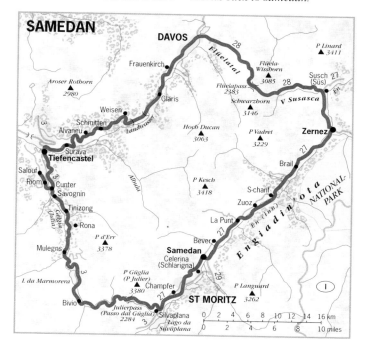

ZERNEZ

MAP REF: 111 F3

The old and attractively sited village of Zernez stands at the foot of the Ofenpass, midway between Scuol and Zuoz, close to the point where the upper and lower stretches of the Engadine valley meet. Although its chief distinction is its proximity to the Swiss National Park, it has some intrinsic features of interest of its own. The beauty of the surrounding landscape is one, another is the legacy of the ubiquitous Planta family, which stamped its influence on the Engadine for the better part of 1,000 years.

Among a number of fine, 16th-century houses lining the narrow, cluttered streets, the Planta-Wildenberg Castle with its 13th-century corner tower, ornate iron grilles and geometric wall patterns, stands out as the most impressive. This was one of the principal residences of the family for over 400 years. On a slope to the northeast of the centre stands a fine, early 17th-century mountain church with a tall, slender clock-tower. At the end of the village is the National Park House with a permanent exhibition and audiovisual show about the nearby nature reserve.

In addition to some of the best rambling terrain in the country, Zernez also offers extensive cross-country skiing trails, tennis and an indoor swimming pool.

The village of Zuoz in the Schons valley

SWISS NATIONAL PARK

Zernez stands at the gateway to the huge Swiss National Park, 169 sq km of unspoilt, natural landscape in the Ofenberg area between the Lower Engadine valley and the northern Italian border. Established in 1914, this is one of the world's most spectacular nature reserves in a setting of extraordinary, solitary beauty. The mountains and valleys are among the most rugged and untamed in Switzerland. Entrance is free, but the rules are rigidly enforced by 10 permanent wardens. Walkers must keep to the marked paths, motorists may not deviate from the Ofenbergstrasse, flowers must not be picked or minerals collected, wood may not be cut or fires lit. Campers, cyclists, climbers and cross-country skiers are banned and all that is really permitted is to walk or drive and enjoy the scenery and wildlife. That is compensation enough. About one third of the park is forest, another third is covered with Alpine meadows, and the remainder is rock, scree and water. Six-hundred-and-fifty species of plants are protected within the park with Alpine rose, Alpine poppy, dwarf willow, juniper, crowberry and edelweiss predominating. There are over 30 species of mammals, 100 species of birds, and 5,000 species of invertebrates. Marmots, red deer, ibex and chamois proliferate, and occasionally white hares, foxes, marten and ermine can also be spotted.

ZILLIS

MAP REF: 111 E3

The village lies midway along the Schons valley. It is chiefly celebrated for its Romanesque church, which contains one of the most valuable series of ceiling paintings of its type in the world. The 153 square panels, painted in the 12th century, are attached to the cross beams. Arranged in an inner and outer section, they depict scenes from the Apocalypse, the Last Judgement, and the Life of Christ. Near the church is a pastoral museum in a 16th-century peasant dwelling, with a collection of agricultural implements, furniture and textiles dating from the same period.
Nearby Five kilometres south is the principal village of the valley,

Andeer. For centuries an important spa, it is now a popular sports resort offering a wide range of summer and winter facilities. Above the little village of Donath, just south of Zillis on the western bank of the Rhine, stand the ruins of Fardun Castle, formerly the seat of the governors of the valley. One of their number in the mid-15th century, a man of particularly brutal disposition, is said to have entered the home of a peasant named Johann Caldar and spat in his broth. Caldar seized him by the throat and, plunging his head into the scalding liquid, cried: 'Eat thyself the soup thou hast seasoned!'. He then strangled him.

ZUOZ

MAP REF: 111 F3

The influence of the Planta family in this old Engadine village is again clearly seen. The cobbled streets are very narrow, admitting little sunlight and lined by ancient, 16th-century buildings, shuttered and painted in the distinctive Engadine style. The fountain in the main square is surmounted by a bear, the heraldic symbol of the Plantas, and one which is repeated throughout much of the valley. The family coat of arms comprises a severed bear's paw with the sole (*planta* in Romansch) turned upwards. This is seen to interesting effect in the decorations of the village's Romanesque church, rebuilt in the early 16th century, and providing a distinctive landmark with its tall, finely tapered spire. On the northern perimeter of the square is the most imposing building in the village, the former Planta residence with its 13th-century tower connected by arcades.

Formerly the capital of the Upper Engadine, Zuoz is now a summer resort of some importance. It is also traditionally a centre of education, now the home of the Lyceum Alpinum, and the 19th-century location of the Engiadina boarding school – for 'delicate' boys.

MOUNTAIN WALK

Allow 3 hours

From Zernez drive east for 17km through the centre of the Swiss National Park, past Il Fuorn, and park in car park No 7 on the left of the road. Take the forest path north through the Val dal Botsch to the first observation point in a clearing, reached after a brief climb. At the fork ahead turn right, where after a delightful climb through Alpine flora, the path skirts the summit of Margunet, which is just to the south. From this splendid vantage point there is a sweeping panorama which frequently includes herds of chamois and red deer. To the south rises the flat summit of the 2,586m Munt la Schera, to the east the 3,009m Piz Nair, and the west the 2,906m Piz dal Fuorn. Behind are some remarkable dolomite pillars. The path then descends through Alpine meadows to the park wardens' hut at Stabelchod. Here the meadow is permanently occupied by a resident marmot colony. Continue the descent via the righthand path over more meadows to car park 8, on the other side of the road.

From here follow the nature trail through the forest until the right-hand turning for car park 7.

MOTOR TOUR

Distance 180km

This tour covers half of the lovely Upper Engadine valley, crosses into northern Italy via the Bernina Pass, includes two of the most spectacular Italian Alpine valleys, re-enters Switzerland via the Pass Umbrail and traverses the Swiss National Park via the Ofenpass. Do not forget passports.

From Zernez travel southwest up through the Upper Engadine valley. After 13km turn right off the main road into the old village of S-chanf and from there follow the old road into Zuoz. Rejoin the main road, signed St Moritz, after 7km at La Punt, bypassing Samedan and following the signs to Pontresina and Passo del Bernina. Immediately after Punt Muragl take the first left turn into Pontresina, driving through the town and rejoining the main road up through the Bernina valley. This is a gradually ascending, scenic route past the splendid Morteratsch glacier on the right to the cable-car station at the foot of the Diavolezza.

Diavolezza

The 2,973m peak of Diavolezza offers some of the most scenic skiing in the Swiss Alps. If time permits, take the 9-minute journey by cable-car to the top station for an outstanding view of the Bernina massif.

The road continues past the cable-car station to the 2,959m Piz Lagalb on the left. Three mountain lakes shortly come into view just to the right of the road before the Bernina Pass.

Bernina Pass

Lying at an altitude of 2,328m, this is one of the most scenic of all Swiss mountain passes. To the south stretches the Val Poschiavo, with the 3,604m Piz Cambrena and its glacier prominent to the southwest.

The pass road descends to the southeast in a series of wide curves. Take the lefthand road at the border post signed Livigno, through the valley of the same name. From the centre of the town turn right for the passes of Eira and Foscagno, signed Bormio. From Bormio turn north, re-entering Switzerland after 17km at the Passo Umbrail (Giogo di Santa Maria).

Passo Umbrail

At 2,501m this is the highest of the Swiss mountain passes, offering views north over the Val Muraunza to Santa Maria. The 3,032m Piz Umbrail rises to the west.

The steeply winding pass road down to Santa Maria is little more than a tarmacked track, 16km long. At Alpenrosli there is a fine panoramic restaurant with outstanding views.

Santa Maria

The old village is notable for its traditional houses with façades painted in the Engadine style. The 15th-century, late-Gothic church has a tower that dates from 1400, and exterior and interior murals dating from 1492.

If time permits, make the brief 5km excursion east off the circular route to the charming frontier village of Müstair.

Mustair

Tradition suggests that Charlemagne founded a monastery here at the end of the 8th century. This was converted into a Benedictine nunnery, an impressive group of buildings that rank among the oldest in Switzerland, in the 12th century. The adjacent church of St John, rebuilt in the 15th century, is triple-apsed with Carolingian wall paintings from the 9th century.

Return to Santa Maria and, follow signs for Zernez through the Val Müstair to the Ofenpass, and through the Swiss National Park back to Zernez.

·*FLORA & FAUNA*·

The Swiss Alps have been described as a botanist's paradise, and it is difficult to imagine a part of the world more worthy of the description. From the subtropical islands of Brissago on Lake Maggiore to the fringes of the eternal snows on the High Alps, the region has virtually every form of plant life common to the European continent.

Irrespective of the season, the Alps – their foothills valleys and lakesides – offer an extraordinarily rich and varied collection of flora. In winter, the dark-green spires of Norway spruce are silhouetted in silent, white-tipped ranks against a backdrop of snowy peaks; in autumn the deciduous leaves cover the ground with a carpet of

The small Alpine flower edelweiss – characterised by its white woolly leaves and rocky position. Resilient to its harsh habitat, the edelweiss is all too often the victim of human interference

gold. However, it is in the spring and summer that the mountain-scape comes alive with colour.

Spring is often delayed at altitude, and it is therefore possible to see a range of plants at different stages of growth between high and low-lying ground. In the valleys early Alpine flowers are quickly hidden from view beneath taller plants but, progressively,

they reappear at higher levels as the snows recede up the mountainside. By late June and early July, the full range of conditions is visible from the lower grasslands (which are not yet cut) to the Alpine zone where the flowers are in full bloom. By late summer only the most resilient species of high-Alpine flora are still found, and these tend to be congregated almost exclusively by the snowline.

The Alpine zone provides the most humbling reminder of the miraculous power of nature. Above the tree line, the scree slopes and loose moraines are the highest habitats supporting plant life before the bleak mountain-scape of permanent snow and ice is reached. Here, in inhospitable surroundings, flowering plants somehow contrive to exist and flourish in freezing conditions – covered for more than half of the year by a blanket of snow. This frosty layer is a mixed blessing to Alpine flora; insulating them from the worst excesses of swirling winds, it also deprives the plants of the light essential for growth.

With the thaw in late April and early May, the slopes burst into riotous colour with sturdy Alpine snowbells pushing their way impatiently through the melting snow. Following their example, coltsfoot, crocuses and spring gentians make their first appearance – the latter studding the mountainsides with their distinctive blue flowers. Large blooms and deep shades of colour are distinctive features of Alpine flora, a factor which is entirely due to the increased ultraviolet content of light at high altitude. Various other species proliferate in the Alpine zone as well, many of them 'dwarfed', or of the creeping variety, to protect them from the raking mountain winds. The alpenrose is a particularly notable and colourful example; a dwarf rhododendron, its smooth leaves are as tough as leather. Another less common Alpine plant is the famous edelweiss, equally resilient, but sadly far too frequently victim to collectors – notwithstanding its protected status. Its distinctive white 'fur' is seen less and less throughout the Alpine region, and is increasingly supplanted by the no less appealing dwarf willows, saxifrages and sandworts, Alpine toadflax and moon daisies often sprouting from clefts in rocks. The rare musk orchid may also be found in clumps of short turf. Even in the zone of eternal snow Alpine plant life does not completely disappear; the glacier buttercup is frequently found at heights of over 3,000m and many exposed rockfaces are frequently adorned with intricately patterned lichens.

If the Alpine zone offers the most dramatic of settings for flora, it is unquestionably the lower-lying meadows that offer the greatest variety in the most tranquil surroundings. Against the impressive background of white peaks and glaciers, these pastures – grazed by cattle during the summer – provide an exquisite mosaic of contrasting colours. Bellflowers, daisies, knapweeds, bladder campions, yellow monkswood and hay-rattles proliferate, and in damp hollows, clumps of butterworts amd marsh marigold lend an extra splash of colour. Burnt orchids and the creamy spikes of elder-flowered orchids are also widespread, and in mid-summer the round-headed and black vanilla members of the species add to the variety. Not surprisingly with such a banquet of flower heads on offer, the air literally hums with insect life in search of nectar. Butterflies are numerous; blues, skippers, fritillaries, apollos and whites flutter dreamily among the kaleidoscope of changing colours.

The animal and bird life of the Swiss Alps is largely similar to that of other central European countries. Alpine marmots, large rodents with coarse fur, are ubiquitous, their burrows lining mountain paths or set in tussocks of grass in meadows. The marmot's shrill, bird-like call is heard frequently throughout the Alps, and can be quite unnerving in the absolute silence of the mountains. Another of the most familiar sounds in summer is that of screaming Alpine swifts. Larger than their lowland relatives, they are often seen swooping around rocky cliffs, vying for air-space with Alpine accentors and snow finches. High above the peaks, golden eagles, peregrine falcons and griffon vultures can occasionally be seen circling – ever on the alert for small rodents. The Alpine chough, is the most commonly seen bird at high

Pink camellias

altitude. Distinguished by their yellow beaks and red claws, their inquisitive nature has given them a virtual monopoly of mountain restaurants.

Among the larger animal species commonly found in the Alps, the nimble chamois are the most abundant of those living at high altitude. Frequently seen crossing impassable rock-faces, their sure-footedness is a defiance of natural law. The rarer ibex is also occasionally seen. At lower altitude roe deer and red deer proliferate, especially in the parks and nature reserves. In winter, skiers are often surprised by the sight of ermine stoats scampering across the piste and, very occasionally, polecats and foxes will be seen prowling through trees. Mountain hares are also sometimes seen bounding through the snow.

The best places to see indigenous wildlife at close quarters are the parks and nature reserves. Of these, the huge Swiss National Park in the Graubünden stands out as an exceptional monument to the extraordinary beauty and power of nature.

NORTHEAST SWITZERLAND

Although it is the lowest of the country's Alpine regions, the northeastern area of the Swiss Alps none the less offers striking mountain scenery – softened in parts by the rolling green hills of the Appenzell district and the broad flat plains of the Rhine valley. Comprising the cantons of Glarus, St Gallen and Appenzell – the latter subdivided into the two half cantons of Innerrhoden and Ausserrhoden – and the tiny principality of Liechtenstein, the area lies at the eastern end of the central Alpine chain.

Bordered to the north by the huge Bodensee (better known to English speakers as Lake Constance), across which lies Germany, to the south by the Graubünden, and to the east by Austria, this is where the Swiss Alps assume a less awe-inspiring appearance and become instead more benevolent and by Alpine standards, almost tame. Many of the peaks in the northeast are accessible by foot on marked paths, requiring equipment no more sophisticated than a pair of good walking shoes. There are two distinct massifs. The Alpstein, the most northerly, stands alone between the Toggenburg and Rhine valleys and includes the splendid vantage point of the 2,502m Säntis. Immediately to the south the seven prominent peaks of the beautiful Churfirsten range brighten the north bank of the gloomy Walensee and provide some excellent skiing runs on their north-facing slopes. The range known collectively as the Glarner Alpen (Glarus Alps) form the largest group of mountains, almost completely encircling the small canton of Glarus and culminating in the highest peak of the northeast, the 3,614m Tödi on the border with the Graubünden. The Tödi also marks the point

where the eastern section of the Alps converges with the great watershed of the St Gotthard massif to the west.

One of the most distinctive features of this area is its rich variety of picturesque medieval towns and villages. Lying at an average height of about 500m, rising to the highest altitude settlement of Wildhaus at 1,080m, many of them bear the stamp of the pervasive influence of a strong monastic tradition – as powerful here as in any other part of the country, if not more so. In the delightful town of St Gallen, for example, the monks of the famous 8th-century abbey (founded in 612 by the Irish missionary St Gallus) were tireless builders, erecting innumerable chapels, churches, priories, castles and ecclesiastical residences throughout the northeast. Their visible legacy remains in the cathedral and abbey buildings of St Gallen itself, the ancient abbey of Mariaberg near Rorschach, and even Rorschach's vast baroque granary numbers among a fine collection of architectural gems.

St Gallen was, and remains, the natural focus of cultural and economic activity in the region, and during the Middle Ages was one of the leading educational

centres in Europe. In 1212 the settlement that had grown up around the abbey was recognised as a free city, enjoying a degree of autonomy that encouraged its rapid growth as a trading centre. In 1454 it joined the Swiss Confederation and in 1524 adopted the Reformation, a step that significantly reduced the influence of its monastery.

The conversion to Protestantism also led to the creation of one of the most curious features of the Confederation – the farming canton of Appenzell being divided into two 'half' cantons according to the peoples' religious convictions. This arrangement still exists today. In 1803 the area around St Gallen became a canton in its own right, with the city as its capital, and with the additional curiosity of the split canton of Appenzell contained within it. The hilly countryside around Appenzell is one of the most beautiful parts of Switzerland with rich pastures lending themselves equally to fruit growing, grazing, and vineyards. The architecture of the area is quite unique, with many of the houses gaily painted and surmounted by distinctive curved gables. Like the neighbouring canton of Glarus, Appenzell also retains the Landsgemeinde – the purest form of democracy where voters meet once a year in the open air to elect their representatives by a show of hands. This part of Switzerland is also the centre of the country's textile industry, which has been the foundation of the local economy since the Middle Ages. A visit to any of the many textile museums, particularly that in St Gallen, is recommended.

No visit to the northeast would be complete without a swim in one of the many thermal pools of Bad Ragaz. This famous old spa town has the added advantage of a splendid site in the Rhine valley, surrounded by snow-capped peaks, and close to the southern border of Liechtenstein.

Linked to Switzerland by a common currency, diplomatic expedience and an absence of custom formalities, Liechtenstein is in fact a sovereign state with its own constitution and a ruling family whose origins can be traced to the time of the Holy Roman Empire. The delightful irony of the world's oldest democracy living hand in glove with what is effectively a thriving remnant of feudalism is not infrequently the source of bemused comment.

Liechtenstein, however, is rather more than a playground for an

Monte Säntis

admittedly very rich royal family. It is an enlightened, democratic monarchy with power vested equally in the people and their Prince. The fact that Prince Franz Joseph II, the twelfth ruler since the founding of the principality in 1719, rules only 29,000 subjects living in an area of 160 sq km – less than the smallest of Switzerland's cantons – does not diminish the importance of Liechtenstein as a prosperous and dynamic independent state that enjoys the highest standard of living per capita in Europe. Not surprisingly perhaps, in view of its relaxed tax system, it is also the base for thousands of international holding companies which bring in a revenue hugely disproportionate to the size of the territory and its influence on the world economy.

The history of the principality is traced to the Neolithic age, with clear signs of a settlement at that time; later, it was colonised by the Rhaetians in the 8th century BC who remained in occupation of the area until the Roman invasion of 15BC. There are remains of Roman villas in the villages of Schaanwald and Nendeln. The Romans, in turn, were dislodged by the mass migration of the Germanic peoples, and it is their descendants who make up the bulk of the native population of Liechtenstein. Still part of the Roman Catholic diocese of Chur, the majority of the state's citizens are Catholic. For many years the area that comprises today's country was part of the German Dukedom, divided into the two domains of Vaduz and Schellenberg. In 1712 both domains were bought by a wealthy Austrian prince, Johann Adam of Liechtenstein, and his lands were granted the title of Principality some seven years later by Kaiser Karl VI. Made part of the

Rhine Confederacy by Napoleon in 1806, the newly sovereign state duly became part of the German Confederation in 1815. When that was dissolved in 1866 the princedom entered a loose alliance with the Austro-Hungarian Empire, wisely reviewing that relationship at the end of World War I and deciding that its future lay with Switzerland. The present set-up has existed since 1923.

Since the end of World War II the country has experienced an economic and cultural development unsurpassed, in relation to its size, by any other western nation. In the course of 50 years it has undergone a remarkable transformation from being a predominantly agrarian state to a highly industrialised producer of a range of goods from dentures to textiles. In that time the proportion of the working population involved in farming has shrunk from over 60 per cent to just 2 per cent. However, any idea that the country is blighted by belching chimney stacks and ugly sprawling factories is misplaced. Liechtenstein has achieved the commendable feat of disguising its industrial buildings in such a way that they blend unobtrusively with the surrounding scenery. That doubtless is one of the advantages of having a keen conservationist as its monarch.

The country is divided geographically into three distinct parts: a hilly region in the north around Nendeln and Eschen leading to a dramatic mountain ridge above Gaflei; a flat, narrow ribbon of land bordering the right bank of the Rhine from Ruggell in the north to Mäls on the southern border, and another high ridge of mountains forming the border between Austria to the east and the canton of Graubünden to the south. Vaduz, the capital, lies midway down the plain with the mountain partition rising immediately behind it. It is the natural base for excursions in the country, and has fine walks along the Rhine and a beautiful mountain drive up through the ancient villages of Triesen and Triesenberg to Malbun at the end of the valley of the same name.

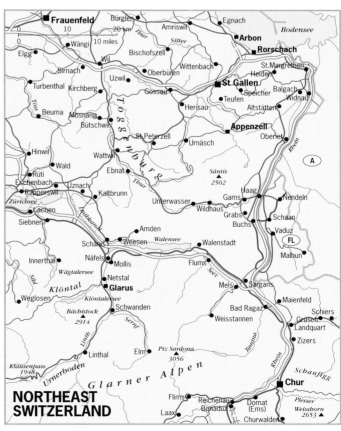

NORTHEAST SWITZERLAND

ALTSTATTEN
MAP REF: 111 E4

A pretty medieval town, typical of this lower Alpine region, Altstätten occupies an agreeable position at the foot of the Appenzell Hills on the western perimeter of a fertile plain divided by the Rhine and the Austrian border. Its most appealing feature is the distinctive Marktgasse, a picturesque arcaded street lined with 18th-century houses characterised by tall, rounded gables. Two anomalous structures disturb the harmony of the sweep of raised and pillared arcades. The small mid-17th-century Placidus chapel was erected by the monks of St Gallen long before the main part of the street was planned; opposite is a late 15th-century building which, although much altered, is still clearly identifiable as belonging to an earlier period. The Engelplatz is the natural heart of the old town, and retains one of the four original town gates. The square also has an attractive fountain and a cluster of pleasingly asymmetrical old buildings.

APPENZELL
MAP REF: 111 E4

This colourful town is capital of the Catholic 'half-canton' of Innerrhoden, which, together with its Protestant other half of

Ausserrhoden, forms part of the canton of St Gallen. This curious idiosyncrasy is one of many odd features that distinguish Appenzell from other Swiss towns. Numerous anachronisms survive from the relatively recent period when the area remained resolutely resistant to external influences. Ancient customs, traditions and institutions are kept very much alive in the form of festivals, ceremonies, and the annual Landsgemeinde – an open-air meeting held on the last Sunday of every April, when the men of the town (wearing swords indicative of their right to vote) elect their administrators. Women are not allowed to participate.

The town is set in delightful pastoral countryside, bordered to

Appenzell townscape

the south by the foothills of the Alpstein massif. Orchards, meadows and vineyards rise in serried ranks up their sides.

The bustling Hauptgasse, the focus of the town's activities, offers something of a contrast to the rustic surroundings. Lined with brightly painted wooden houses, with the distinctive steep gables typical of the region, it also has a variety of shops doing a brisk trade in embroidered goods and the famous and distinctively decorated Appenzell cakes.

Of the many buildings that catch the eye, one in particular commands attention. This is the quaintly painted Lowen-Drogerie, with its panelled façade bearing a series of illustrations of medicinal herbs and an inscription roughly translated somewhat ominously as: 'many plants curing sickness; none death'.

Many of the buildings date from the mid-16th century when a fire devastated the town. The Rathaus, built in 1561, is a particularly fine example of the Gothic style with exterior frescos added in the 1920s. Another striking example of Gothic architecture is an imposing private residence of 1563, standing next to the early 17th-century Capuchin convent on the south of the street. The town's main church, high above the west bank of the river, was founded in the 11th century and although it was extensively rebuilt in 1823, it retains some 16th-century features, notably the choir with its splendid frescos. There is also a Capuchin monastery on the west of the town centre, with a church dating from the late 16th century, and rebuilt in 1688.

Nearby Just north of the town, in the hamlet of Mettlen, is a small 17th-century chapel. There is also

Floral detail on a painted building in Appenzell

a pretty, roofed wooden bridge over the Sitter River.

The best Alpine panorama in the immediate vicinity is from the 1,640m Ebenalp, reached via a two-stage cablecar from Wasserauen, 7.5km south of Appenzell. Close to the midway station is a former 17th-century hermitage in the Wildkirchli caverns, where prehistoric remains have been discovered.

BAD RAGAZ

MAP REF: 111 E3

One of Switzerland's most famous old spa towns, Bad Ragaz occupies a narrow plain on the left bank of the Rhine, surrounded by snow-dusted peaks and conifered hills. Its lovely setting is well complemented by an agreeable combination of modern resort facilities (including a golf course) and a variety of charming old buildings. Just to the northwest of the town, high above the main road to Zürich, are the ruins of the 13th-century Freudenburg Castle destroyed in 1437 by the Swiss Confederates. Below them is St Leonard's Chapel, an early 15th-century structure with a beautifully painted choir of the same period. The other two churches, in the centre of town, are 18th- and 19th-century. The former, St Pancraz, retains a medieval tower.

Bad Ragaz owes its fame to the thermal springs that rise in the Taminaschlucht (Tamina Gorge) to the southwest of the town. These are piped from the nearby village of Pfäfers, and feed a large number of private and municipal baths. The Tamina spa has two indoor baths (one panoramic, one historic) and an excellent new open-air, all-year pool linked to a modern sports centre. More recently, the town has acquired a reputation as a winter sports resort as well, with a cable-car mounting the 1,630m peak of Pardiel to the west of the town, and leading on to the extensive snowfields of the Pizol area. From Pardiel, and the higher station of Laufböden at 2,224m, there are magnificent views of the Ratikon massif to the east and the Rhine valley. There are also excellent summer walks from the latter. Nearby In Pfäfers, 4km south, there is a former Benedictine abbey founded in 730. The church dates from the late 17th century, and the former monastery buildings (of the same period) are now used as a sanatorium.

A highly recommended excursion from Bad Ragaz is up the wooded Taminatal south of the town. Beyond the lovely old baroque spa of Bad Pfäfers is the remarkable Tamina Gorge where the hot springs emerge. A narrow path winds down through a cleft in the rock to the point where, centuries ago, patients were lowered on ropes into the steaming and turbulent waters.

GLARUS

MAP REF: 111 D4

Capital of the small canton of the same name, the industrial centre of Glarus is an interesting example of mid-19th-century town planning in Switzerland. In 1861 a disastrous fire, fanned by the ferocious winds that frequently sweep down the Linth valley, destroyed most of the former medieval buildings and led to the creation of a new town laid out on a grid pattern regularly interspersed with large – sometimes disproportionately large – squares. The Spielhofplatz, north of the centre, is one of the most striking of these comprising a wide-fronted courthouse and a series of houses of uniform style overlooking an attractive green. The central Rathausplatz is dominated by the Rathaus, one of the first buildings of importance to be erected in the wake of the fire and completed in 1865. Further

The town of Glarus beneath the gigantic Ridge of Glarnisch

south the Landsgemeindeplatz (the location for the annual open-air elections that are still traditionally observed in parts of central and eastern Switzerland) retains some of the few buildings that survived the great fire. Notable among them is the Haus Brunner im Sand, built in 1770, which has the curved gables typical of the region. Next to the town's pleasant park, the Stadtpark, is the Kuntshaus with permanent exhibitions of Swiss art and some fascinating fossilised fish. One of the town's most obvious attractions is the dramatic nature of its setting. Almost completely encircled by a high mountain chain, it looks southwest to the mighty peak of the 3,614m Tödi. Nearby Six kilometres west through the village of Riedern is the Klöntalersee (Klöntal lake), lying beneath the huge granite precipices of the Glärnisch. The best view of the lake is from its western end, reached by a road that follows the northern bank. There is also a fine view from the 1,100m Schwammhöchi, reached by a winding road immediately before the lake on the left.

Braunwald, the area's main sport resort, is 16km south of Glarus at the head of the Linth valley.

RAPPERSWIL

MAP REF: 111 D4

This enchanting little town lies at the northern end of a causeway between the Zürichsee and Obersee, about 30km southeast of Zürich. Founded in the late 12th century, Rapperswil retains a distinctly medieval flavour which is enhanced by an imposing 13th-century castle offering fine views of the Glarus Alps. Inside are two museums, one recording the development of Swiss castles, the other, founded by descendants of Polish refugees who settled here in the mid-19th century, devoted to Polish history and culture. The church adjoining the castle dates from the same period, but underwent extensive rebuilding in 1883. In the town itself a number of buildings stand out – notably the 15th-century Rathaus in the central Hauptplatz, and the early 7th-century Gothic Bleulerhaus in the arcaded Hintergasse. In the Herrenberg, installed in the 15th-century Breny-Haus (13th-century tower) is a small regional museum.
For children A children's zoo (Kinderzoo) is located behind the railway station close to the lake front. Among its attractions are a whale aquarium and a dolphinarium.

RORSCHACH

MAP REF: 111 E4

An ancient port on the southern shore of Bodensee (Lake Constance), Rorschach has traditionally been a conduit of maritime trade with Germany. Founded in the 9th century by the monks of nearby St Gallen, the

The snow-clad Säntis

attractive lakeside village reflects much of its neighbour's medieval charm. One of the ecclesiastical benefactors' most enduring legacies is the baroque Kornhaus, a splendid and imposing old granary built in 1746 close to the harbour. It now houses a fascinating local museum illustrating in colourful detail the history of the region, with particular attention to the lace and weaving industries. The village is beautifully positioned in a sheltered bay against a backcloth of pine-covered hills, the highest of which is the Rorschacherberg at 883m. The main street, the Hauptstrasse, has several notable 16th- to 18th-century buildings, with the late 17th-century Rathaus standing out as a particularly fine example. Close by is the church of St Columba and St Constance, dating largely from the early 15th century but altered in the 17th.

On the southern outskirts of the village, on a hillside, lies the ancient Benedictine abbey of Mariaberg – another inheritance from the monastery at St Gallen. Now a school, it is notable for the curious interwoven vaulting of its 15th-century Gothic cloister. On the nearby Rorschacherberg stands the castle of St Anna, a fine 15th-century structure with a Gothic chapel. There are two other castles on the mountainside, the Wartegg (dating from the mid-16th century) and the Wartensee, substantially rebuilt in the 19th century in neo-Gothic style.

ST GALLEN

MAP REF: 111 E4

This ancient city, the cultural and economic centre of eastern Switzerland, owes its name to the Irish missionary St Gallus whose early 7th-century hermitage in the Steinach valley led to the foundation of a monastery in 719. The small settlement that grew up around it had, by the early

St Gallen's baroque cathedral

medieval period, achieved a reputation as a place of learning and as the hub of the Swiss textile industry. Today the city remains the major producer of cotton and embroidered goods in the country, although its once world-famous linen industry is now extinct. Notwithstanding its industrial heritage and the removal of the ancient town walls in the early 19th century, St Gallen is one of the finest and best-preserved medieval cities in Switzerland with a collection of 15th-, 16th- and 17th-century Gothic buildings grouped in a perfect circle around the monastery precinct. In the southern half, surrounded by the former abbey buildings, stands one of the most splendid baroque

cathedrals in Switzerland. Built over a period of 14 years from 1755, the massive edifice with its distinctive, twin rococo towers has a sumptuously decorated interior, surpassed only by the lavish décor of the nearby Abbey Library (Stiftsbibliothek). This two-storey rococo hall, with its rare inlaid floor of walnut and cherry wood, magnificent ceiling paintings and gilded wooden carving, houses over 100,000 volumes and illuminated manuscripts, many of which date from the 7th to 12th centuries.

On the western side of the cathedral is the ancient Gallustrasse leading on to the Gallusplatz, a delightful square with a number of 15th-century houses. Opposite is the narrow

Schmiedgasse (note the early 18th-century Haus zum Pelikan with its distinctive wooden oriel), and running parallel to the north, the Multergasse with its fine balconies and Gothic façades. The Marktgasse and Spisergasse, in the top right segment of the old town circle, also reward exploration.

St Gallen's historic association with textiles is faithfully recorded in the Textile Museum in Vadianstrasse, on the western circumference of the old town. Among its fascinating collection of embroidered fabrics and lace are a number of period garments. Nearby The Freudenberg (884m) offers fine views of the Säntis and Lake Constance.

The Wildlife Park of Peter and Paul is 3km north of the city.

MOTOR TOUR

This 175km tour leaves from the historic town of St Gallen, skirts the southern bank of Bodensee (Lake Constance) and passes through the pastoral region of Appenzell before circling the Säntis and the Alpstein massif.

Leave the centre of St Gallen by the St Jakob-strasse, signposted Konstanz. Arbon, bordered to the south and west by meadows and orchards, and to the north by Lake Constance, lies 14km ahead.

Arbon
The lakeside town of Arbon has a number of fine old buildings. Known as 'Arbor Felix' by the Romans, the former Celtic settlement still retains signs of Roman fortifications. The medieval castle, built on the site of the original fort, has a mid-13th-century keep, but was substantially rebuilt in the 16th century. Inside, the local museum has a collection of Roman relics.

Follow the south bank of Lake Constance through Rorschach, and stay on the 7-13 route until the frontier village of St Margrethen. Continue south on Route 13 to Altstätten. Drive through the centre following the signs for Appenzell. Just after Gais, take the minor road on the left for Appenzell 5km ahead. From the centre, follow the signs for Gonten and Urnäsch. At Urnäsch take the pass road south for Neu St Johann and Nesslau, past the Säntis on the left.

Neu St Johann
The ancient village, beautifully

sited in lush green hills, takes its name from the Benedictine abbey founded in Alt St Johann in 1150 and transferred here in 1626. The church, designed by Alberto Barbieri, was constructed between 1641 and 1680 and is notable for its blending of late-Gothic and baroque architectural features.

Continue through Nesslau and remain on Route 16 for 25km through Wildhaus with Gams. Continue straight on for a further 4km until the road rejoins Route 13 at Haag. Turn left here and drive north for 22km through a succession of small villages until you enter Altstätten once again. From the centre take the steep, winding

mountain road to Trogen.

Trogen
Capital of the half-canton of Ausser-Rhoden, the Landsgemeinde assembles here on the last Sunday of April in years with even numbers. The town is the home of the Kinderdorf Pestalozzi, a children's 'village' founded after World War II for war orphans from all over the world. Notable buildings include the neo-classical, late 18th-century church and the nearby Zellwerger Palace, built by the town's main family in the late 18th century.

From here continue through the Speicher. Re-enter St Gallen from the south a short distance ahead.

URNASCH

MAP REF: 111 E4

A small and pretty village 11km west of Appenzell, Urnasch is an interesting place to visit for a number of reasons: its excellent local museum, its fine traditional 17th- to 18th-century timber buildings, and its proximity to the best Alpine vantage point in the region – the summit of the Säntis. The museum is housed in an old timber-frame building and is notable for its comprehensive collection of ancient hats and costumes. Some of the hand-painted ceremonial head-dresses are so unwieldy that they have to be hung from the ceiling. One floor is entirely devoted to a reproduction of a typical Appenzeller living space. In the quaint village square, a number of buildings stand out, particularly the mid-17th-century church, and the wooden Zurchersmuhle, notable for its roofed windows and doors.

Nearby The 2,501m Säntis, the highest peak of the Alpstein range, is reached after a 10km drive south from the village, and thence by funicular from Schwagalp. It offers what is unquestionably the finest panorama in eastern Switzerland and, arguably, one of the finest in the country. The summit is gained after a short walk from the top station and commands outstanding views of lakes Constance and Zürich to the north, the Grisons Alps to the south and the Bernese Oberland to the southwest. An observatory, restaurant and hotel are situated close by.

VADUZ

MAP REF: 111 E4

Capital of the Principality of Liechtenstein, Vaduz is a modest town of square modern blocks and chalet-style buildings offering little in the way of architectural merit. Its one distinguishing feature is the huge and impressively sited castle, home to the Liechtenstein royal family, which dominates the town from its position on a rocky shelf overlooking the Rhine. The castle's origins date back to the 12th century, and the keep and the buildings on the eastern section are the oldest surviving parts. The walls of the northeast round tower, built at the beginning of the 16th century, are 4.5m thick. Like the medieval Rotes Haus on the Schloss-Strasse, the town's only other building of interest, it is closed to the public, but its position immediately next

Vaduz Castle, home of the Liechtenstein royal family

to the winding mountain road up to the ancient village of Triesenberg means that it can be viewed at close quarters.

Surprisingly, in view of its size, Vaduz has three world-famous museums (all on the town's main street, the Stadtle): the Liechtenstein State Art Collection in the *Englanderbau* ('Englishmen's building'), with works by Rubens and Van Dyck; the National Museum, devoted to the history of the principality and its geology; and the Postal Museum recording Liechtenstein's considerable (albeit somewhat disproportionate) significance in the world of philately. For this latter reason, the town's post office, also in the Stadtle, is as much a focus of interest for stamp collectors as the museum itself. As a base for entertainment and excursions, Vaduz has much to recommend it, with an open-air swimming pool, squash and tennis centre, minigolf, billiard hall and a

network of picturesque paths through delightful countryside. A fine, well-marked walk from the centre of town is to the ruins of the old robber barons' castle of Wildschloss, a steep but scenic hour-long route through the Schlosswald woods to the north.

Nearby Of the many villages in the vicinity that reward exploration, the old celtic settlement of Triesen, 4km south, with a fine 15th-century, Gothic chapel, stands out. So, too, does Triesenberg above it, distinguished by a picturesque onion-domed church tower and splendid views west over the Rhine valley. From here the road continues up to the little ski resort of Malbun, where members of the British royal family learned to ski. Off this road to the north is a splendidly sited hotel at Gaflei, base for the Furstensteig mountain walk.

WALENSEE

MAP REF: 111 E4

One of the most frequented tourist spots in the eastern Swiss Alps, the lake of Walensee is splendidly situated beneath sheer, green cliffs, which border its northern shore. Behind them lies the precipitous Churfirsten range and, to the south, the Glarus Alps. At each end of this 15km stretch of emerald water lie two popular holiday resorts. Weesen, on the west bank, is a charming little town with a delightfully shady lakeside promenade. The 13th-century church of the Heiligkreusz has late-Gothic alterations and forms an imposing group with two other late-Gothic buildings – the Schlossli and an old chaplaincy – southeast of the Buhlerstrasse. From the north of the town a minor road leads steeply up to the small, all-year resort of Amden lying high above the lake on sunny Alpine meadows; a chair-lift ascends to the 1,285m Alp Walau with fine views over the lake and the Glarus Alps.

The garrison town and holiday resort of Walenstadt lies on the lake's eastern extremity. Not quite as appealing as Weesen, it has, none the less, some fine old buildings – notably, the Grosse Haus and the 17th-century Zugenbuhlerhaus opposite. Parts of the old town wall remain.

The ancient settlement of Flums lies 5km south. Just before it on the left, on a rocky crag above the village of Berschis, is the St George Chapel – the oldest chapel in the

Black and white buildings in Wildhaus contrast with a fresh green valley of pasture land

region and formerly part of a medieval fortified church. Northwest of Flums is the ruined Burg Grapplang, a 13th-century former administrative seat, impressively framed by the jagged teeth of the Churfirsten. In the town itself, by the Seez canal, is the church of St Justus, rebuilt in the 12th century with a 15th-century tower and choir. Beneath the latter is an Alemannic necropolis. Other notable buildings include a former dower house (just south of the church) built in 1524 and, near by, the 1624 Haus Zingg. A rewarding excursion from the town is to the

Flumserberge, a delightful region of meadows much frequented during the summer and winter sports seasons.

WILDHAUS

MAP REF: 111 E4

The old village is now one of eastern Switzerland's largest ski resorts. Framed spectacularly by the seven jagged peaks of the Churfirsten range to the south and the great ridge of the Alpstein massif to the north, it is a marvellous base for some predominantly gentle skiing in the middle of beautiful scenery. There is ample scope as well for long summer walks, well served by an efficient network of mountain lifts. These link Wildhaus to the smaller resorts of Unterwasser and Alt St Johann 3km and 8km respectively to the west by road. From Unterwasser there is a funicular to the midway station at Iltios, and from there a cable-car to a breathtaking viewpoint at the 2,262m Chaserugg. From the restaurant terrace there are fine views over the Walensee and Flumserberg to the south.

Wildhaus village is an unpretentious, rather straggling arrangement of hotels and old chalets. Its chief distinguishing feature is the Zwinglihaus, reputedly one of Switzerland's oldest timber houses, and the birthplace of Ulrich Zwingli, the famous 16th-century reformer, in 1484. Note also the 18th-century baroque church of St Bartholomew.

MOUNTAIN WALK

Allow 3 hours

This is an high-altitude hike which requires a reasonable level of fitness, good hiking boots, and a head for heights. It involves walking along part of the Furstensteig, a marked footpath said to have been cleared on the orders of Prince Johann II in the late 19th century and now offering competent walkers an opportunity to marvel at a magnificent view of the principality of Liechtenstein and the Rhine valley.

Drive up to Gaflei from Vaduz, via the famous castle, and up a winding road through Rotenboden and Masescha. Park by the hotel (which is effectively all there is to Gaflei) and walk back out of the car park following the path up to the left of the road. Turn sharp left

at the sign for Furstensteig and Bargella, following the path round to the right and then turn sharp right where the path actually meets the Furstensteig descending by the side of the Alpspitz. That is the final part of the walk, but at this stage continue south and up through a clearing following the path round to the left and via a series of switchbacks up to Kamin.

At the end of the switchbacks turn left, ignoring the first two paths off to the right, and following the next righthand path to Kamin and the Furstensteig. It now becomes steeper as it passes beneath the 1999m Hehlawangspitz peak immediately to the east. At the next fork it levels out. Keep to the left path for a further 500m or so until the next fork. This is where it joins the Furstensteig. Turn left along the high ridge beneath the

Alpspitz and continue along the winding mountain path southwards. From here, and throughout the final descent to Gaflei, the views over the valley are magnificent. At the next fork turn right, following the path down until it meets the original intersection for the return to Gaflei. The hotel terrace is a fine place to recuperate.

CENTRAL SWITZERLAND

The region of central Switzerland has proved to be a powerful lure for visitors to the country since the very beginning of the Swiss tourist industry. Long before the winter sports boom, the majority of the early tourists headed directly for the ancient city of Lucerne and its immediate environs. It was, and remains, incontestably the finest excursion centre in the Swiss Alps. The city and its canton, and the neighbouring cantons of Uri, Schwyz, Unterwalden (divided into the half-cantons of Obwalden and Nidwalden) and Zug, not only form the physical heart of Switzerland, but also represent the historical embryo of the modern Confederation.

The three founder 'forest' cantons of Uri, Unterwalden and Schwyz resolved in 1291 to throw off the yoke of Hapsburg oppression and by 1315 had the Austrians on the retreat. In 1332 Lucerne joined the 'Confederates', followed by Zug 20 years later, and the Swiss Confederation grew quickly thereafter taking the name of the new country from the founding canton of Schwyz.

Not surprisingly this central region is frequently referred to as the 'cradle' of Switzerland, with Lucerne as its focal point.

The surrounding countryside of this delightful city varies from the fertile pastures of the Central Plateau to the steep mountain meadows of the Lower Alps, culminating in the sheer precipices overhanging the southern part of Lake Lucerne.

The Lake of the Four Forest Cantons, known to the Swiss by its German name, Vierwaldstättersee, but most familiar to English speakers as Lake Lucerne – is the most famous lake in Switzerland, and deservedly so. Generally glass-like and placid, but occasionally swept by a violent storm known as the Fohn (once, according to

legend, delivering William Tell from his Austrian captors), the beautiful and constantly changing waterscape stretches for 38km from Lucerne to the little resort of Flüelen on its southeastern extremity. Divided into seven distinct bays, it covers an area of 114sq km at a mean altitude of about 434m above sea level.

There are many other lovely lakes in the Swiss Alps, but none can claim the same extraordinary variety of scenery, nor so comprehensive a cruising network as that operated by the Lake Lucerne Navigation Company. Eighteen steamships and motor vessels, including five elegant old paddlesteamers, carry more than 2 million passengers a year to every point on the lake – summer and winter.

Of the many charming resorts that they visit, the triumvirate of Weggis, Vitznau and Gersau on the northeastern arm stand out as exceptional. The small town of Gersau was for 400 years a tiny independent republic, before being incorporated into the canton of Schwyz. A wonderful relic of that period remains in the shape of the 'Zur Gerbi', the

'tanner's house', built in 1577 and which still represents the typical architectural style of central Switzerland. Further along the shore is the town of Brunnen – after Lucerne the second largest resort on the lake. From its elegant lakeside promenade the view southwards down the part of the lake known as the Urnersee is outstanding. Opposite is the Boatman's House at Treib, another typical old building in the regional style erected in 1657 and faithfully reproducing the original 14th-century house, which had been destroyed by fire. Close by is the famous Rütli meadow where, according to tradition, the Confederates of the three founder cantons met in 1307 to swear the oath confirming the Everlasting League of 1291.

In truth, there are few parts of this lake where the shores are not steeped in the history of Switzerland. One of the country's most enduring folk heroes, William Tell, is popularly believed to have lived in this area and the 'Tell's Chapel' stands on the banks of the Urnersee to lend substance to the tales of his exploits. In the same part of the lake is the famous Schillerstein, a natural rock formation rising from the lake in the form of a 24m-high obelisk. It bears a gold inscription dedicated to Frederick Schiller, the writer of the play that has immortalised William Tell.

There are two other compelling reasons to visit Lucerne and its lake. On either side stand the great rocky sentinels of Mount Pilatus and Mount Rigi. The former is the unmistakable landmark of the city, a vast pyramid of rock soaring to a height of 2,129m on the western bank of the lake. Its summit offers one of the great Alpine panoramas and since 1889 the ascent has been made easier by the steepest cog-wheel railway in the world – at times reaching a gradient of almost 1 in 2.

At the mid-way point down the lake is the 1,797m Rigi, reached via cable-car from Weggis or the oldest cog-wheel railway in Europe from Vitznau. Known as the 'Queen of Mountains', it is small by Alpine standards but none the less attractive for that. Its fabled sunrises are said to be a remarkable spectacle, but at any time of day the mountain offers splendid views (in fine weather), and lovely walks through Alpine meadows.

Of the other lakeside mountains that have traditionally attracted visitors to the region, the Bürgenstock has earned an

The massive Unteraar Glacier fronted by Lake Grimsel

exclusive niche in fashionable society. Since the end of the 19th century, the shoulder of this sheer rock wall immediately abutting the lake has been one of the most stylish venues in the Swiss Alps – known locally as the 'film star's mountain' because of the preponderance of international celebrities who haunt its luxurious hotels. One of the most scenic cliff paths in the country – the 'Felsenweg' – encircles the mountain, and leads to the fastest outdoor lift in Europe.

The history of central Switzerland is indivisible from that of its major city which, like so many of Switzerland's great cities, grew up around a monastery. By 1450, because of its strategic position on the great St Gotthard trade route between southern and northern Europe, it had become one of the most important trading centres on the continent.

The 18th century witnessed the beginning of educational travel, or the 'Grand Tour', and Lucerne was deemed to be an integral part of the itinerary. However, it was with the construction of the railway network in the 19th century that the region experienced the beginning of its boom period. Within a short time, Lucerne became one of the most desirable destinations in Europe. Emperors and kings, philosophers and poets, artists and writers flocked to the

beautiful city, establishing a trend that has made it one of the world's premier resorts. The celebrated Lucerne International Festival, held every August, ensures that it remains high on the list of international centres of culture.

The highest part of the region lies immediately south of Lucerne around the delightfully sited skiing and climbing resort of Engelberg at the foot of the 3,239m Mount Titlis. This is the loftiest peak in the Central Alps, and since 1967 an aerial cableway has brought a marvellous panorama of the Bernese, Valais and Graubünden Alps within reach of non-climbers. The section stage of the journey

provides a thrilling glide over the Titlis Glacier. Between the Titlis and the Sustenhorn to the south lies the newest of the splendid Alpine passes, which are another distinguishing feature of central Switzerland. This is the Sustenpass, completed in 1946. Together with the famous Furkapass, linking the cantons of Uri and Valais, and the pass roads of Klausen, Oberalp and St Gotthard, it provides some of the most scenic high altitude motoring in the country. The ancient town of Andermatt, in the heart of the St Gotthard massif, is near the meeting point of the Furka, St Gotthard and Oberalp passes, and also marks the point where the Rhône and Rhine valleys meet. North of Andermatt, following the route of the old St Gotthard railway, is the equally old town of Altdorf – scene of William Tell's legendary feat of marksmanship. A huge bronze statue of the archer and his son dominates the town square and supposedly marks the spot where the apple was spliced.

About 20km further north along the side of the Urnersee is the historic town of Schwyz, sheltering beneath the twin peaks of the Mythen, and one of the oldest settlements in the country. Any tour of Central Switzerland should also include the nearby monastic town of Einsiedeln, home of one of the most beautiful baroque buildings in Europe, and the ancient and beautifully preserved medieval town of Zug on the banks of Lake Zug. However, it is to Lake Lucerne that many visitors will want to return, for there can be few more romantic experiences than taking the slow boat to the Alpine tableau at its eastern end.

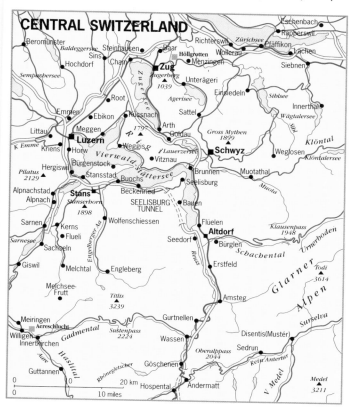

CENTRAL SWITZERLAND

ALTDORF

MAP REF: 111 D3

The capital of the Uri canton, Altdorf lies in a fertile valley on the main St Gotthard Pass route. It is a charming, old-fashioned town closely associated with the legend of William Tell who, according to legend, is said to have accomplished his feat of apple-splicing here. The intrepid archer is commemorated by a massive bronze statue in the main square, his hand protectively on his son's shoulder. The inscription is taken from Schiller's famous play and reads: 'The story of William Tell will be told as long as the mountains stand'. Erected 1895, it stands beneath a 13th-century tower, surmounted by a dome that was added in the early 19th century. Above the town is the conspicuous Bannwald (literally, 'banned woods') carefully preserved to protect it from the avalanches that have threatened for centuries. Throughout Altdorf's narrow streets, the architecture of many of the 17th- and 18th-century houses show decidedly Italian influences – a reminder of the important commercial significance of the town's location. The Capuchin friary on the northeast perimeter, founded in 1591, is the oldest in Switzerland. South of the main square on the Gotthardstrasse is a regional historical museum.

William Tell statue, Altdorf

Nearby Close to Altdorf are three villages of considerable charm. In Seedorf is a Benedictine monastery with a decorative baroque chapel. Near by is a little 16th-century gabled castle, A Pro. The ancient and picturesque settlement of Bürglen, 3km southeast, is reputed to have been the birthplace of William Tell, and the Tell Museum is housed here in an old medieval tower. Bauen, 10km north, is a delightful little hamlet on the west bank of Urnersee (Lake Uri) directly opposite Tell's Chapel.

Andermatt in the Urseren valley, junction of four main Alpine roads

THE LEGEND OF WILLIAM TELL

In 1307 the Austrian Governor of Uri and Scwyz, the infamous Gessler, had a pole erected in Altdorf's main square. His hat was pinned to the top and orders were given that all passers-by should kneel and pay homage to it. William Tell, a freeman of nearby Bürglen, failed to do this when he was visiting the town with his son, Walter. Gessler had him arrested and, knowing of Tell's reputation as a marksman, decided to torment him by ordering that he shoot an apple from his son's head. Informed that his son would be executed if he refused, Tell withdrew two arrows from his quiver, placing the first in his belt and the second on his crossbow. Offering a prayer, he pierced the apple through the centre. Demanding to know the significance of the *first* arrow, Gessler was calmly assured by Tell that it was destined for him should he have killed his child, adding 'Believe me, I would not have missed my mark a second time'. Infuriated, Gessler had the archer bound and taken by boat to his castle in Küssnacht, where he was told he would spend the rest of his days in a dungeon. During a storm on the lake, Tell overcame his captors and disappeared into the forest. Awaiting Gessler in the 'hollow lane' near Küssnacht, he shot the tyrant as he was about to ride down a peasant woman and her children. This famous deed marked the liberation of the country from its Austrian oppressors, and the Confederation came into being in the same year.

ANDERMATT

MAP REF: 111 D3

At first sight this ancient village at the northern end of the St Gotthard Pass appears to be oppressively bleak and gloomy, an impression lent further substance by its dark, narrow streets, military barracks, steep bare hillsides and the fact that it is almost permanently in shade. Closer inspection reveals it to be a place of considerable charm, with a collection of handsome old buildings and a seductive air of faded grandeur.

The main street runs from the square through the heart of the old village, and is flanked by 16th- and 17th-century residences with their façades decorated with curious scale-type cladding. The parish church, situated between here and the lower Reuss, is a baroque building dating from 1695.

Apart from its strategic significance as the meeting point of the 'Three Passes' of Susten, Furka and Grimsel, Andermatt is also well known as an expert's skiing resort and a centre of ski-touring. The skiing is divided into two areas – Gemsstock and Nätschen. From the top station of the former, reached by a two-stage cable-car, there are magnificent views from an altitude of 2,963m. Nätschen is a sunnier area, with a better choice of mountain restaurants.

Nearby Eleven kilometres north, the little village of Wassen on the old St Gotthard road repays a visit. Its early 18th-century baroque church has a fine inlaid wooden altar.

BRUNNEN

MAP REF: 111 D4

This former fishing village is reached from the south by the famous Axenstrasse, a scenic road on a shelf cut deep into sheer rock on the eastern bank of Lake Uri. On the northeastern elbow of Vierwaldstättersee (Lake Lucerne), it enjoys an enviable setting framed against a densely wooded mountain backdrop, which gives it an almost fjord-like appearance. This impression is particularly true of the view from the quayside down towards Lake Uri, and it is perhaps unsurprising that Hans Christian Andersen felt so much at home in this Scandinavian setting during his regular visits.

Brunnen is now the next largest holiday resort on these lakes after Lucerne, and paddlesteamers stop here regularly on their tour of the historic lakeside villages near by. Near the chestnut-lined lakeside promenade, by the landing stage, is a delightful baroque chapel built in 1632. The centre, a short walk away, has an interesting selection of elegant shops and lively bars. Overlooking the lakes are a number of luxurious 19th-century hotels, built in the grand style, and the waterfront is

cluttered with attractive cafés shaded by gaily coloured awnings. Sports facilities include mountain biking, bowling, tennis and a lido.

MOTOR TOUR

A circuit of about 120km, the 'Three Passes' tour traverses three of the great Swiss mountain passes – the Furka, Grimsel and Susten – in the heart of the Alps. The tour circles the Winterberg and Sustenhorner mountain ranges, with peaks reaching an average height of 3,500m. Skirting the spectacular Rhonegletscher (Rhône Glacier), it also threads the beautiful Urseren, Hasli, Gadmen and Meien valleys.

From the centre of Andermatt follow Route 19 west to the village of Hospental which lies just off the main pass road.

Hospental
The old village of Hospental takes its name from a 13th-century hospice which has long since disappeared. A tower, dating from the same period, dominates the village. The lovely old St Gotthard Hotel was briefly occupied by the Russian general Suvarov and his staff during the 1799 campaign.

From this point the road climbs gradually for a further 6km to the village of Realp, after which it

starts its winding ascent up the Urseren valley to the Furkapass.

Furkapass
A short distance past the austere but impressively sited Furkablick Hotel, the Furka ('fork') is a high mountain saddle, falling steeply away on each side between the 3,026m Kleines Furkahorn and the 2,757m Blauberg. Forming the boundary between the cantons of Valais and Uri, it affords spectacular views.

The road descends steeply past the magnificent Rhône Glacier to the town of Gletsch. From Gletsch turn north on the Grimselpass road.

Grimselpass
Lying at an altitude of 2,165m, the Grimselpass, forming the boundary between the cantons of Berne and Valais, offers stunning views of their respective mountain ranges south and west. The khaki-coloured Totensee (the 'Lake of the Dead'), just to the left of the pass, is one of the eeriest places in the Alps. It earned its name from the massive slaughter which took place here during the bitter fighting between Austrian and French forces in 1799.

The road continues past the bleak and fjord-like Grimselsee and Räterichsbodensee on the left. Between them is the Grimsel Hospice. The road descends to Innertkirchen, past the Handegg Falls (right). At Innertkirchen turn right on Route 11 for the ascent through the lower valley of the Gadmental to the old village of Gadmen. The 3,239m peak of the Titlis is clearly visible on the left. From Gadmen the road continues to climb, zig-zaging through woods and tunnels until it reaches the Steingletscher Hotel on the right.

The Sustenpass Road
Most of the mountain road between Gadmen and the Sustenpass was built between 1938 and 1946 by refugees from the countries of war-torn Europe. There are splendid views over the glacier, dominated by the 3,447m Tierberg and the 3,420m Gwatchenhorn. One of the best is from the Swiss Touring Club viewing table 2km before the summit of the pass on the right. This stretch of road, between the Himmelrank Gorge and the tunnel under the pass, is the most scenic of the tour. Just before the tunnel entrance there is a large car park. From here a 5-minute climb leads to the summit of the pass where a restaurant offers fine views.

From the Sustenpass, named after a 'sust' - a toll or custom house - the descent to the village of Wassen is through the pastoral Meien valley (Meiental), enclosed by steep mountain walls and offering glimpses of the St Gotthard railway below. At Wassen take Route 2 south to the village of Göschenen at the mouth of the St Gotthard railway tunnel. From here the road ascends through the Schollenen Gorge, over Devil's Bridge where a cross commemorates the battle between Russian forces and the French in 1799.

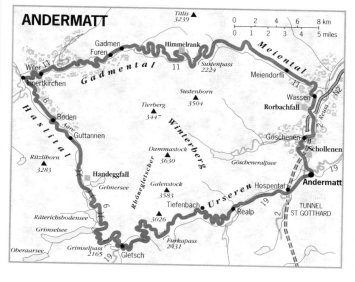

BURGENSTOCK

MAP REF: 110 C3

Less of a community and more of a massive and luxurious hotel complex, Bürgenstock is also the name given to a cliff rising abruptly from the southern bank of Lake Lucerne. On a plateau at about 500m is a purpose-built holiday resort created by Franz Joseph Bucher-Durrer at the end of the last century. Today it is still privately owned, and the palatial hotels have become a popular and exclusive retreat for the fashionable and famous.

Not least of the resort's obvious attractions is a magnificent panorama of the lake, the distant Jura, and Lucerne's twin sentinels of Rigi and Pilatus. There are many lovely footpaths through woods and Alpine pastures, and a famous circular cliff path – the Fersenweg – which is about a ¹/₂hour walk around the mountain. At the midway point is the highest and fastest mountain lift in Europe, which ascends, intermittently, through the cliff-face, to the Hammetschwand at a height of 1,128m. The view from the summit is magnificent, and there is a small restaurant and a couple of bars from which to enjoy it.

Bürgenstock can be reached by car or by funicular in 6 minutes from Kehrsiten at the lakeside.

The last of the great Alpine passes to be cut – the snow-speckled Sustenpass at 2,946m. The road passes beneath the pass in a tunnel

EINSIEDELN

MAP REF: 111 D4

Known as the 'jewel' of the Schwyz canton, this is a summer and winter resort of special appeal. Its site is particularly beautiful, deep in a basin in the green ring of the lower Alps with their rugged foothills, rolling meadows and dark, scented pine forests. However, its fame springs chiefly from its reputation as one of Western Europe's most important places of pilgrimage.

The huge Benedictine monastery, rebuilt between 1704 and 1735, which dominates the town from the main Klosterplatz is remarkable for the force of its visual impact. More than one respected authority has been moved to observe that its power lies not so much in its undoubted architectural merit, as in the scale and grandeur of a structure of this

The Benedictine grandeur of the Abbey of Maria Einsiedeln

sort in such an improbable setting. A 136m façade presides over the large, graceful square with its semi circular sweep of arcades around an ornate baroque fountain. A broad flight of steps leads up to the central one of three simple portals, set between twin clock-towers surmounted by distinctive, citron-shaped cupolas. These flank a convex frontispiece, itself crowned by a monumental statue of the Virgin and child. The whole ensemble constitutes what is arguably the largest and most impressive masterpiece of baroque architecture in Switzerland.

The interior of the church is equally grandiose with its abundance of richly coloured frescos, countless gilt adornments, and finely detailed stucco and rococo decorative features. However, unquestionably the most arresting interior feature, and the goal of the estimated 250,000 pilgrims each year, is the Lady Chapel, destroyed by French marauders in 1798 but rebuilt in 1816. This black marble obelisk, in the centre of the octagonal nave, contains the famous Black Madonna – a surprisingly small black statuette of the Virgin holding a black infant Jesus. The colouration owes its origin to the effect of candle smoke on the original Madonna, destroyed by fire in 1465. Since 1600, both figures have been clothed in the style of the Spanish court.

The town of Einsiedeln lies below the monastery and is surrounded by glorious countryside of pleasing contrasts. The peaks of Nüsellstock, 1,479m, and Gschwandstock, 1,616m, lie immediately to the south; and the lake and pleasant pasturelands of Sihlsee to the east. Many of the fields are occupied by horses bred by the monks – a tradition that dates back to the 15th century.

THE GREAT THEATRE OF THE WORLD

One of the world's great amateur theatrical productions takes place every five years in the unique setting of the abbey square in Einsiedeln. The Great Theatre of the World, written by Don Pedro Calderón, was first performed before the Court of Spain in 1685. A religious drama dealing with miracles, life and death, it is held under the night sky between June and September with a cast of 600 – all residents of the town coached by the monks of the monastery. The last performance was in 1987. For visitors who miss the five-yearly repeats, the Festival of the Miraculous Dedications, which takes place every 14 September, is a fascinating and impressive occasion that also involves the townsfolk, who participate in a torchlight procession.

ENGELBERG

MAP REF: 110 C3

A popular health and mountaineering resort since the 19th century, Engelberg is 34km south of Lucerne, delightfully set in a wide, steep-sided valley shadowed by the dark precipices of the Titlis massif. Since the mid-1960s, when the two-stage cable-car to Klein-Titlis was installed, it has also increased in popularity as a major winter sports resort. This latter factor has occasioned one of the most incongruous sights of Alpine life – the spectacle of monks in full habit mingling with colourfully dressed skiers in the town's old streets. For Engelberg has had a Benedictine monastery since 1120, and the present imposing buildings, which date from 1730, are still the dominant feature of the community.

Located on the western side of the town, the great structure dwarfs nearby chalets and hotels, and includes a religious college and an impressive church which contains one of the country's largest organs. Even for the non-religious, the services are said to be a fascinating experience. Queen Victoria was sufficiently persuaded of this to attend her first Catholic mass here in 1868, a decision that caused consternation among the British Establishment of the day.

The town centre has some attractive old wooden buildings, elegant 19th-century hotels and a busy, cosmopolitan main shopping street. Inevitably, there are also

The small mountaineering resort of Engelberg dwarfed beneath the impressive Spannort Group

some unattractive examples of the 'neo-Alpine' architecture popular in the 1960s and 1970s, but not enough to impoverish the traditional nature of the resort, which retains considerable charm.

The skiing area is divided into the two sections of Brunni and Titlis, with the latter providing the most interesting and varied skiing. In summer, and in winter for non-skiers, the resort offers a comprehensive range of facilities, including marvellous walks through picturesque Alpine scenery, indoor and outdoor skating and curling, tennis, swimming and the varied possibilities of a large sports hall.

The trip to the Titlis top station at 3,239m by an elaborate system of lifts starting from the south of town is recommended – summer or winter. This involves a thrilling aerial journey over the Titlis Glacier and a tremendous view of the Bernese and Valais Alps, and the Jura to the far west. There is a large, panoramic restaurant on the summit.

Titlis, rising 3,239m above Engelberg, provides the highest viewpoint in central Switzerland

LUZERN (LUCERNE)

Lucerne is a cornucopia of delightfully contrasting images in a magnificent mountain and lakeside setting. Not many world cities can offer a combination of freshwater beaches, tree-lined promenades, paddlesteamers plying clear waters overshadowed by great pyramids of rock, glittering casinos and risqué cabarets, and – most memorably – a marvellous medieval legacy.

The city (map ref: 110 C4) is justly celebrated for all of these things, but its old town is arguably the *coup de grâce*. Bisected by the River Reuss flowing turbulently out of the Vierwaldstättersee (Lake Lucerne), it still retains a powerful flavour of its fascinating past. The surest way of familiarising oneself with this is to amble leisurely across the 14th-century Kapellbrücke – an elegant, roofed footbridge which curves invitingly across a more placid stretch of water upstream of a foaming weir. Dovetailed neatly into its roof trusses are over 100 triangular, early 17th-century paintings recording in colourful story-board fashion the history of the city and its legends. Originally a small fishing village, Lucerne grew to prominence as a result of the founding of a Benedictine monastery in the 9th century. What had been intended to be no more than an annexe of an abbey in Murbach, Alsace, found itself a key staging post by the time the St Gotthard Pass had linked northern and southern Europe in the 13th century. In 1291 the Benedictines sold their possessions to the House of Hapsburg, and the people of Lucerne found themselves reluctantly forced into a series of bloody feuds with their mountain neighbours. Unwilling pugilists or not, the martial instinct was clearly strong and over the

years Lucerne acquired a reputation for providing fearless mercenaries of unshakeable loyalty. In 1792, the Swiss Guards who lost their lives to a man in defence of the French royal family were almost exclusively recruited from Lucerne. Their bravery is

commemorated by the city's powerfully evocative lion monument.

By 1450, the city had shaken off its Hapsburg overlords, and settled down to become an important mercantile centre with thriving markets and over 400 inns and restaurants. During the following centuries it continued to grow in prosperity, although it never quite attained the same degree of influence and power as cities of Berne and Zürich. That doubtless goes some way to explaining why Lucerne still retains a welcome air of intimacy and seclusion.

The city and its surroundings offer an unrivalled choice of activities and excursions. Its rocky guardians, Pilatus and Rigi, two mountains 15km and 24km respectively each side of the centre of town, provide superb walks and matchless views over the Alpine massif and the winding waters of the Vierwaldstättersee – the Lake of the Four Forest Cantons. This irregularly shaped and endlessly fascinating stretch of water is one of the most beautiful lakes in Europe. If the visitor to Lucerne does nothing else during his or her stay, the 3-hour trip by steamer to the town of Flüelen on its southeastern arm will provide, at the very least, a potent taste of the intoxicating pleasures of the city and its delightful environs.

Ceiling paintings on the Chapel Bridge, Lucerne

TOWN WALK

Start from the south bank of the Reuss on the Bahnhofstrasse and cross the famous 13th-century wooden Kapellbrücke.

1 Kapellbrücke (Chapel Bridge)
The series of paintings under the gabled roof show historical events and the legends of the city's two patron saints, Maurice and Leger. The octagonal Wasserturm (water tower) was first used as a watch tower.

Walk up between the baroque Zur Gilgen house and the 12th-century St Peter's chapel, into Kapellplatz with its Fritschi fountain (1918). Double back by the rear of the chapel on to the Rathausquai, and turn right just before the Rathaus (town hall).

2 Rathaus (town hall)
This fine old Renaissance building dates from 1602 and is notable for its unique roof and gable-shaped wooden canopies over its upper windows. The hall is flanked by a tower built in the 12th century but enlarged in the early 1500s. In the adjoining Am Rhyn-Haus, built in 1618 and also Renaissance in style, is a permanent Picasso collection.

Continue through the Kornmarkt, and back down on to Rathausquai via the side of the Rathaus. Cross over a footbridge, back on to the Bahnhofstrasse and turn right.

3 Jesuitenkirche (Jesuit church)
Begun in 1666, the outer shape of this rococo masterpiece was much changed in 1895 with the addition of two 'onion-domed' towers. The original building was the first baroque church in Switzerland and remains one of the most beautiful.

Continue past Renaissance-style Regierungsgebäude (1556), the seat of local government, and turn left into Franziskanerplatz, to find the impressive Barfusser (barefoot) fountain of 1519 and the Franziskanerkirche.

4 Franziskanerkirche
The Franciscan church of St Mary was built between 1270 and 1280. A substantial reconstruction programme in 1561 has left it with a predominantly Gothic flavour.

Return to the river and walk past the old Arsenal, left (1567), now the Historical Museum, and climb to the Spreuerbrücke.

5 Spreuerbrücke
This beautiful roofed bridge was built in 1408. The roof paintings date from 1625.

Walk into the Mühlenplatz, and bear right into the Kramsgasse, then left into the Weinmarkt.

6 Weinmarkt
This is the most impressive of the city's many squares. Bordered by 16th- and 17th-century houses (note particularly the ancient pharmacy) it has as its centrepiece an enchanting copy of a Gothic 15th-century fountain. The original is now in the government palace (Regierungsgebäude).

Continue into Hirschenplatz, a classically contoured courtyard with painted Renaissance buildings, and then into the Weggisgasse. Cross Löwengraben and climb the Mariahilfgasse towards the rampart walls. You will pass the Cysat House, built 1578. At the Museggstrasse turn right and then left up steps, along a path and then under one of the nine Musegg Towers, built between 1291 and 1513. Turn right into Brambergstrasse and down steps to Museggstrasse, left of an arch in the wall. Walk through the busy Löwenplatz up to the Lion Monument.

7 The Lion of Lucerne
This famous monument was sculpted in 1821 in memory of the Swiss Guard who were killed in 1792 protecting the French royal family from the revolutionary mob. The nearby Glacier Garden, discovered in 1872, is a fascinating natural wonder tracing 20 million years of the Earth's history.

Walk back down the Weystrasse to the Hofkirche, founded 768 but burnt down in 1633 and rebuilt in Renaissance style. Skirt the side of the church, through a cloistered terrace on to Zinggentorstrasse, thence on to the quayside to Schweizerhofquai. Cross the Seebrücke back to Kapellbrücke.

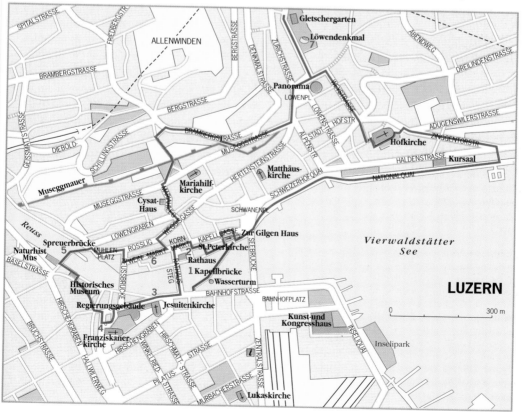

is 4.5km with a minimum gradient of 19 per cent and a maximum of 48 per cent (or nearly 1 in 2) – said to be the steepest in the world. The journey up to Pilatus-Kulm takes about $^1/_2$ hour each way.

From the top station, where there are two hotels, it is a short walk to either of the two peaks of Esel or Oberhaupt up steep, well-prepared paths and steps. The openings in the Oberhaupt tunnel offer glorious views of Lake Lucerne, spread-eagled far below with the surrounding countryside laced with silver, thread-like rivers. The highest projection of the mountain, the Tomlishorn, can be reached in under $^1/_2$ hour by a scenic cliff path. In all directions the panorama is overwhelming. To the north the view extends over the Swiss lowlands, dotted with sparkling lakes, to the Black Forest; to the east, over the lake and beyond Rigi, the Säntis range; to the south and west, the ice-capped giants of the Bernese Oberland.

THE LEGEND OF PONTIUS PILATE

It is said that after the Crucifixion of Christ, Pontius Pilate – then Roman procurator of Judaea – was so stricken by remorse that he travelled to the solitary mountain now named after him, and drowned himself in its lake. Less charitable interpretations suggest he did indeed commit suicide, but only because he suspected that he was to be executed himself for failing to prevent disorder in Samaria. According to local tradition, whenever his spirit was disturbed he would rise up in wrath and call down storm, tempest and flood on the town of Lucerne. Not surprisingly, to prevent any such catastrophe taking place, the town banned anyone from climbing the mountain. The ban lasted until the late Middle Ages.

Leisurely 'mountaineers' at the Mount Pilatus viewing station

PILATUS

MAP REF: 110 C3

The mount of Pilatus is one of the great attractions of the Swiss Alps. The huge pyramid of rock, 2,132m tall, presides like a massive watchtower over Lucerne some 15km to the northeast. Detached from the main range of the Alps, it stands as a solitary giant in the centre of the country, and its forbidding precipices and jagged peaks have been the source of countless legends over the centuries. No visit to this part of Switzerland is truly complete without making the rewarding ascent to its summit.

Its name is popularly believed to be derived from the Roman procurator, Pontius Pilate, who was thought to have drowned himself in its small lake. More prosaic interpretations suggest that the name comes from the Latin word pileatus, or 'hair-covered', because of the scrub that covers even its highest points. Either way, it was the first Swiss mountain to be named and more has been written about it by botanists, historians and geologists than about any other mountain in the country. The ascent can be made in a number of ways: by foot from Hergiswil – a gruelling 5-hour climb of about 1,700m ; 40 minutes by gondola lift from the suburb of Kriens, changing to a cablecar at Fräkmüntegg; or the most popular route by the steepest cogwheel railway in the world, from Alpnachstad, a small village on the lakeside. In 1868 Queen Victoria ventured to the summit on the back of a mule but, sadly, this form of transport is no longer available. The rack railway from Alpnachstad must rank, however, as a similarly memorable experience and, by any standards, it is a remarkable engineering achievement. Built between 1886 and 1889, the total length of track

Newly fallen snow, moulded to Mount Rigi like icing on a cake

RIGI

MAP REF: 111 D4

Some 21km east of Lucerne, the mighty 1,797m-high cliffwall of the Rigi is as enchanting and friendly as Pilatus is stern and forbidding. Separated by Lake Lucerne, the two mountains have vastly different personalities, with Rigi traditionally earning greater affection from local people. In the 19th century it became the goal of what appeared at times to be every tourist in Switzerland, doubtless lured by tales of spectacular sunrises and magnificent views. Then, many of them had to be turned away from the limited number of mountain inns and hotels; today, there are

countless hamlets and small resorts scattered about the mountainside – detracting little from its considerable appeal. The main resort is Rigi-Kaltbad, some 300m beneath the summit and reached by cablecar from the charming lakeside resort of Weggis, or by railway from Vitznau. The latter is the oldest railway of its type in Europe, built 1871. It continues up to the resort of Rigi Kulm, the mountain's highest point, which is also accessible by mountain railway from Arth-Goldau, inaugurated four years later. Both journeys take about 35 minutes. From this point the radius of the remarkable view stretches about 150km in clear weather. There are many delightful, easy walks through Alpine pastures and, in winter, some fine intermediate skiing.

• RIGI

85

MOUNTAIN WALK

Allow 2¹/₂ hours

Take the mountain railway from Arth-Goldau to Rigi-Kulm, and from the top station walk up to the cross on the summit. The magnificent Alpine panorama takes in the Säntis range to the east, the Titlis and the Bernese Oberland to the south, Lucerne and the Jura to the west, and the lowlands and the Black Forest to the north.

Return back along the path and walk down about 500m beyond the station to the Kulmhütte. Turn right here along the level, attractive path through woods to Rigi-Staffel. Continue down to Rigi Staffelhöhe keeping the Vitznau-Rigi railway to the right. At Staffelhöhe, cross the tracks and walk down the path on the Grat ridge to the viewing platform at Känzeli (or Chanzeli). Turn back here taking the wide pathway signposted Kaltbad. At Kaltbad,

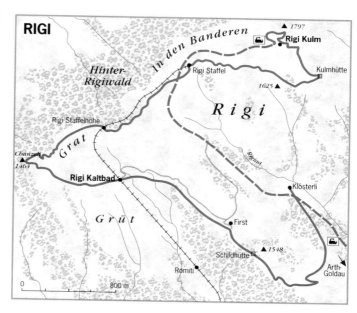

cross the tracks again and bear right towards the Hotel First. At the old, disused Sheidegg railway line take the Felsenweg path through woods to Schildhütte. Following the signs to Rigi-Klösterli, pass the shooting range

on the way down, before arriving at Klösterli station. Take a few minutes to wander about this pleasant little village, a place of pilgrimage since the 18th century and famous for its baroque chapel. Return by train to Arth-Goldau.

SALCHSELN

MAP REF: 110 C3

A charming old village on the eastern bank of the Sarnersee, Sachseln is best known as the final resting place of the only Swiss man ever to have been canonised. Nicolas von Flüe was a prosperous farmer who retreated to a hermit's cell in nearby Ranft at the age of 50 for a life of contemplation. He emerged briefly in 1481 to save the Swiss Confederation from fragmenting at the Diet of Stans, and died in 1518. He is buried under the altar of the church of St Theodul, rebuilt in 1672. The church's interior is a masterpiece of baroque extravagance, with a black marble, galleried nave contrasting vividly with the predominantly white marble chancel. The ossuary adjoining the Romanesque tower contains the slab from the hermit's original tomb.

In the Dorfstrasse in the village centre there is a museum in a late 18th-century house, dedicated to Von Flüe's life and works. Two other houses of interest are the Alte Krone, a half-timbered building dating from 1673, and the Brunmatthaus built in 1750 for a descendant of Von Flüe and notable for its fine exterior plasterwork.
Nearby Flüeli-Ranft is a small hamlet 3.5km northeast of Sachseln. It was here that Von Flüe was born and later retired to his hermit's cell. His original 14th-century home still stands, and is reputed to be the oldest wooden building in the country. His descendants lived in a separate 15th-century house, showing similar characteristics to the earlier building. The hermit's cell can be seen in its original condition next to the oldest of three pilgrim chapels in Ranft.

Schwyz below twin-peaked Mythen

SARNEN

MAP REF: 110 C3

The historic capital of the forest canton of Obwalden, Sarnen was founded in 1210 and played an important part in the early days of the Swiss Confederation. It is attractively situated at the northern end of the pretty lake of Sarnersee, in the middle of the lush Alpine pasture between Interlaken and Lucerne. Conspicuous on a hill above the town to the southwest is the twin-towered parish church of St Peter, founded in the 11th century, but dating in its present form from 1742. Next to it is a 15th-century ossuary.

In the town centre, the Rathaus is a fine baroque structure rebuilt on 16th-century foundations in 1729. It contains 15th-century documents relating to the struggle for independence from Austria, and several portraits of local worthies, including the hermit-hero Nicholas von Flüe (credited

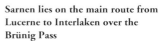

Sarnen lies on the main route from Lucerne to Interlaken over the Brünig Pass

with saving the embryonic Confederation). On a small hill opposite stands the few remains of the castle of the Austrian governor, Heinrich von Landenberg, destroyed by popular revolt in 1308. Near by is the imposing Schutzenhaus with its onion-domed twin towers, built in 1752.

The town is home to two major religious institutions, the St Andrew Convent and the Benedictine college, dating from the early 17th and mid-18th centuries respectively. Both have modern churches built in the 1960s.

There are a number of other historic buildings of interest, including the former arsenal (1599) on the outskirts of the village on the road to Lucerne, now the location of the local museum.
Nearby The Melchtal is a fertile pastoral valley leading south from Sarnen to the tiny resort of Melchsee-Frutt on the bank of the Melchsee. The road passes first through Kerns with some interesting old buildings, among them what is thought to be the oldest stone house in the canton, built in the early 16th century. Four kilometres south is the 14th-century St Nicholas chapel with its unusual timber ceiling comprising 100 decorative panels depicting scenes from the Old and New Testaments. There are cablecars at various points along the valley for hikers taking the mountain route to Engelberg.

SCHWYZ

MAP REF: 111 D4

The ancient town of Schwyz, capital of its canton, is famous for giving its name to Switzerland and also for having one of the most ornate rural baroque churches in the country. Built by the brothers Jakob and Johann Anton Singer between 1769 and 1774, the church of St Martin is an impressive building that dominates the town from the northern side of the Hauptplatz. The two-storey underground crypt in the churchyard dates from 1512. The main church's interior is sumptuously decorated in baroque style, with a notable marble pulpit and many fine frescos. Across the square is an elaborately decorated town hall, built in 1645, and containing some fine decorative woodwork and stained glass in its public rooms. Behind this is a fine 12th-century tower, the Archivturm, now a museum with a collection of cantonal artefacts. In the Herrengasse leading west off the Hauptplatz is the Capuchin monastery, built in 1620. Between the Herrengasse and the Bahnhofstrasse is the Zeughaus, built in the early 18th century as a cornstore, but used subsequently as the town's arsenal.

Other noteworthy buildings include several patrician houses dating from the 16th century, some of which are still inhabited by families that trace their roots back to the foundation of the Confederation. They include the wooden, 16th-century Haus Bethlehem and the early 17th-century Ital-Reding Haus, a curious combination of baroque and rustic architecture with two domed turrets. In the Schmiedgasse, running south of the square, is the early 17th-century Redinghaus – another baroque residence built around a central courtyard. In the splendid pre-World War II Bundesbriefarchiv on the Bahnhofstrasse there is a collection of federal documents dating from the 13th century, including a collection of excellently preserved 14th-century banners. The building is also attractively decorated, inside and out, with some unusual frescos painted in the 1930s.

The town is located in a beautiful position at the foot of the twin peaks of the Mythen, rising to a height of 1,811m and 1,899m respectively. To the west is the Urmiberg, the eastern spur of the Rigi, and to the east the truncated cone of the Fronalpstock.

Nearby On the eastern outskirts of the town, reached via a narrow road, is the small village of Rickenbach notable for its 17th-century chapel with baroque and Gothic interior features, and the ruins of an 11th-century fortress. A cable-car leads up to just below the Grossemythen, from where there is a fine view.

Twelve kilometres south of Schwyz is the old village of Muotathal, with a cluster of attractive wooden houses, a late-18th-century rococo church, and a Franciscan convent dating from 1684. A mountain lift ascends to the summit of Stoos, and thence to the 1,922m Fronalpstock, from where there is an extensive panorama over the Urnersee towards the peaks of central Switzerland.

CYCLE TOUR

Allow a full day

From the Hauptplatz in the centre of Schwyz, turn left up by the side of St Martin's church and ride through the small village of Rickenbach, about 1.5km southeast. This is a winding mountain road which becomes progressively steeper as it makes its tortuous way through thick forest for about 10km up to the splendid viewpoint of Ibergeregg at 1,406m. The most difficult part of the tour is now over, and from here the road descends steeply at first, then more gently by the right bank of the Minster to the small hamlet of Tschalun. At the larger village of Oberiberg just ahead, follow the main road round to the left through Stöcken and Unteriberg. Continue around the south bank of the Sihlsee, through the hamlet of Euthal and cross over the bridge on the left just past it. Turn right at the end and follow the road along the west bank of the lake through Gross, and turn left at the first opportunity into the centre of Einsiedeln. Ride past the huge monastery on the left, bearing right into the main street and take the first road southwest to Alpthal on the left. This crosses over the

Alp River just before the village of Trachslau, and then climbs gently along the west bank of the river until Alpthal. At the end of the village on the right a bridle-path climbs steeply to the Haggenegg Pass at 1,414m. It will probably be necessary to dismount for part, if not most, of this section – particularly if the bike is not equipped with fat tyres. The climb lasts a little over 3km, but from Haggenegg the path rejoins a good mountain track for the 6km descent to Schwyz. (If the Haggenegg Pass route does not appeal, it is possible to return to Schwyz on the main road from Einsiedeln via Biberbrugg, Rothenturm and Sattel.)

SEELISBERG

MAP REF: 111 D3

This secluded resort, on a mountain terrace high above Lake Lucerne, is one of the most exclusive summer retreats in central Switzerland. Facing the twin peaks of the Mythen and, beneath them, the delightful towns of Schwyz and Brunnen, Seelisberg occupies a remarkable and attractive site. The village is set in semi-Alpine pasture and woods, and affords beautiful views over the lake and surrounding mountains. Among its many amenities is a network of charming wooded paths, one of which leads to the idyllically situated hunting castle of Beroldingen which was founded in 1530. The resort is reached by a scenic lakeside road from the lovely village of Beckenried 11km to the west, or by 8 minute funicular from the Treib landing stage.

Nearby A path leads from the village down to the historic lakeside meadow of Rütli, about a $1/2$-hour walk away. A few kilometres further up the lakeshore is the famous old boatman's house of Treib, the meeting place of the Old Confederates. Although the original was destroyed by fire in 1657, it was immediately rebuilt in the same style and has since been sensitively restored a number of times – most recently in 1982.

RÜTLI – THE CRADLE OF SWITZERLAND

It was on this sacred meadow that the Confederates of the Three Founder Cantons are said to have met in 1307 to take an oath confirming the Everlasting League of 1291 and throw off the yoke of their Austrian oppressors. Every year thousands of Swiss children visit the Rütli to re-enact the solemn oath and recall the more recent occasion when the Swiss affirmed to the world their determination to defend their neutrality at all costs.

On 25 July 1940, when Switzerland was entirely surrounded by the Axis powers, General Henri Guisan summoned his highest-ranking commanders to this field, not simply as a symbolic gesture but also to agree the national defence plan.

Now, in November of every year, a national shooting competition is held here, in part as an excuse for a huge national party, but also to remind potential aggressors of the unerring accuracy of Swiss marksmen.

Weggis on Lake Lucerne. The cable-car transports people to the top of the Männlichen – where winter ski runs are numerous

STANS

MAP REF: 110 C3

This is an old and historic cantonal capital nestling under the tree-covered peak of the 1,898m Stanserhorn on the southern perimeter of Lake Lucerne. It is also, incidentally, a cradle of the purest form of democratic life. Once a year, on the last Sunday in April, the citizens meet to elect their cantonal government by a show of hands. The splendid 17th-century baroque church is the town's most impressive building. Rebuilt in 1647, it has a fine Romanesque belfry and contains the unusual pilgrim's chapel of St Mary Under-the-Hearth situated

Seelisberg above Lake Lucerne

beneath the left aisle. Several important 18th-century buildings are near by, including the town hall, the Historical Museum, and the Rosenburg manor house known as the 'Höfli'.

The summit of the Stanserhorn is reached by funicular and cablecar from the town centre. It offers fine views of Lake Lucerne, and the peaks of the Titlis and the Jungfrau massif to the south and southwest.

Stans is famous for its association with three of Switzerland's great historical figures. On 9 July 1386, during the decisive Battle of Sempach between the Austrians and the Swiss Confederates, one Arnold von Winkelried (a citizen of Stans) hurled himself into the massed ranks of the Austrian spear-carriers in an heroic sacrifice to breach a path through them for his compatriots. This single action is said to have turned the battle in the Swiss's favour. Nearly a century later, in 1481, Niklaus von Flüe, the Hermit of Ranft, saved the Confederation at a critical time when it threatened to dissolve through a combination of good sense and expert diplomacy. More recently, Heinrich Pestalozzi, who is known as the father of modern education, started his famous orphanage in the town for the children of the 400 men slaughtered in a courageous stand against the French in 1798.

ZUG

MAP REF: 111 D4

On the banks of the second largest lake in central Switzerland, the Zugersee, Zug is an ancient walled city with a well-preserved medieval centre distinguished by ruined fortifications and delicate spires. This is clustered around the old Kolinplatz. On the side of the square is the 16th-century Rathaus (town hall) and a fine old clock tower (the Zytturm) with a blue-and-white tiled roof crowned by a slender belfry. There are picturesque rows of houses dating from the 16th century in the Ober-Altstadt and Unter-Altstadt between the Kolinplatz and the lake, and to the east up the Aegeristrasse is the 1526 Capuchins' Tower, close to the 16th-century chapel of a Capuchin convent. The other medieval tower of interest is the Pulverturm (Powder Tower) on the southern extremity of the old town on the Zugerbergstrasse. The town's most outstanding structure is the late Gothic church of St Oswald, just to the south of Kolinplatz. Built between 1478 and 1515, it is dedicated rather curiously to the English St Oswald, whose remains were said to have been brought to Zug at the time of its foundation. The choirstalls date from 1484.

The handsome church of St Michael, on a hill to the east, was erected in 1902.

The quaysides from the Seestrasse to the Alpenquai offer delightful views of the mountains of central Switzerland, including Rigi and Pilatus, and the peaks of the Bernese Oberland. The town's own mountain, the 1,039m Zugerberg, is a tall, wooded plateau reached by car through the Schonfels, southeast of Zug. From there it is a short climb to a terrace with impressive views. **Nearby** Five kilometres east of Zug are the Höllgrotten (Hell's Grottoes). These stalactite caves are well worth an excursion.

MOTOR TOUR

This 155km tour skirts the rocky mountain sentinels of Pilatus and Rigi and also includes the historic cities of Lucerne, Schwyz and Zug.

From the centre of Stans take the minor road northeast, under the N2, to the pretty lakeside town of Buochs. Continue 5km east along the south bank of Lake Lucerne to Beckenried.

Beckenried

Beckenried has considerable historical significance as the original venue of the Diet of the Old Confederates, who held their assemblies here between 1350 and 1554. The church of St Heinrich was built between 1790 and 1807, and the pilgrim chapel of Maria im Ridli, high above the lake, was built in 1701. A cable-car leads from the village to the 1,593m summit of Klewenalp, where there are splendid summer walks (and skiing in winter).

Follow the lakeside road east through St Anna. Just after, join the eastbound carriage of the N2, which will shortly enter a 10km tunnel. At the end of the tunnel follow the signs for Altdorf. The town is a 3km diversion south of the circular tour. From the central square take the same road back, through the small resort of Flüelen on the banks of the Urnersee and thence towards Brunnen on the Axenstrasse, a beautiful lakeside road cut into the rock-face and passing through a series of short tunnels. At Brunnen follow the lake road round to the left to Gersau, Vitznau and Weggis.

Weggis

Known as the 'vegetable garden of Lucerne', Weggis is arguably the most attractive of the lake resorts. The chapel of Allerheiligen was built in 1623 and is notable for its late Renaissance frescos. Note also the neo-classical Hotel du Lac, built in 1838. A cable-car leads from the village to Rigi Kaltbad.

Continue ahead to Küssnacht and remain on Route 2, travelling for 2km northeast towards the Hohle Gasse.

Hohle Gasse

Legend has it that it was here in the 'Hollow Lane' that William Tell shot the Austrian tyrant, Gessler, who had forced him to shoot the apple from his son's head. The scene is marked by the Tell Chapel, built in 1638, with a painting recording Gessler's death.

Head south on the old road through Arth and Goldau to Schwyz. From the centre of this historic town (which gave its name to the country) take Route 8, signed Sattel and Einsiedeln. At Sattel turn left on the road back to Goldau and then immediately right towards the resort of Unterägeri, following the east bank of the Agerisee. From Unterägeri remain on the same road until Zug. From the centre of this lovely medieval town take Route 4 around the northern perimeter of the Zugersee.

Continue on Route 4 to Lucerne. From the city centre follow the signs for the N2 back to Stans.

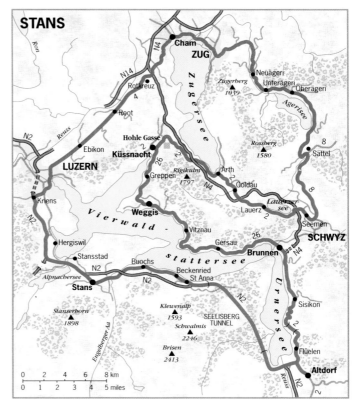

BERN (BERNE) & THE BERNESE OBERLAND

The second largest of Switzerland's cantons, the 6,050 sq km area is more than two-thirds mountainous with the great rocky spine of the Bernese massif traversing the area from the Wildhorn range in the west to the Sustenhorn on the border with central Switzerland. The southern flanks of these great mountains form part of the neighbouring canton of Valais, but the magnificent peaks of the Jungfrau, Eiger, Mönch and Finsteraarhorn are all part of the Bernese Oberland.

This dramatic mountain region has been instrumental in establishing some of the world's most famous climbing and skiing resorts – Mürren, Wengen and Grindelwald foremost among them. The latter share what is arguably the most scenic skiing terrain in the world on the slopes beneath the Jungfrau range. Just to the north lies one of Switzerland's oldest-established holiday destinations, the splendidly sited town of Interlaken, set midway between the delightful lakes of Thun and Brienz and commonly referred to as the 'Gateway to the Bernese Oberland'. The range of facilities that this major holiday centre offers rivals that of any other of the leading resorts in the country.

Beyond it to the north lie the 'Pre-Alps' of the Oberland, which precede the area known as Mittelland, at the heart of which lies Switzerland's capital, Berne. If not the gateway to the Bernese Oberland, this charming and historic old city might justifiably call itself the gateway to the entire Alpine region which unfolds invitingly before it over the rich pasture of the Emmental and Aare valleys.

It is often said of Berne that no other capital in Europe provides such swift and unimpeded access to the countryside, but it might be added that few other capitals exercise such a powerful incentive to stay. Listed by UNESCO as one of the world's major cultural assets, the romantic medieval streets of the Old Town are lined with row upon row of sandstone arcades, providing, as long ago as the 17th century, the world's first covered shopping 'mall'. Remarkably, the 6km-long 'Lauben' remains the world's longest covered promenade. The entrancing mixture of cobbled streets, elegant patrician houses, intricately sculpted, 16th-century fountains, bustling street markets – not forgetting the famous bearpits (which the shaggy city mascots have occupied for centuries) – represents one of the most genuinely pleasing experiences that Switzerland has to offer.

Founded by Berchtold V of Zähringen at the end of the 12th century, Berne expanded considerably under the protectorate of Peter of Savoy a century later. In 1353 it joined the Swiss Confederation, but continued to pursue an independent policy of hegemony against non-Swiss states. Between the years 1536 and 1798 the Bernese ruled much of what is now western Switzerland, including most of the area around Lake Geneva. Berne became the Swiss capital in 1848.

In due course the lure of the Swiss Alps, enticingly visible from the south-facing terraces of the Münster and the Bundeshaus, will provide persuasive enough reason to depart this lovely city. A fast road leaves south, following the course of the Aare River, to the equally historic town of Thun just 22km away. Lying on the northwest bank of the lake of the same name, this ancient Celtic settlement vies with Interlaken as the premier resort of the Bernese Oberland. In its favour is a collection of splendid medieval buildings, particularly in the Hauptgasse with its extraordinary arrangement of elevated pavements, and an imposing 12th-century castle.

The town's surroundings may be impressive, but they cannot match that of Interlaken's which were described by the German composer, Mendelssohn, in 1842 as 'the most wonderful of all in

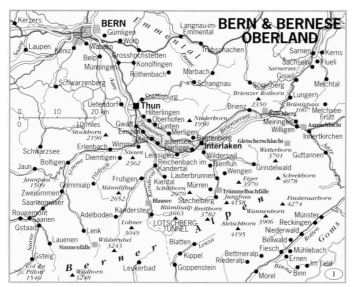

this unbelievably beautiful country'. The view of the Jungfrau massif from the town's elegant and leafy boulevard, the Höheweg, is one of the most memorable in the Alps, and is even further enhanced by a trip via funicular to the summit of the Harder Kulm just north of the town's centre.

Also close to the town is the idyllic and peaceful little lakeside resort of Bönigen, just one of the many beautiful villages on Lake Brienz. Ringgenburg on the north bank, and Iseltwald on the south are two of the more exceptional. At its eastern end, the old town of Brienz is not only a well-equipped holiday resort, but also one of the most famous centres of wood-carving skills in the world. From here the romantic days of rail travel are recalled by Switzerland's last surviving steam-powered cog-wheel railway. The distinctive red carriages are nudged to the top of the 2,350m Brienzer Rothorn by a miniature, green steam engine. Another nostalgic experience is a moonlight cruise by paddle-steamer over the still, deep waters of Lake Brienz from Interlaken Ost. Of the two lakes, Lake Thun is the larger and more frequented, surrounded by orchards of fig trees, vineyards and lush pastures. It is bordered by similarly charming lakeside villages, of which Spiez and Oberhofen with their medieval castles stand out as two of the finest. Offering a wide choice of watersports, these lakes are almost unique in their ability to provide a summer morning's windsurfing or swimming, followed by an afternoon's glacier skiing beneath the Jungfrau.

This flexibility, and variety of climate and scenery, is one of the great advantages of the Bernese Oberland and helps to explain why it has been such a popular tourist destination since the mid-19th century. However, it was the arrival of the skiing pioneers in the early 20th century that really marked the beginning of the Bernese Oberland's incalculable impact on the winter sports industry. Predominantly British adventurers, with primitive hickory planks strapped to their feet, they were enormously influential in transforming the sleepy Alpine villages of Mürren, Wengen and Grindelwald from mountaineering centres into the world-famous ski resorts they have become.

One man in particular was instrumental in effecting this change. Sir Henry Lunn, a one-time tennis racquet salesman, organised the first package tours to the region in 1910. Blatantly exploiting British class-consciousness, he insisted on certain 'social credentials' before accepting a booking. His son, Arnold, continued to promote the resorts – particularly Mürren – and the result is that they remain to this day popular British enclaves. Any tour of the Swiss Alps would be incomplete without visiting all three, not only because of their superb settings but because of one outstanding individual attraction that each possesses. At Mürren it is the remarkable revolving restaurant on the summit of the Schilthorn, offering a superb circular mountain panorama that simply defies description. In Wengen, it is the trip by cogwheel railway first to Kleine Scheidegg, and from there through a tunnel behind the north face of the Eiger to the Jungfraujoch – Europe's highest railway station – with views that are similarly stunning. In Grindelwald, the 'glacier village', it is the two magnificent glaciers that give every impression of waiting to roll remorselessly over the resort before discharging their icy waters into the Lütschine River. Wengen and Mürren, both dramatically located on mountain shelves, face each other across the spectacularly deep Lauterbrunnen valley – famous for the splendid waterfalls of Staubbach and Trümmelbach, the latter one of the most impressive falls in the Alps.

The rumble of waterfalls is a recurring feature throughout much of the Bernese Oberland. Other captivating examples of this natural wonder include the Giessbach Falls, plunging through the thickly wooded slopes on the south bank of Lake Brienz; the famous Reichenbach Falls close by in the precipitous Hasli valley, where Sherlock Holmes and Moriarty met their fictional watery deaths; and the Engstligen Falls southwest of the charming resort of Adelboden. Mountain lakes are another compelling attraction of the region and there can be few more beautiful than the Oeschinensee above the

Idyllic Brienz on Lake Brienz

traditional resort of Kandersteg, lying at the head of the Kander valley south of Spiez.

Needless to observe in such a mountainous region, valleys are also a conspicuous feature of the scenery. West of Kandersteg as the crow flies lie the Engstligental, the beautiful Simmental and the remote Lauenental. At the foot of the latter is Gstaad, the exclusive winter sports resort, which ranks with St Moritz as one of the most fashionable destinations in the Swiss Alps, and yet further reason to take time to explore this remarkable part of the world.

ADELBODEN

MAP REF: 110 B3

A quaint old village at the head of
the broad, sunny valley of
Engstligental, Adelboden lies
below the towering 3,243m
Wildstrubel on the western
extremity of the Bernese Alps. To
the east it is well-sheltered by the
3,049m Lohner. At 1,356m it is one
of the Bernese Oberland's highest
altitude resorts and, since its link
with the nearby ski resort and spa
town of Lenk, it has moved
progressively up the league of
winter sports resorts in
Switzerland. It has been a popular
summer resort since the mid-19th
century. To date it has not suffered
too much in the way of new
development, and its long main
thoroughfare still retains a
traditional Alpine feel with an
attractive cluster of ancient timber
houses leaning precariously into
the street. The village church dates
from 1433 and has a weather-
beaten, 16th-century mural of the
Last Judgment still clinging
resiliently to an exterior wall.
One of the most attractive features
of the resort is its proximity to
abundant waterfalls. These are
plainly visible all the way up the
beautiful Engstligental valley on
the right, but the best is kept until
beyond Adelboden below the
Engstligenalp. The Engstligen Falls
drop about 150m in two leaps
over a rocky shelf and provide a
striking spectacle with the icy
anvil-shaped Wildstrubel in the
background.

The best panorama (for non-
climbers) is from the summit of

The Niederhorn above Beatenburg

the Laveygrat at an altitude of
2,209m . This is reached by a long,
three-stage gondola lift from the
south of the village up to Geils,
then by triple chair up a steep
slope which, for skiers, is a very
tough black run dropping over
500m back to Geils. There are fine
views down into Lenk, and across
much of the Alpine range. In
summer there are many delightful
walks around Adelboden, through
Alpine pastures richly carpeted
with rhododendrons – particularly
above the small hamlet of Boden.

The village of Adelboden

BEATENBURG

MAP REF: 110 C3

This is an impressively sited resort
perched on a terrace on the
southern flank of the 1,950m
Niederhorn. Consisting mainly of
holiday chalets, apartments and
hotels straggling along a forked
road for about 5km, it has little
community focus but, by way of
compensation, some spectacular
views of Interlaken below it, and
across Thunersee (Lake Thun) to
the shining glaciers of the Jungfrau
massif.

It has all the amenities one might
expect of one of the leading
summer resorts in the Bernese

Oberland, including tennis and swimming, and a marvellous natural wonder in the shape of the St Beatus's Caves (Beatus Höhlen) off the main cliff road beneath the village. According to legend, an Irish missionary named Beatus lived here in the 6th century, having evicted a dragon. Certainly there is some indication of human habitation many centuries ago, but to date archaeologists have failed to find any evidence of occupation by a pyrogenic reptile.

A trip by chair-lift to the summit of the Niederhorn is strongly recommended. This offers one of the great Alpine panoramas, sweeping across the entire southern Alpine range to Mont Blanc which is clearly visible in fine conditions.

BRIENZ

MAP REF: 110 C3

Brienz is one of the most charming villages in the Bernese Oberland, attractively located on the northeastern shore of the pretty cobalt-blue lake named after it. It faces the Giessbachfälle (Giessbach Falls) cascading through woods 2km across the lake, generally considered to be amongst the most beautiful waterfalls in the Alps.

The village itself is the centre of Switzerland's woodcarving industry, and amongst the fine old vine-covered timber buildings lining the streets are a number of woodworkers' shops with freshly carved figures, models and furnishings in their windows. There is also a world-famous school that specialises in teaching the art of making stringed musical instruments. The church on a hill on the western fringe of the village is 16th-century, and contains a fine carved altar dating from 1517. The Romanesque tower is early 12th-century, and the view of the Meiringen valley from the churchyard beneath it is impressive.

Behind Brienz to the north is the stately 2,350m peak of Brienzer Rothorn. More waterfalls tumble down its side, and the summit is reached by the last steam-driven cog-wheel railway in the country, built in 1892. The splendid view embraces the Bernese and Valais Alps, and the northern peaks of central Switzerland.

Nearby The village of Ballenberg, a few kilometres east, is an attractive wooded park with an open-air museum that houses a unique display of old rural architecture. Buildings from all over the country have been

dismantled, transported and re-erected here, complete with the sort of furnishings typical of their period. Even their surroundings have been carefully arranged to simulate their original environment.

ERLENBACH

MAP REF: 110 B3

Many fine examples of typical extensively decorated Bernese houses, with low-pitched roofs and wide eaves, are to be found in this interesting village. Ten kilometres south of Spiez, at the mouth of the Simmental valley, it is approached from the east on an attractive road that follows the course of the Simme River with its quaint roofed bridges. The church dates from the 10th century and, although much altered, it retains a number of appealing features. It is set on a terrace, raised above the village, and is reached via a wooden, covered stairway leading off the main street. Inside are a large number of murals dating from the early 15th century. Further along the main street is a cablecar station, from where a two-stage, 25-minute journey can be made to the top of the 2,190m Stockhorn. From the mid-station at Chrindi, the cablecar glides directly over the pretty lake of Stockenseen up through rich Alpine flora to one of the most breathtaking spots in the Bernese Oberland. The panorama from the summit, about a 10-minute walk from the top station, ranks among the most impressive in Switzerland. To the north lies the

The chair-lift on the Niederhorn

glittering Lake Thun, and beyond it the Emmental valley; to the south, the broad green valley of the Simmental with its lovely Alpine meadows. Beyond that lie the great white peaks of the Valais Alps and Mont Blanc, and to the southeast the awesome giants of the Jungfrau massif.

Nearby South from the small village of Latterbach, 2km from Erlenbach, is the entrance to the Diemtigal valley. This is one of the most unspoilt pastoral regions of the Bernese Oberland, liberally blessed with beautiful meadows and thick pine forests. The village

Autumnal sunshine, Brienz

of Diemtigen is passed through on the way to the tiny old health resort of Grimmialp. Surrounded by towering peaks, this is a popular starting point for keen hikers. The 2,652m Männliflue, a somewhat strenuous ascent from the small hamlet of Filderich, offers just one of the many fine views from this ring of mountains.

THE CITY OF BERN (BERNE)

Lying at the gateway to the Swiss Alps on a rocky peninsula in the River Aare (map ref: 110 B3), this delightful city is, arguably, the most enchanting of world capitals. Few other centres of government can begin to emulate its distinctive blend of medieval beauty and quiet charm. In some senses it is a living museum where 16th- and 17th-century buildings play host to a variety of long-standing uses, and where ancient customs are still rigorously observed.

However, in other ways it somehow contrives to be a modern, prosperous cultural and business centre where embassies, legations and international organisations operate from the heart of the old town. Perhaps the secret of Berne's enduring appeal is that there is little of the functional architecture that blights other historic capitals – not, at least, in the centre of the city. It is possible to walk down narrow, cobbled streets, through magnificent medieval arcades, past splendid Gothic buildings, gilded fountains and lavishly decorated towers, and imagine with little difficulty what it must have been like to walk those same streets 300 and 400 years ago. There is nothing artificial about Berne; it is a microcosm of genuine Swiss history.

The city was founded by Berchtold V, Duke of Zähringen in the late 12th century. According to legend, he resolved to name it after the first animal felled in a hunt through the thickly wooded outskirts of the new settlement. Happily, it was a bear (in German *bär*, pronounced 'barn' in local dialect); no doubt *schwein* would not have denoted the same qualities of dignity and fortitude. The bear remains the symbol of the city to this day, and its ubiquitous image is even found in the flesh in Berne's famous bear-pits. In the 13th century, under the protectorate of Count Peter of Savoy, further expansion took place, but in 1405 the greater part of the town was gutted by fire. The buildings that replaced those destroyed were themselves replaced by the greenish sandstone masterpieces of 16th- and 17th-century design which now characterise the city. They remain barely altered – at least in external appearance.

Although it joined the Swiss Confederation in 1353, Berne continued to pursue its own policy of territorial expansion with considerable vigour. Between the years 1536 to 1798 it enjoyed its greatest influence, mostly at the expense of the House of Savoy. Bernese rule at that time extended as far as the Vaud Alps and the northern banks of Lake Geneva. Indeed, without this period of continuing hegemony it is unlikely that much of the French-speaking part of Switzerland would today be part of the Confederation.

With the Napoleonic invasion of 1798, Berne's authority was temporarily extinguished and in the new country that emerged from the ruins of the French emperor's imperial vision, the city had surrendered almost half of its territories. None the less, it became the cantonal capital and in 1848 was chosen to be the seat of the Swiss Parliament and capital of the Confederation. In a touching acknowledgement of the benevolence of the earlier period of Bernese rule, its former vassal states were unanimously in favour of this choice.

Today Berne is the natural centre of a culturally and linguistically diverse nation. A pleasing symbiosis of Germanic and Gallic influences, it is a rewarding city to explore at leisure and on foot, both from the point of view of the beauty of its buildings and the rich treasures which, on closer inspection, many of them yield.

Market stalls in Berne

TOWN WALK

Whichever route the walker takes, three distinctive features of this ancient medieval city stand out: its arcades, fountains and towers. The 7km of *Lauben* (15th-century arcades) that flank its narrow, cobbled streets are in some ways the precursor of the modern shopping mall. The 11 intricately crafted thematic fountains are largely the legacy of the sculptor, Hans Gieng, who erected them in the mid-16th century. Berne's famous towers date from the earliest days of the founding of the city, and the impressive clock tower – one of the most enduring images of Switzerland – is as good a place as any to start a walk.

1 Zeitglockenturm (clock tower)

Built in 1191, this was the city's west gate until 1256. Its present appearance dates from the late 15th century. The astronomical clock was installed in 1530, and four minutes before each hour a mechanical figure-play takes place in an alcove next to the clockface.

Walk eastwards down the Kramgasse. Pass first the Zähringer Fountain, raised in 1542 in memory of the city's founder and surmounted by the heraldic bear, and then, a short distance further along on the righthand side at No 49, the former home of Albert Einstein (the upper floor is now a museum). After the Samson Fountain take the next left down Kreuzgasse for the Rathaus .

2 Rathaus (Town Hall).

This is a beautiful, late-Gothic building dating from 1406. Still the seat of both city and cantonal government, it is notable for its splendid old council chamber. In front of the town hall is the Rathausplatz, a perfectly preserved medieval square at the centre of which is the Venner Fountain.

Walk back to the Kramgasse and continue left past the Fountain of Justice on Gerechtigkeitsgasse. Bear left at the bottom and walk down the steep Nydeggstalden, keeping the Nydeggkirche to the right. The church dates from 1341. This is the site of Berchtold V's original fortress. Turn left and cross over the Untertorbrücke. At this point you have the option of turning left for the Rosengarten, a climb up the Aargauerstalden for fine views, or turning right and following the signs for the Bärengraben (Bear Pits).

3 The Bear Pits

Animal rights' supporters might claim with some justification that these 10m deep soulless dug-outs, built in 1857, are aptly named. However, the bears seem content, not least because they are shamelessly pampered with titbits.

Cross back over the Nydeggbrücke and continue up the Junkerngasse to the Münster (cathedral and chapter house). Turn left behind it for a view over the River Aare.

4 Münster (cathedral)

This masterpiece of the late Gothic period in Switzerland was begun in 1421. The 100m steeple, added in 1893, is reputedly the highest in Switzerland. The cathedral is otherwise notable for its figurative depiction of the Last Judgement above the main portal dating from 1495. Inside, the beautiful stained-glass windows date from 1441, and the finely carved choirstalls from 1523.

Continue up Münstergasse, until you reach the Casinoplatz. A possible extension to the walk is to cross the Kirchenfeldbrücke into the New Town to visit Berne's museum quarter in Helvetiaplatz (including the Natural History, Swiss Rifle and Bernese Historical museums). Otherwise turn right just before it and take the walkway to the terrace fronting the Bundeshaus.

5 Bundeshaus

This imposing, late 19th-century building is the seat of Swiss government. Its most obvious attraction is a broad terrace with sweeping views over the Aare.

Taking the steps up the left side of the Bundeshaus, cross the Bundesplatz into the Bärenplatz – the site of a street market on Tuesdays and Saturdays. At the Käfigturm (prison tower, 1256) turn left up Spitalgasse past the Piper Fountain as far as the Heiliggeistkirche (church of the Holy Ghost, 1729). Retrace the route back past the prison tower, down Marktgasse, past the Anna Seiler and Musketeer fountains and back to the clock tower.

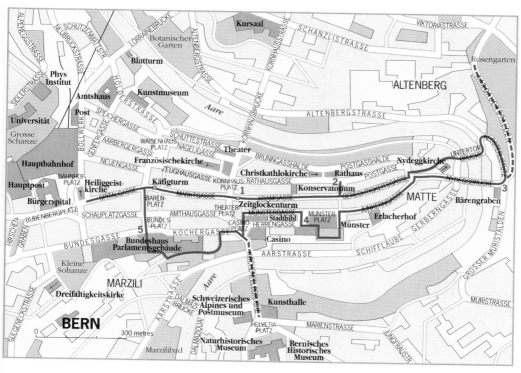

·THE PEAKS·

The Alps were the natural cradle of mountaineering, and the beauty and unpredictable nature of the Swiss Alpine ranges have traditionally drawn the best and boldest of climbers. As long ago as the 16th century men were exploring the highest passes, but few ventured far beyond the permanent snow-line to the summits of the great mountains.

The reason for their timidity was simple; they knew that the peaks were dangerous, and that they supported no human life. This latter consideration held an additional and powerful disincentive to explore further. As recently as the early 18th century some of the most learned authorities on Alpine conditions persisted in their belief that the world above the snow-line was occupied exclusively by dragons. In 1708 one Professor Schenchzer, a Fellow of the Royal Society, even went to the extent of classifying the types and relative ferocity of different Alpine fire-breathing reptiles. Less scholarly opinion, notably that of sections of the Church and the peasant classes, insisted that the eternal snows were also home to the spirits of the damned. Shortly before the first successful ascent of the Matterhorn in 1866, local people in Zermatt were still speaking of a ruined city on the summit where evil spirits dwelt.

The prevailing mood of the time was therefore decisively against incurring the wrath of the mountain spirits. But there were notable rejections of the received wisdom of contemporary experts. The first recorded ascent of any Alpine peak was by six monks in 1387 who toiled successfully up to the summit of the 2,129m Mount Pilatus above Lake Lucerne. But it

was the attempts to scale the great peaks of the Monte Rosa range and the successful ascent of Mont Blanc in 1786 which provided the real spur to Alpine exploration. The 4,158m Jungfrau was climbed by the Meyer brothers in 1811, and most of the peaks of Monte Rosa had been conquered by an assortment of international climbers by 1842. At this point, the interest of British climbers had been attracted and in 1854 the ascent of the Wetterhorn by Alfred Wills on his honeymoon – although not the first – is seen as the birth of mountaineering as a sport. In the succeeding 11 years, known as the 'Golden Age' of mountaineering, the British climbed virtually every remaining peak of significance in the Alps. In 1857 the Alpine Club was founded in London for an exclusive membership of those who had ascended above 3,962m, and the remaining years of the decade witnessed an astonishing series of ascents throughout the Alps – at times with almost casual disregard for the danger.

But it was the attempt on the Matterhorn in 1865 which really captured world attention, and simultaneously signalled the end of the Golden Age. A young British artist, Edward Whymper, commissioned in the early part of the 1860s to draw a series of sketches for the *Alpine Journal*, became obsessed by the desire to be the first to conquer the Matterhorn. It was, by common consent, the last of the great challenges in the Alps. On a number of occasions he attempted the ascent from the Italian side in the company of the famous guide Jean-Antoine Carrel, but he was defeated each time. Returning to the Italian town of Breuil in 1865 for a renewed attempt, he was horrified to discover that Carrel had already been hired by a rival Italian party. A chance meeting with another British climber, the 18-year-old Lord Francis Douglas, led to the discovery that a Zermatt guide called Taugwalder had decided that the ascent was also possible from the Swiss side. Whymper and Douglas then hastened to Zermatt to hire him. There they discovered that Taugwalder and his son were available, but that another British party led by the Reverend Charles Hudson had already planned an ascent with the celebrated French guide Michel Croz.

Deciding to join forces in the interests of national pride (and, incidentally, to reduce the risks involved in having two parties make a simultaneous climb) they set out on a summer morning in mid-July to climb the last of the great Swiss peaks. Later, Whymper conceded, there was some dispute between he and Hudson about who was leading the expedition and also – more critically – Hudson's companion, Douglas Hadow, proved to be completely inexperienced. On the morning of 14 July they reached the top in triumph – an achievement made more satisfying by the sight of the Italian party still toiling up the southern flank hundreds of feet below. On the descent an hour later – disaster struck. Hadow slipped, knocking Croz below him from his holds. Hudson and Douglas above them also lost their grip, and then the rope which had tied the climbers together snapped between the elder Taugwalder and the four hapless climbers beneath.

Taugwalder, his son, and Whymper watched helplessly as their companions plunged 1,219m to their deaths. Three of the bodies were later recovered, but that of Lord Francis Douglas was never found. It proved to be the most controversial incident in the history of mountaineering, and the consequences plagued Whymper for the rest of his life. Speculation grew that Taugwalder had cut the rope to save himself, his son and Whymper from certain death, and despite grudging exoneration by

the subsequent enquiry the guide and members of his family eventually left Switzerland to escape a continuing spiral of gossip.

For a short period the sport of mountaineering came into serious disrepute throughout the world. Quickly recovering, another series of firsts was achieved during what has become known as the 'Silver Age' of mountain climbing. The first ascent of the Matterhorn by a woman was made by Lucy Walker on 22 July 1871 in the company of her 63-year-old father. The spell was broken, and mountaineering was now a pursuit open to all peoples of all sexes and all callings. Once all the major Swiss peaks had been conquered, the new challenge was to conquer them in different ways. A new ideology embraced the sport, and by the 1930s only two great challenges remained – the near-vertical north faces of the Matterhorn and the Eiger (known as the Eigerwand). Both were climbed successfully by Germans (in the case of the Eigerwand, a joint Austro-German party).

The Eigerwand continues to exercise a fascination for climbers

from all over the world and, despite attempts in the 1930s to ban climbing on it (a move which was guaranteed to increase its attraction), it is still seen as one of the ultimate tests of mountaineering skill. In a scathing criticism of the compulsion which drives climbers to risk their lives scaling it, the editor of the *Alpine Journal* wrote shortly before the first successful ascent: 'The Eigerwand – still unscaled – continues to be an obsession for the mentally deranged of almost every nation. He who first succeeds may rest assured that he has accomplished the most imbecile variant since mountaineering first began'.

Opposite: the Matterhorn, seen from the Gornergrat near Zermatt. Above: the awesome Jungfrau massif, with its group of three famous peaks. From left to right, the Eiger (3,970m), the Mönch (4,099m) and the Jungfrau (4,158m)

GRINDELWALD

MAP REF: 110 C3

This is a large, cosmopolitan and busy year-round resort spread over a wide area at the head of the Lütschine valley some 20km southeast of Interlaken. It is one of the three great mountaineering and skiing centres of the Jungfrau region, and is famed for its spectacular views of the Oberer and Unterer glaciers and the great peaks of the Wetterhorn and the Schreckhorn rising majestically above them. However, it is unquestionably the vertical north face of the Eiger that provides Grindelwald's seductive mixture of enchantment and notoriety. This sheer, dark wall of rock glowers menacingly down on the village, and for well over a century it has acted as a magnet for mountain climbers, many of whom have discovered to their cost that its magnetic qualities do not include a sure grip on the rock-face.

The first recorded mention of Grindelwald is found in a document dated 1146, when it enjoyed the protection of the monastery in Interlaken. Its subsequent history has been chequered: destroyed by the Bernese in the mid-16th century for resisting the Reformation, all but wiped out by plague in 1669, and suffering almost total destruction by fire in 1892, the little farming village had more than its fair share of disasters. Its recent history has been kinder, helped in part by the early patronage of British tourists and ski-pioneers in the late 19th century. The village has since grown into a major international sports resort with a comprehensive range of leisure facilities including skating, curling and swimming in its large sports centre. It also offers long and beautiful walks, particularly from the top of the 2,168m First (pronounced 'fierce') down through gentle, wooded slopes looking over towards the stunning turquoise-coloured glacier of Oberergletscher.

As a result of this natural phenomenon, and the equally spectacular Unterergletscher which runs parallel to it on the western flank of the Mättenberg, Grindelwald has traditionally been known as the 'glacier village'. These two great rivers of ice creep imperceptibly down towards the village. The former can be seen at close hand by walking up the main street past the station and following the path on the right of the church of St Mary (built in

1793, with a late 19th-century tower) for just over an hour. At the end is the precariously sited Chalet Milchbach, a restaurant with magnificent views of the ice fall.

Less energetic visitors can make the slightly shorter journey to the famous Gletscherschlucht, or Glacier Gorge, well signposted from the village centre, over the river and about a $1/2$ hour by foot. Here there is a spectacular wooden gallery above the raging milky torrent flowing down from the Unterergletscher. The great ice wall of the glacier is seen after a short walk through a tunnel in the rock.

Grindelwald shares much of its skiing with Wengen in the delightful (and largely intermediate area) below the Kleine Scheidegg and around Männlichen. It also has its own large area on the northeastern side of the village below First and Bort, well-known for its wide and sunny pistes.

GSTAAD

MAP REF: 110 B3

Like St Moritz, Gstaad has become almost a byword for the ultimate in fashionable winter playgrounds. It is a surprisingly small, albeit very attractive, cluster of traditional timber buildings with a few modern additions. Set in a wide, flat-bottomed grassy arena at the junction of four valleys, close to the border of the cantons of Berne and Vaud, it enjoys a beautiful position in what has come to be known as the White Highlands. Cynics may argue that the description is applied more in hope than in expectation. For all Gstaad's jet-setting, exclusive image, its relatively low-altitude skiing means that winter whiteness is never guaranteed. However, as more than one contented winter holidaymaker has observed, people do not come to the resort solely for its skiing;

The Imperial Palace Hotel, Gstaad

the real attraction is the town itself, its atmosphere, and its excellent range of leisure and excursion possibilities. Perhaps the opportunities to spot the legion of stars and celebrities is another.

Until the railway arrived at the beginning of the century, Gstaad was little more than a church and a few farmhouses. With little left of historical interest, today it is a compact, well-ordered and charming holiday resort arranged (appropriately enough) around a star-shaped network of roads. Only two of them lead anywhere. The main road connects it with the nearby village of Saanen to the north and the growing resort of Les Diablerets 20km to the south. The other winds up the pretty Lauenental valley before forking into two narrow lanes, both petering out under unpassable peaks.

In the fashionable main street, cluttered with luxury shops and expensive restaurants, the small early 15th-century chapel of St Nicholas stubbornly survives (if not entirely in its original form). Gstaad's most imposing building though is some way out of the village on a tree-covered bluff to the east. Dominating the village like a fairy castle, the famous Gstaad Palace is one of Europe's most unashamedly ostentatious hotels, masquerading as a neo-baroque fortress. An army of security guards lends further substance to the impression of impregnability.

The resort's skiing is divided into three separate areas: the Eggli, the Wispile and the Wasserngrat. The Eggli, reached by gondola from the south of the village, interconnects with the lovely village of Rougemont via the top of La Videmanette, but summer and winter visitors may be content to remain on its sunny plateau, where there is a fine mountain restaurant. The larger White Highlands ski region includes the areas of Schonried, Saanenmoser, St Stephan and Zweisimmen.

Nearby Saanen is an attractive old-fashioned village some 3km to the north of Gstaad. Popular with holidaymakers unwilling to pay the latter's prices, it has the added bonus of some fine wooden chalets, and the Gothic church of St Mauritius dating from 1444. The Lauenental valley running directly into the southeast of Gstaad provides a fascinating excursion. Six-and-a-half kilometres up it is the charming village of Lauenen with some lavishly carved and painted 18th-century wooden houses and the 16th-century Gothic church of St Petrus. The road continues past the delightful Lake Lauenen, to the waterfalls of the Dungelschuss below which it ends. Immediately to the south rises the 3,248m Wildhorn, and to the southwest the 2,807m Spitzhorn.

MOUNTAIN WALK

Allow 3 hours

Take the three-stage new gondola lift from Grindelwald up to the summit of First, past the splendid Oberer Glacier descending between the Wetterhorn and Schreckhorn to the right, and take the path signed Bachsee. After a slightly steep beginning this is a lovely walk of about an hour along a fairly level path, forking right along the northern bank of a tiny lake, to the edge of Bachsee itself. Turn left along the northern shore of the lake following the signs for Waldspitz. This is a gradual descent of about 40 minutes, through a few scattered farm buildings where there is a choice of paths – each leading to the restaurant at Waldspitz. From here follow the main path down through a forest to a sharp left turn after about 15 minutes. Continue down through the trees, bearing left at all times, until the landscape opens up and the path leads through a meadow beneath the First gondola, just south of the Bort lift-station.

Weary walkers can return by lift at this point. Otherwise the hour-long descent continues through pleasant Alpine pastures with magnificent views of the glacier. The path curves round to the right towards Milibach (Mühlebach), and after about 10 minutes it reaches a crossroads where there is a surfaced track leading left. Continue straight ahead until the path rejoins the track at Mühlebach. Shortly it joins a narrow road, from where it is approximately a 15-minute walk back down to the bottom lift-station.

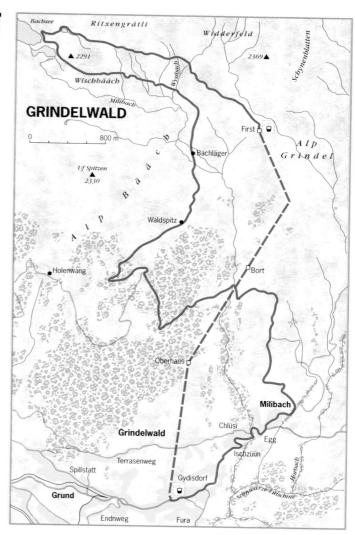

INTERLAKEN

Interlaken (map ref: 110 C3) is one of the oldest and most traditional of Swiss resorts, exquisitely located (as its Latin name implies) between the lakes of Thun and Brienz. It is notable for its elegant 19th-century hotels, wide tree-lined esplanades, and striking lake and mountain views. It is also known as an unrivalled excursion and entertainment centre, with a wide range of leisure facilities, and easy access to the Jungfrau region and the many beautiful lakeside resorts of the Bernese Oberland.

Formerly known as 'Aarmuhle',

because of its position on the banks of the River Aare, the town traces its history to the founding of an Augustine monastery at the beginning of the 12th century. This was abolished at the time of the Reformation and all that remains of the original buildings are the east walk of the 1445 cloister, the chapter-house, and the 13th-century Gothic chancel of the present church of St Mary. Adjoining this is the Landvogteischloss, a baroque castle dating from 1747, now the cantonal administration centre. These are located on the east side of the delightful Höhematte, a 14-

hectare 'meadow' of sprawling lawns and flowerbeds in the centre of the town on the south side of the main thoroughfare – the Höheweg. This famous boulevard must rank as one of the most attractive streets in Europe, bordered on its northern side by palatial Victorian hotels overlooking the wide green expanses of the Höhematte and, beyond that, a dazzling panorama of the snow-clad peaks of the Jungfrau massif. A suitably nostalgic note is struck by the horse-drawn carriages which constantly trot along this shady avenue, evoking memories of a time in the late 19th century when one caustic traveller was prompted to observe that the town had become 'a sort of Swiss Margate', so popular was it with English visitors.

Between the Höheweg and the

River Aare is aother of Interlaken's major attractions, the Kursaal – a casino built in 1859 and set in magnificent gardens, the centrepiece of which is a huge flower clock. The Kursaal also doubles as the town's 'cultural meeting point', and regularly holds concerts, festivals and theatrical performances. These have been a traditional feature of Interlaken for many years, and an open-air performance of Schiller's *William Tell* has taken place every summer since 1912 in the natural amphitheatre in the Rügen, a wooded park south of the Höhenmatte.

Some of the town's most attractive buildings are found on the north bank of the Aare, having crossed a slender island traversed by two parallel bridges. Here in the suburb of Unterseen is an attractive Gothic church, built in 1674, surrounded by charming 17th- to 18th-century wooden houses with ancient latticed windows in the medieval style. Near by, in an exceptionally well-preserved 17th-century house in the Oberegasse, is the town's museum tracing the growth of tourism in the area since the beginning of the last century. Further to the west, on the north bank of Lake Thun, is one of the world's most attractive golf courses – 18 holes of 'relentless scenic distraction' as described by one professional golfer after a poor round. To the east, following the river promenade and past the indoor swimming pool, is the funicular for the 15-minute journey up to the summit of the Harder Kulm. From here, at a height of 1,323m is a splendid view of the surrounding mountains and lakes. South of the town, on the edge of the Rügen park, is another funicular taking sightseers up to an equally impressive vantage point on the shady Heimwehfluh, albeit from a lower altitude of 670m. The journey time is about five minutes.

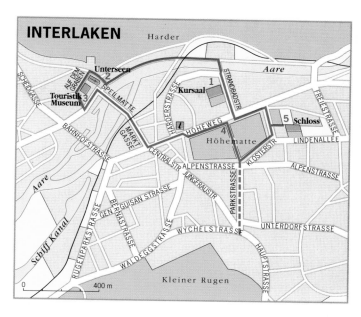

TOWN WALK

Start at the town's casino, the Kursaal, on the north side of the splendid Höheweg. There is a car park on the right of the Strandbadstrasse which runs parallel to the casino and its landscaped gardens.

1 The Kursaal
A curious hybrid of architectural influences, this rambling building dates from the mid-19th century. Framed by the rocky green precipices of the Harder to the north, it is set amidst beautiful gardens with fountains and a celebrated flower clock. Actually rather more than a casino, it is also a congress hall and cultural centre.

Walk north up the Strandbadstrasse and over the bridge to the lovely Goldey Promenade. Turn left along the river bank, passing the huge lido on the right, and continue along the leafy Untere Goldey. Turn right at the end up the Beatenburgstrasse and then left into Auf dem Graben.

2 Gothic Church, Unterseen
This is an imposing building retaining a tall medieval tower, with the main structure rebuilt in 1674. Extensively restored in the mid-19th century, it is particularly notable for its magnificent location. The peaks of the Jungfrau massif rise behind it, providing a dramatic backcloth.

Continue down the Auf dem Graben and turn left into the Obere Gasse.

3 Museum
Housed in a fine 17th-century house, this small regional museum records the history of the town and the development of the Jungfrau region. There is a section devoted to Alpine climbing and the growth of winter sports.

Walk east down the Untere Gasse, turning right over the bridge into the Spielmatte on a narrow island in the middle of the Aare. Cross over another bridge and walk down the busy Marktgasse to the Postplatz. Turn left here and walk east into the famous Höheweg. Cross the road and walk along the shady Hohe-

Promenade, passing the palatial hotels on the left. Turn right into the Peter Ober Alle, which bisects the Höhematte.

4 The Höhematte
This delightful 14-hectare central park is one of the great attractions of Interlaken. It has been a protected area since 1864 when 37 local citizens entered an agreement to purchase it from the town and prevent any future development of it. It is still privately owned.

At the end of the park there is a choice of continuing south for about 10 minutes down the Parkstrasse to the woody Kleiner Rugen, another lovely park, which is home to the open-air William Tell Theatre. There is a circular walk around the tree-covered summit in the centre. Alternatively, turn left into the Spielplatz on the southern perimeter of the Höhematte and continue walking east through a shady avenue. Bear round to the left, leave the park, and cross the north-bound Klosterstrasse.

5 Former Augustinian Monastery
On the right side of the Klosterstrasse, traces of the 12th-century priory remain in the Protestant church of St Mary, notably the east walk of the 15th-century cloister. The adjacent castle, now the cantonal administration centre, is a mid-18th-century baroque structure.

Return to the Klosterstrasse and turn right. Turn left at the top, back on to the Höhe-Promenade, and then cross the Höheweg, turning right up the Strandbadstrasse back to the Kursaal.

JUNGFRAUJOCH
MAP REF: 110 C3

This shoulder of the Jungfrau peak is both a monument to the ingenuity of the Swiss and a confirmation of the awesome beauty of their mountain home. It merits the former accolade because it is made accessible by a miracle of engineering, and the latter because of the extraordinary panorama that rolls out beneath its unique belvedere. The Jungfraujoch has the highest railway station in Europe cut into the rock at an altitude of 3,475m in eternal snows. It has an hotel, two restaurants, an ice palace, an observatory and a view that defies description.

To the south the icy expanses of Switzerland's largest glacier, the Grosser Aletschgletscher, stretch away to the south between the Mönch and the Jungfrau itself. To

Subterranean splendour, the Ice Palace deep within the glacier on the Jungfraujoch

the north, best viewed from the platform terrace of the permanently manned Sphinx Observatory, the lakes of Thun and Brienz shimmer in the distance like two fluttering blue ribbons either side of Interlaken. Beyond them, over the peaks of central Switzerland, the Black Forest is clearly visible in fine conditions.

A leisurely walk through the Ice Palace, deep inside a glacier, is a memorable experience, but, understandably, warm clothing is advisable if the fascinating sculptures are to be appreciated in comfort. In summer the Jungfraujoch has a celebrated ski school, and dog-sleigh rides are available throughout the year, weather permitting.

A railway from Kleine Scheidegg to the towering peak of the Jungfrau was one man's dream in the late 19th century. A Zürich engineer, Adolf Guyer-Zeller, resolved to bring the 'top of Europe' within reach of the common man, and his ambitious plans for a mountain railway tunnelling up through the Eiger were finally approved, after understandable scepticism, in 1896. It was completed in 1912, at a cost of Sfr714,000 and a number of human lives, including that of Guyer-Zeller himself. The strain of the

project was thought to be a contributory factor to his early demise and, sadly, he never lived to see the realisation of his dream. Because of rising costs the initial plans to continue the railway up to the summit of the Jungfrau were shelved, and it was decided to make the Jungfraujoch the terminus. The total length of track is 9.5km, of which the last 7km are via a tunnel cut through the Eiger and the Mönch. The steepest gradient is 1 in 4 and the journey time is about 40 minutes from Kleine Scheidegg. En route, the train stops at two stations where windows are cut into the rock walls for views from behind the treacherous north face of the Eiger.

Above, right: buildings growing out of the Jungfraujoch – reached by subterranean passageways. Left: picturesque Kandersteg beneath one peak of its mountainous ring

KANDERSTEG

MAP REF: 110 B3

Famous for its dramatic setting in glorious mountain scenery, Kandersteg is a major mountaineering and winter sports centre at the head of the Kandertal valley. There is little of historical interest remaining in the resort apart from the Rüedihaus, built in 1753, and easily distinguished from neighbouring buildings by its overhanging saddleback roof and colourfully painted exterior walls.

However, the real appeal of Kandersteg is less to do with the architecture of the village than the remarkable beauty of its setting. Above it to the southeast are the great peaks of the Doldenhorn, Fründenhorn, Oeschinenhorn and Blümlisalp, a huge mountain group streaked by impressive glaciers. To the southwest lie the smaller, but no less striking, peaks of Lohner and Bundespitz behind which lies Adelboden, about 8km as the crow flies.

In winter, Kandersteg has a small skiing area and a good selection of cross-country trails. In summer it has all the usual amenities associated with a major Alpine resort.

Nearby The Oescheninsee, accessible part way by chair-lift from the centre of the village, is a beautiful mountain lake set in an amphitheatre of imposing mountains and glaciers. The walks around the lakeside are strongly recommended.

There is another attractive lake some 6km down the valley in a delightful forest setting just off the main road to the left. This is the remarkable Blausee or 'Blue Lake', so-called because of its extraordinary shade of blue, thought to be caused by the chemical effects of minerals.

KLEINE SCHEIDEGG
MAP REF: 110 C3

Kleine Scheidegg is a tiny mountain resort at an altitude of 2,061m reached by railway from either Wengen or Grindelwald. For most visitors it is either the starting point for altitude walks or skiing beneath the peaks of the 3,970m Eiger, the 4,099m Mönch and the 4,158m Jungfrau (the 'ogre', the 'monk' and the 'maiden'), or as the midway point on the rail journey to the Jungfraujoch. The small resort commands one of the most dramatic views in the Alps.

COUNTRY WALK

Allow 3 hours

Walk north down through Kandersteg, past the Hotel Bernerhof on the left, and continue for another kilometre until just before the 'Institut' on the right. Here, turn up the Forstweg (forest path) running beside it, signed 'Oeschinensee'. Follow it until the first right turning, by a bench, where it becomes narrow and starts climbing steeply by the side of a gully. Shortly, a series of zig-zags begin, after which there is a junction with the left path signed Port and Libige. Turn right and continue to climb, pass through a gate, and then the path emerges into an open meadow with a dramatic view of Kandersteg and the Oeschinen valley spread out

below.

Traverse the steep slope, under the chairlift, beyond a chalet on the right, and continue straight ahead at the next junction following the signs to Läger. Turn left across a little bridge, then turn right and walk down the steep path along a gully. The path then levels out, with occasional glimpses of the lake below through the forest. Turn right at the next junction, following the path around to the hotels on the side of the beautiful turquoise Oeschinensee, dominated by great rock towers streaked with waterfalls. The recommended walk back to Kandersteg, which can be shortened considerably by following the signs to the chair-lift, is the path via the Grüenenwald. Take the main path to the point where it diverges, bear right, and stay on the right bank for the descent through woods back to the village.

MOUNTAIN WALK

Allow 2^1/$_2$ hours

From the station at Kleine Scheidegg, reached by rack railway from either Grindelwald or Wengen, cross the tracks and head in the opposite direction to the Jungfrau. Take the Bustiglen/ Männlichen path and make the gentle descent in the shadow of the north face of the Eiger to the farm buildings of Bustligen. Keep left, and after 5 minutes take the left fork signed Männlichen. This climbs through trees, and then out into pastures with the Schwarzi Flue escarpment on the left. The path continues under a short chair-

lift and then climbs more steeply beneath another chair-lift. It then runs up to join the slightly higher route back to Kleine Scheidegg. At this stage there is a choice of either keeping along the ridge to the restaurant at the top station of the Grund-Männlichen gondola – about a 10-minute walk – or returning via the high path to Kleine Scheidegg. Either way, this is the route back and there can be few more dramatic high altitude walks. Below, right, is Wengen; across the Lauterbrunnen valley, Mürren perches on its shelf; ahead, to the right are the peaks of Tschuggen and, behind it, Lauberhorn. Ahead is the Jungfrau massif. The path is virtually level,

with no deviations until a sharp right bend at Honegg after which it climbs gradually until the final descent to Kleine Scheidegg.

LAUTERBRUNNEN

MAP REF: 110 C3

The name of the town, located in the centre of a beautiful valley directly south of Interlaken, means 'nothing but springs' and its origin quickly becomes apparent. Down the sheer rocky precipices on the western side of the narrow Lauterbrunnen valley cascade several waterfalls and mountain streams. The most celebrated of the former is the Staubbach ('spray brook'),which descends from a jutting rock beneath the village of Mürren in a spectacular leap of 305m. It dissolves into a silvery mist during its long downward journey and, caught by the morning sun (or indeed the moonlight), it is an arresting sight. Lauterbrunnen is frequently dismissed as little more than a car park for the high-lying, traffic-free resorts of Wengen and Mürren above it. However, that description does a cruel disservice to this scattered collection of unpretentious, rather shabby old hotels and attractive darkwood chalets lying on both banks of the Lütschine. The town has a definite charm, but one that will probably appeal only to connoisseurs of unassuming railway towns in remarkable mountain settings. The old schoolhouse has a local history museum.

Nearby Isenfluh is a beautifully situated hamlet 4km north of Lauterbrunnen up a mountain track. Set in woodland and fields of wild flowers, it enjoys a spectacular view of the Jungfrau massif.

Lauterbrunnen and its valley of waterfalls

The road south from Lauterbrunnen opens up a scenic banquet of increasing grandeur, with the distinctive 3,782m Breithorn ahead, clearly detached from the neighbouring Grosshorn on its eastern side. Before the hamlet of Stechelberg at the road end is a path leading up to the Trümmelbachfälle (Trümmelbach Falls). These are arguably the most impressive in the Bernese Oberland. Caused by the swollen Trümmelbach forcing its way through a narrow gorge, the three foaming plumes of water make a captivating spectacle. The highest fall is the most dramatic.

The Staubach Falls, Lauterbrunnen

LENK

MAP REF: 110 B3

A splendidly sited, all-year resort in a wide sunny basin at the head of the Simmental valley, Lenk is a health and winter sports resort famed for its sulphurous springs and rugged, glacial scenery. The village is a successful symbiosis of the old and new, with pretty flower-decked chalets softening the sharp lines of some extensive new development. One of its chief attractions is its proximity to two fine waterfalls, the Iffigenfälle (Iffigen Falls) and the Simmenfälle (Simmen Falls), 4km south and southeast respectively from the centre. Both involve short walks at the end of good mountain roads where there is ample car parking. The best vantage point for the Iffigen Falls requires a walk of about 20 minutes up a steep track; the Simmen Falls, thundering down the northern face of the impressive 3,243m Wildstrubel, is only about 5 minutes from the car park.

Lenk shares its highly rated skiing with Adelboden in the area below Metschberg and Geils on the east of the village, but summer visitors keen on mountain panoramas would be better advised to take the two-stage gondola lift, just to the right of the road to Iffigen, for the ascent to the Betelberg at 1,960m. This is the starting point for Lenk's other ski area, and there is a short walk (or ski) down to the chair-lift at Mülkerblatten, where there is a marvellous view of the Wildhorn range to the south. The chair-lift returns to the western outskirts of the village and, naturally, the journey can be reversed.

Nearby Thirteen kilometres north, down the Simmental valley, is the old village of Zweisimmen with a mid-14th-century Gothic church notable for its interior and exterior frescos painted in about 1500. The village is also part of the White Highlands ski area, sharing its skiing with Gstaad among others. A two-stage gondola lift leaves from the south of the village to the 2,011m peak of Rinderberg, from where there are spectacular views.

MERINGEN
MAP REF: 110 C3

The town is the main tourist centre of the precipitous Haslital valley, east of Lake Brienz. Many of its buildings were destroyed in two serious fires in the late 19th century, but the church of St Michael, rebuilt in 1684, survived along with the few wooden houses that are all that remain of the old town. The detached, late-Romanesque tower (built in 1351), surmounted by a wooden spire, is the oldest in the canton. The lower church dates from the 12th century and has been incorporated into the present structure. A few fragments of some 14th-century frescos remain. There is a local museum near by.

Meiringen is a time-honoured excursion centre for a number of very good reasons. The famous Reichenbach Falls, immortalised as

the place where Sherlock Holmes and Moriarty were believed to have plunged to their deaths, are just to the south of the town. A funicular leaves from a station to the right of the road to the Grimselpass.

The eery Aareschlucht (Aare Gorges), an impressive cleft through limestone cliffs, are also on the southern outskirts of the town just before Innertkirchen. Viewing galleries are located at various stages along its course.
Nearby The 12km drive up the

Aare Gorge, Meiringen

narrow Rosenlauital valley makes a fascinating excursion. The serpentine road leaves the small village of Willigen, 1.5km south of Meiringen. There are tremendous views of the great peaks of the Engelhorn, and close to the mountaineering resort of Rosenlaui itself are the intriguing Gletscherschlucht (glacier gorges) – great troughs in the rock gouged out by the Rosenlaui Glacier.

MOUNTAIN WALK

Allow 2¹/₂ hours

On the northern perimeter of Meiringen, past St Michael's church, take the cable-car which ascends to the small hamlet of Reuti at 1,055m on the Hasliberg. Near the top station there is a splendid view of the Alpbach Falls. Take the main road south out of the village following the signs to Innertkirchen, and after approximately 1km turn right down the forest path signposted Wylerli and Appigen (Aeppigen). This is a gradual descent, becoming steeper just before Wylerli, where the path briefly doubles back on itself before continuing down to the tiny hamlet of Appigen (Aeppigen). Here it rejoins the road that weaves down to Innertkirchen. Turn right at the crossroads, cross the bridge over the River Aare and take the path along the riverbank following the signs for the Aareschlucht (Aare Gorge). The path threads the length of the daunting gorge, and has a series of galleries with impressive views of

the sheer, sometimes overhanging walls, and the green waters surging in the dim depths below. At the end of the gorge the path rejoins the road, where after

0·5km, there is a footbridge on the right over the river into the hamlet of Sand on the outskirts of the town. From there it is a 10-minute walk back to the centre.

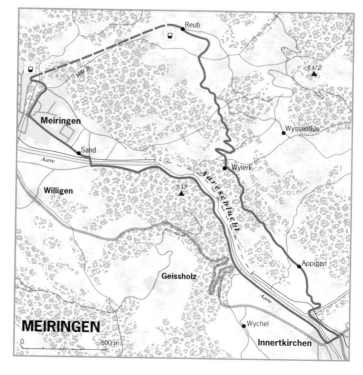

MÜRREN

MAP REF: 110 C3

Set at an altitude of 1,638m, Mürren is the highest and most impressively sited village in the Bernese Oberland, accessible only by funicular from Lauterbrunnen or cablecar from Stechelberg. Perched precariously on a shelf, high above the Lauterbrunnen valley, it offers unrivalled views over the Jungfrau massif and the Breithorn. It is also a remarkably pretty, car-free cluster of old wooden chalets and 19th-century hotels set in glorious Alpine pastures. In winter, it is one of the most charming and traditional ski resorts in the world; in summer it is a botanist's paradise. The village owes its prominence in large part to the British, who first 'colonised' it in the mid-19th century, popularised it in the early 20th, and today still represent the largest body of skiers. Overlooking the Lauterbrunnen valley is a statue of Sir Arnold Lunn, the 'father' of modern downhill skiing, who founded the famous Kandahar Ski Club in 1924 in Mürren's Palace Hotel. The world renowned 'Inferno' race from the summit of the 2,970m Schilthorn first took place here in 1928.

The resort has a fine modern sports centre on the upper road with an indoor pool, squash courts, gymnasium, icerink, sauna and whirlpool. There are indoor and outdoor tennis courts, and an extensive network of excellent rambling paths.
Nearby No visit to Mürren is complete without the journey by two-stage cable-car to the magnificent Piz Gloria revolving restaurant on the summit of the Schilthorn. It was made famous as the mountain eyrie of the villainous Blofeld in the James Bond film, *On Her Majesty's Secret Service.*

A Mürren restaurant with a position and view that would surely be the envy of most restaurateurs

SPIEZ

MAP REF: 110 C3

The small lakeside town of Spiez is one of the most appealing on Lake Thun. It lies on the southern shore at the foot of the pyramidal 2,362m Niesen, with the higher peaks of the Jungfrau massif behind. Apart from its idyllic location, it is notable for two striking works of architecture. The castle, standing on a slight promontory jutting out into the lake, dates from the 12th century – although the lower part of the keep is even earlier. Founded by Rudolf II of Burgundy, it was later owned by a succession of families and gradually enlarged. Today it houses a museum containing some fine period furniture and various effects of the Von Erlach family, who used it as their main residence from 1561 to 1875. One of its public rooms contains some notable baroque stucco work dating from 1614. There is a pleasant, tree-lined public garden by the castle entrance, with fine views over the lake.

The detached Romanesque castle church is late 10th-century, and has a unique oval crypt and some interesting medieval murals in the apse. Its spire is early 17th-century, restored in 1950.

Spiez is a pleasant summer resort providing a good range of water-related sports and excursions.
Nearby In Wimmis, 5km southwest of Spiez, there is an early Romanesque church surrounded by trees. Above it is an imposing 17th-century castle, and in the upper village some fine period houses dating from the 17th century.

Six kilometres northwest of the town is the charming lakeside village of Einigen. It has a small Romanesque church dating from the 11th century, with a late Gothic font and some 15th-century stained glass.

MOUNTAIN WALK

Allow 2 hours

From Mürren's upper road, facing the old funicular station up to the Allmendhubel, turn left and then right after about 100m up the mountain path signposted Im Suppen and Blumental. At a junction after 10 minutes or so take the lefthand path signposted Im Suppen. This is a gentle and pretty climb of just under 1km through trees to a delightful mountain restaurant. From here follow the path south to Im Schilt, climbing beneath the Birg cable-car, then across broad pastures with stunning views across the Lauterbrunnen valley to the Jungfrau massif. Bear left at the huddle of farm buildings at Im Schilt, and follow the path down to some more farm buildings at Gimmela. Take the righthand path down to Spilboden, crossing a small bridge over the Schiltbach, and then walking along its southern bank for about 300m to a sharp left turn. Recross the Schiltbach almost immediately and continue down past barns and storehouses on the left, keeping ahead at the next junction, and then enter a dense thicket from where the path emerges to rejoin a larger track that descends to the bottom station of the Birg cable-car. From there it is a 10-minute walk back to the centre of the village.

THUN

MAP REF: 110 B3

This ancient and picturesque town has retained much of its medieval character over the years, which, combined with its delightful mountain and lakeside setting, makes it a worthy rival to Interlaken as a suitable base for excursions within the Bernese Oberland. The name 'Thun' is said to derive from the Celtic *dunum*, meaning fortified hill, suggesting that the town was founded long before the Middle Ages.

The hill, the Schlossberg, is still crowned by a spectacular four-turreted fortress, built by Berchtold V of Zähringen after 1182. The hipped roof was added in the 15th century. There are magnificent views from each of the turrets. The castle is now home to an historical museum, exhibiting some fine 15th-century tapestries and a miscellaneous collection of weapons, armour, furniture and ceramics. Covered steps lead down to the Rathausplatz, with a central fountain, and a late 16th-century town hall distinguished by its attractive arcades. Arcades are also a striking feature of the busy Obere Hauptgasse which leads southeast from the square beneath the Schlossberg. Even more striking is this old street's extraordinary arrangement of paved walks actually on the roofs of the shops. From the upper end of the street there are more covered steps leading up to the baroque church of St Maurice, founded in the early 10th century, but with most of the exterior structure, except its 14th-century octagonal tower, dating from 1738. The interior frescos are early

15th-century. There is a fine view of the town, the lake and the Alps from the churchyard.

The town has two delightful parks. The Jakobshübeli, south of the town centre on the eastern bank of the Aare, is a hilly, densely wooded public space with marvellous views reached by steps from the Hofstettenstrasse. Across the river, over the covered Obere Schleuse bridge, is the Schadau Park laid out in the mid 19th century in the style of the great parks of Victorian London. It is especially notable for its splendid castle, built at the same time, and a circular linen painting of early 19th-century Thun housed in a building near by. Just north of the park is the church of St Mary, in the Romanesque style, retaining a 14th-century tower and some fine frescos dating from the 13th century.

The Eiger, Mönch and Jungfrau

Spiez, on the southern shore of Lake Thun

WENGEN

MAP REF: 110 C3

A beautifully sited and long-established resort high on the eastern side of the Lauterbrunnen valley, Wengen is a charming cluster of slightly faded Victorian hotels and elegant shops. Like Mürren on the opposite side of the valley, it is set on a mountain shelf in dramatic mountain scenery, but it is a larger, more sophisticated resort with access to a greater skiing area – much of it beneath the magnificent peaks of the Jungfrau massif. The village centre is compact, attractive and refreshingly free from cars. The only access is by train up from Lauterbrunnen, or from Grindelwald and then down via Kleine Scheidegg. There is also a cable-car link with Grindelwald via Männlichen.

Wengen has had a long association with the British, illustrated by its traditional pubs and the presence of an English church. Perhaps unsurprisingly, there is intense rivalry between it and the other British enclave of Mürren – each attracting fierce loyalties from different sections of the skiing fraternity. The exclusive DHO (Downhill Only Club) was founded here in the 1920s in direct opposition to Mürren's Kandahar Club. The resort also hosts the historic Lauberhorn World Cup, one of the most famous and traditional downhill races on the international skiing calendar.

In summer, there are excellent mountain walks along well-kept paths through peaceful Alpine woods and meadows.

• FOOD & DRINK •

In Switzerland the visitor will discover a fascinating variety of tastes and influences concentrated within a relatively small area. The 26 cantons each have their own regional specialities.

There is a body of opinion in gastronomic circles which maintains that a so-called 'Swiss' cuisine does not exist; instead there is a hybrid of national influences drawing in varying measures from Switzerland's neighbours. But evidence indicates otherwise. Switzerland has given the world *fondue*, *raclette*, *rosti*, meringues, *zabaglione*, muesli, Emmental and Gruyère cheeses, and the celebrated chocolates of Nestlé, Lindt and Tobler. And if further proof were needed that the Swiss know a thing or two about cooking, their master chefs have earned a reputation through-out the world's great kitchens.

The meat dish is the focus of the Swiss meal. Veal tends to be the most favoured with the Zurich dish *geschnetzeltes kalbsfleisch* (ground veal served in a cream sauce with butter, white wine and mushrooms) a perennial favourite. Another celebrated meat dish is *Berner Platte* – a huge plate of bacon, sausages, ham, boiled beef, sauerkraut, potatoes and haricot beans. Also worth trying are *gegmsenbraten* (roast chamois) and *pied de poro au madere* (pig's trotters in madeira sauce).

Accompanying meat dishes, or often served on its own, is the delicious *rosti* – vying with *fondue* as the 'national' dish of Switzerland. The basic version is diced boiled potatoes, fried and then baked with bacon cubes, but it comes in a variety of types.

The two areas of Switzerland's cuisine where the Swiss really

come into their own are cheese and confectionery. The most famous of Swiss cheeses are Emmental and Gruyère, and it is these which are the main components of *fondue*. Another cheese-based Swiss invention is *raclette*, originating in the Valais and made from special Valais cheeses like Bagnes or Goms.

Famed worldwide for their chocolate, the Swiss also make delicious cakes and sweets and have earned similar acclaim for their pastries and desserts – the Kirsch cake from Zug, the *Leckerli* from Basel (honey and almond biscuits) and *zabaglione* from the Ticino (whipped eggs with sweet Marsala wine) being just a few of the tempting variety on offer.

Swiss wine is little known outside the country, but in general terms it rivals the best of the great European vintages. The important wine regions are in the west of the country, particularly in the Valais and Vaud, which produce 'Fendant' – a heady white with a musky bouquet, and the various reds from the Gamay and Pinot Noir grapes, branded in the Valais as 'Dole', in Vaud as 'Salvagnin' and 'Pinot Noir' in Neuchatel. The wines of Ticino should not be overlooked either. A full-bodied Ticino Merlot is as good, if not better, than any wine from the Merlot grape in the world.

At the end of the meal, try another national speciality – a distilled stone-fruit brandy. Most famous of these is Kirsch (made from cherries).

Map symbols

A4	Motorway - dual carriageway
A7	Motorway - single carriageway
A1	Toll motorway - dual carriageway
A6	Toll motorway - single carriageway
	Motorway junction
	Motorway junction restricted access
S	Motorway service area
	Motorway under construction
	Primary route
	Main road
	Secondary road
	Other road
D600 E57 N59	Road numbers
	Dual carriageway or four lanes
	Road in poor condition
	Under construction
TOLL Toll	Toll road

	Scenic route
)==========(	Road tunnel
68	Distances (km)
10-6 970	Mountain pass (height in metres) with closure period
	Gradient 14% and over. Arrow points uphill
	Gradient 6% - 13%
	Frontier crossing with restricted opening hours
V	Vehicle ferry
	Airport
	International boundary
	Viewpoint
	Motor racing circuit
2973 DIAVOLEZZA	Mountain / spot height in metres
	Urban area
	River, lake and canal
■ Jockfall	Place of interest
	Mountain railway
	Car transporter (rail)

PRACTICAL GUIDE

ARRIVING

By air
Scheduled air services operate from more than 110 cities in 70 different countries to Switzerland's five international airports in Geneva, Zürich, Berne, Basel and Lugano. There are through rail services to many major destinations direct from Zürich and Geneva airports. Trains between Zürich Flughafen Railway Station and the main station in Zürich run at least every 20 minutes with a journey time of 10 minutes. Trains between Geneva Aeroport and Geneva Cornavin Station run regularly with a journey time of 7 minutes. Both Basel and Geneva have airport coach links with their city centres.

Fly-rail baggage
Passengers arriving in Switzerland by air via Zürich or Geneva airports can check in their baggage from the airport of origin and have it transported through to their Swiss destination. Customs declaration forms and baggage labels are readily available from the Swiss National Tourist Office (SNTO) in many countries throughout the world, and rail tickets can be bought at the same time.

Home-going air travellers whose flights are booked from Basel, Zürich or Geneva airports can check their luggage through to the final destination from many Swiss towns and resorts. A charge per item of luggage is made for this service. With a rail ticket the charge is less than if the luggage is sent alone. Full details are given in the *Fly-Rail* leaflet published by the SNTO.

By rail
There are several rail routes across Europe to Swiss cities. The EuroCity Express 'Loreley' runs from the Hook of Holland to Basel, Lugano and Chiasso. Another EuroCity train 'Edelweiss' covers the route from Brussels to Basel. From Paris there are highspeed TGV services to Geneva, Lausanne and Berne. Advance booking is necessary for most of these journeys. Contact the SNTO for more details.

By road
Located in the heart of Europe, Switzerland is easily reached by road from all points on the compass. Main routes to the country are helpfully listed (with mileage charts) in the publication *Travel Tips* available free from the SNTO in a number of different languages. Details of cross-Channel ferry and SeaCat services are included in the UK version.

Motorists should carry a valid national driving licence and the vehicle's registration document in the event of Customs' queries.

Entry formalities
A valid passport is essential for entry to Switzerland. Holiday or business visitors to Switzerland and Liechtenstein do not require a visa if they are holders of a valid national passport from any country in Western Europe, North America and Australasia (as well as many others) and are intending to stay for a period not exceeding three months.

CAMPING AND CARAVANNING

There are approximately 450 campsites in Switzerland. Camping guides can be purchased from the Swiss Camping and Caravanning Federation (Schweizerischer Camping und Caravanning Verband, Habsburgerstrasse 35, CH-6004 Lucerne. Tel: 041/23 48 22) and the Swiss Camping Association (Verband Schweizer Campings, Seestrasse 119, CH-3800 Interlaken. Tel: 036/23 35 23).

CHEMISTS

Known variously as *Apotheke* (in German), *Pharmacie* (in French), and *Farmacia* (in Italian), Swiss pharmacists are approachable and generally sympathetic to minor ailments. Most will have at least one English-speaking member of staff but – as in many other countries – serious medication will not be prescribed without a doctor's approval. The name and address of the nearest pharmacist on 24-hour duty is posted in all chemists' windows.

CRIME

Switzerland has one of the lowest crime rates in Europe, but travellers should none the less be on their guard against petty theft (often carried out by fellow visitors). Skiers in particular should take precautions in busy mountain restaurants. For example, do not leave expensive skiing equipment and clothes in unattended piles and, wherever possible, separate or mix skis when left outside. The most desirable skis are worthless if they do not come in pairs.

Always lock cars and ski-racks. In hotels it is always sensible to deposit valuables in house safes. In chalets, entrust valuables to the owners (notwithstanding the fact that they cannot be held liable for theft).

Female visitors travelling alone should encounter few problems; the Swiss are generally courteous, and protective in the event of unwelcome sexual advances. Again, fellow tourists probably represent the biggest threat.

CUSTOMS REGULATIONS

Tourists domiciled in a foreign country may import the following goods into Switzerland free of duty and other taxes: personal effects such as clothing, toilet articles, sports gear, cameras, cine cameras and amateur camcorders with relevant film, video equipment, musical instruments and camping equipment; food provisions (including soft drinks) up to the amount a single individual normally requires for one day; other goods declared on crossing the border and imported for gift purposes (with the exception of meat and meat preparations which are governed by special regulations, butter and quantities of goods intended to be laid in store), provided their total value does not exceed Sfr100. Visitors aged under 17 are entitled to half this limit.

Alcoholic beverages and tobacco may be imported in the following quantities:

Visitors from European countries	Non-European countries
Alcoholic beverages:	
– up to 15% proof	
2 litres	2 litres
– over 15% proof	
1 litre	1 litre
Tobacco goods:	
– cigarettes	
200	400
– or cigars	
50	100
– or pipe tobacco	
250g	500g

The exemption from alcohol and tobacco duty applies only to persons of at least 17 years of age.

CYCLING

The contours of the Swiss Alps' mountain and lakeside areas are a great attraction to cyclists. Bicycles can be hired from Swiss Federal Railway stations and some of the private railway termini. Advance reservations should be made directly to the station booking office. Circulars regarding charges and cycling etiquette are available from the SNTO. Mountain bikes are available for hire in most holiday resorts.

DISABLED TRAVELLERS

The SNTO will provide general details on transport, accommodation, facilities and parking for disabled travellers. More comprehensive information is supplied by the Swiss Invalid Association (Schweizerischer Invalidenverband, Froburgstrasse 4, CH-4600 Olten) and the Swiss Study and Working Group for Disabled Persons (Schweizerischer

Arbeitsgemeinschaft für Körperbehinderte, Feldeggstrasse 72, PO Box 129, CH-8032 Zürich). Brochures published cover holiday accommodation, camping and caravan sites, restaurants, resthouses and toilets on Swiss motorways with wheelchair access, and general hints. There are also lists of excursion resorts and aerial cableways meeting the needs of disabled travellers. The Hotel Guide for the Disabled published by the Invalidenverband, in conjunction with the Swiss Hotel Association, is particularly helpful in its categorisation of facilities for the disabled.

DRIVING

Roads in the Swiss Alps are generally well surfaced and maintained. Many of them are winding and steep and, apart from motorway driving, it is difficult to sustain high average speeds. When estimating travel times, therefore, take careful note of the presence of mountain pass roads where average speeds are unlikely to exceed 50kph.

The minimum age for driving in Switzerland is 18, although car rental companies reserve the right to insist on a higher minimum (and frequently do so). For motorcycles exceeding 125cc, the minimum age is 20 years.

Breakdown
SOS telephones are located at regular intervals along all motorways and mountain pass roads. The emergency breakdown number is 140 and all operators speak English. Breakdown and recovery insurance cover is advisable because the cost of roadside assistance on a remote mountain pass can seriously dent a holiday budget. Most European breakdown organisations are affiliated to the Touring Club Suisse (TCS) which operates a nationwide 24-hour breakdown service. If not insured and the breakdown occurs near an exchange telephone, ask the operator for 'Autohilfe'. Carry warm clothes at all times if driving at altitude; breakdown vehicles can often take more than a couple of hours to reach a car on a mountain road.

Car rental
A circular giving details of rental charges (published by self-drive carhire firms) is available from the SNTO. All the major rental firms are represented in Switzerland,

and cars can be rented from airports, main railway stations and most large towns. The minimum age for driving a rented car is 20 to 25 years (depending on the hire firm) and a valid national or international driving licence (held for at least one year) is usually required. Rates include third-party insurance, but collision insurance is extra. Spare keys are only available on request.

Documents
A valid driving licence and the vehicle's registration documents are the only documents needed by visiting motorists in Switzerland. Domestic insurance policies generally provide the minimum legal cover for driving in Switzerland, and production of a Green Card is not compulsory. However, Green Card insurance is strongly advised.

Fuel
Self-service garages and service stations are located at regular intervals on motorways and main roads. Motorists should take special note, however, not to set out over mountain roads without an adequate supply of fuel.

In towns and resorts many fuelling stations are operated automatically. Notes of Sfr10 and Sfr20 are required for the pumps, and credit cards are not generally accepted.

Motorway tax ('vignette')
An annual road tax of Sfr30 (known as the 'vignette') is levied on all cars and motorcycles using Swiss motorways. An additional fee of the same amount applies to trailers and caravans. Although there are no compulsory checkpoints, it is ill-advised to risk driving without the distinctive permit displayed on the windscreen. Motorway patrol cars are fairly assiduous about checking the windows of cars with foreign plates, and on-the-spot fines are generally heavy. Needless to say, ignorance of the tax is no excuse and, anyway, the relatively modest amount involved represents the cheapest form of toll-road driving in Europe.

Rental cars in Switzerland come with the vignette; vehicles hired abroad do not. The sticker is valid between 1 December of the year preceding and 31 January of the one following the year printed on the vignette. The permits, which are available at border crossings, post offices and service stations throughout the country, are valid for multiple re-entry into Switzerland within the duration of the licensed period. To avoid hold-ups at the frontier it is advisable to purchase the vignette in advance from the SNTO.

Speed limits

On motorways, 120kph; other roads, unless otherwise signposted, 80kph; built-up areas and secondary roads (even when not signposted), 50kph; caravan or trailer (up to 1 ton), 80kph.

Traffic regulations

Drivers and front-seat passengers must wear seatbelts. Children under 12 years have to travel in the back seats. Motor cyclists must wear crash-helmets. Foreign cars entering Switzerland are required to display their nationality plate at the rear of the car and caravan. Driving with side lights only in bad visibility is not permitted under any circumstances and the use of headlights, dipped headlights or twin fog lights is compulsory. Dipped headlights are compulsory in road tunnels.

On mountain roads vehicles ascending always have priority, except for yellow postal buses which have priority at all times. On bends their approach is signified by a blast of their distinctive three-note horns.

Roof-rack loads must not exceed 50kg for cars registered after 1 January 1980, and not over 10 per cent of the vehicle's unladen weight if registered before that date.

The laws concerning speed limits, lighting and seatbelts are strictly enforced and police are authorised to levy on-the-spot fines.

Weather conditions

During winter, driving conditions on Swiss roads are often hazardous, especially on mountain roads and passes (where they are still open). Because conditions can change very quickly at high altitudes motorists are advised to carry snow-chains at all times (a precaution that is obligatory if warning signs indicate that they may be required). If the car begins to slide on a gradient, do *not* persevere in attempts to drive out of trouble. Stop at the earliest opportunity and fit the chains. If they are not carried call for assistance immediately, having ensured that the vehicle's tyres are in good contact with the road surface.

Snow-chains can be hired throughout the country at garages and service stations advertising *Service de Chaine a Neige*, or *Schneekettendienst*.

Information on weather conditions appears on notices at strategic points along roads leading to mountain passes. The following is a list of passes that are open only during summer months: (* = alternative road tunnels open all year).

Pass	Open	Max height	Max gradient
Albula	June–Oct	2,312m	12%
Furka	June–Oct	2,431m	11%
Gt St Bernard*	June–Oct	2,469m	11%
Grimsel	June–Oct	2,165m	11%
Klausen	June–Oct	1,948m	10%
Lukmanier	May–Nov	1,914m	10%
Nufenen	June–Sept	2,478m	11%
Oberalp	June–Oct	2,044m	10%
St Gotthard*	May–Oct	2,108m	11%
S Bernardino*	June–Oct	2,065m	12%
Splugen	May–Oct	2,113m	13%
Susten	June–Oct	2,224m	9%
Umbrail	June–Oct	2,501m	10%

Note also that during the winter months the Bernina Pass is open only between 7am and 6pm, and the Fluela between 7am and 9pm.

ELECTRICITY

Swiss power stations supply current at 220 volts/AC. As the socket outlets require Continental plugs, it is advisable to carry an adaptor for the use of electrical equipment that has British-manufactured fittings.

ENTERTAINMENT

Opportunities for entertainment in the Swiss Alps are limitless. Whatever the time of year, visitors will encounter festivals, folklore performances, concerts, ballet, theatre and opera in the major resorts and cities. Full details of 'what's on' in the vicinity are available in all hotels and most chalets and *gasthofs*. The local tourist office will supply additional information, often in the form of news-sheets.

Evening entertainment ranges from simple fondue evenings in mountain huts to the risqué cabarets of Montreux and Lucerne. At the former, guests are invariably invited to blow into an Alpine horn or attempt a yodel; at the latter, they need do nothing more energetic than watch a floorshow over a cocktail. *Après-ski* in mountain resorts is often lively, generally expensive, and almost exclusively centred around bars and discothèques until the small hours. Most of the larger resorts have bowling alleys, cinemas and

ice rinks as well. Although gambling on sport in Switzerland is restricted to the French game of *boules*, with a maximum stake of only Sfr5, there are casinos in many of the larger cities and resorts. Here also there are ceilings on the size of bets, but high-rollers can wager as much as they like in the little town of Campione in the Ticino – an Italian enclave completely surrounded by Swiss territory.

HEALTH

As a general rule vaccination and inoculation is not required by visitors entering Switzerland from European countries and the western hemisphere. As there is no state medical health service in Switzerland and as medical treatment must be paid for, travellers are strongly advised to take out insurance cover against personal accident and sickness (as well as loss or damage to luggage and personal effects, and cancellation charges). Special winter sports policies are widely available. For full particulars concerning medical insurance ask a travel agent or contact the SNTO.

HEALTH RESORTS

The sun, pure air and mineral springs of the Swiss Alps are renowned for their healing properties, and for centuries the ailing and infirm have sought treatment in private clinics and health establishments throughout the region. Details of clinics, climatic health resorts and spa towns are available from the SNTO.

The leading Alpine spas are: Andeer, Bad Ragaz, Bad Scuol, Bad Tarasp-Vulpera, Lenk, Leukerbad, Saillon, St Moritz and Serneus (near Klosters).

HOLIDAYS (PUBLIC AND RELIGIOUS)

New Year's Day, Good Friday, Easter Monday, Ascension Day, Whit Monday, Christmas Day, 26 December.

Other other public holidays are bserved in various cantons such as 2 January, 1 May, Corpus Christi, and National Day (1 August) among others.

MONEY MATTERS

Swiss currency:
Notes (Swiss francs):
Sfr10 Sfr20 Sfr50 Sfr500 Sfr1000
Coins (Sfr/centimes):
Sfr1 10 centimes
Sfr2 20 centimes
Sfr5 50 centimes

Travellers' cheques
Visitors can buy Swiss currency in the form of travellers' cheques or bank notes from their own national banks. Swiss Bankers travellers' cheques (in Swiss francs) can be obtained from the various overseas branches of Swiss banks and many others. These cheques are accepted in Switzerland at their face value and without deductions.

Traveller's cheques in any foreign currency are cashed by banks or by official exchange offices at airports and principal railway stations, at the current rate of exchange, less commission.

Eurocheques
Backed by the appropriate cheque guarantee card, Eurocheques are widely accepted in Switzerland, both in payment for goods and services and for withdrawal of cash from banks.

Credit cards
Most major stores, restaurants and hotels accept Access, Visa, American Express and Diners' cards.

OPENING TIMES

The usual business hours in towns and resorts in the Swiss Alps are 8am to 12am and 2pm to 5pm, Monday to Friday. Banks open for business at 8.30am and close at 4.30pm, Monday to Friday. Shops are usually open from 8am until 12am, and from 1.30pm to 6.30pm (except in major shopping centres and resorts where they do not close for lunch). On Saturdays they often close at 4pm, re-opening late on Monday mornings.

In major resorts, equipment hire shops are open from 8am to 6.30pm on Sundays. Gift shops and boutiques frequently stay open later.

Post offices in large towns are open from 7.30am to 12am, and from 1.45pm to 6.30pm, closing Saturday at 11am except in major cities where they close later. Bars and restaurants open from 8am (for breakfast, where applicable), often stay open all day, and have discretionary closing times – many staying open until the early hours. Mountain restaurants tend to close at 3pm. Mountain lifts open between 8am and 9am and close between 3.30pm and 4.30pm. All have boards prominently displaying last ascent/descent times.

POLICE

Each Swiss canton and community is responsible for maintaining law and order within its own boundaries. Police uniforms therefore vary considerably from one place to another. All police stations (except for those in the most remote areas) have at least one English speaker. On the whole, Swiss police are courteous, helpful and efficient.

POST OFFICES

Correspondence can be forwarded to Swiss post offices for collection. All envelopes must be clearly addressed to the addressee, marked 'Poste Restante', and include the name of the town preceded by the post code. The sender's name and address should be marked on the back. All unclaimed mail is returned to the sender if not collected within 30 days. On collection, the addressee will be required to produce his/her passport for identification. Delivery is remarkably swift, and mail posted from main post offices will generally reach a destination anywhere in Western Europe within two to three days.

PUBLIC TRANSPORT

For comfort, punctuality and all-round efficiency the Swiss public transport system deservedly enjoys a high reputation. The railway network covers all but the most remote regions, with trains on main routes running in each direction at least once an hour and carrying both first- and second-class carriages. Meals, drinks and

snacks are provided on many services; where there is not a dining car, a 'mini-buffet' trolley with sandwiches, cakes, hot drinks, soft drinks and liquor regularly patrols the gangway.

In the rare places where there is not a railway service, the Swiss Postbus Service fills the gaps – covering all major mountain passes.

The Official Swiss Timetable contains full details of services and fares of railways, Alpine postbuses, lake boats and steamers, international connections, dining-cars and other useful information. A masterpiece of condensation, it is an annual publication issued at the end of every May, and can be bought from the SNTO or at any railway station in Switzerland.

Rail travel
There are various tickets for journeys within the Swiss Alps. It is advisable to consider carefully which type would be the most suitable and to obtain the tickets before travelling. Any person boarding a train without a valid ticket for the journey will be obliged to buy a single ticket with a surcharge.

Group tickets
Tickets for journeys at reduced rates are issued for groups of five or more adults. A free 'conductor' ticket is granted for a group of 15 or more fare-paying passengers. Group fares and full details for adults, children and infants can be obtained from the SNTO.

Children's tickets
Children between 6 and 16 years travel at half rate on Swiss railways, boats and Alpine postbuses.

Senior citizens
Holders of senior citizen railcards from countries participating in the Rail Europe Senior scheme are entitled to reduced rate rail travel to Switzerland and 50 per cent reduction on Swiss railways. The scheme does not extend to private railways, lake boats or bus services. Full details are obtainable from the SNTO.

Swiss pass
This entitles the holder to unlimited travel on Swiss railways, boats and most postbuses. In addition, a reduction of 25 per cent is offered on many privately owned funiculars and mountain railways on production of the pass. It also allows travel on transport services within 24 Swiss cities and is combinable with the

family card (see below) in the free-travel area. Validity is for periods up to four days, eight days, 15 days or one month.

Swiss Flexi Pass

This pass enables holders to choose three individual days within a period of 15 days for unlimited trips on the same basis as the Swiss Pass (above).

Swiss Card

This is a ticket giving greater flexibility allowing same-day transfers from frontier stations or airports to any destination within Switzerland and back free of charge, paying only 50 per cent for additional excursions. Family reductions also apply (see below). Validity one month.

Swiss Half-Fare Card

This card enables the holder to purchase (for his or her own use) an unlimited number of tickets at 50 per cent of the full fare for scheduled rail services (including mountain railways), postbuses and lake boats. Family reductions also apply. Validity for periods up to one month, or 12 months.

Day Cards

These entitle holders of the Swiss Half-Fare Cards and Swiss Cards to unlimited travel, on freely chosen days within the validity period, on the rail services shown on the transport map provided and on all postbus services. Validity period 6 (separate or consecutive) days.

Swiss Transfer Ticket

This is a ticket of particular benefit to winter sports travellers. A flat-rate price allowing same-day transfers from frontier stations or airports to your destination in Switzerland and back. Family reductions also apply (see below). Validity one month.

Family Card

This is obtainable free of charge from the SNTO or any Swiss railway station. Either or both parents have to be in possession of a full-fare ticket or any of the afore-mentioned tickets. Children aged between six and 16 years travel free and unmarried young people between 16 and 25 travel at half-fare. The Family Card can also be used for most excursions on Swiss public transport.

Regional Passes

These passes are popular with visitors who intend to remain within a particular region of Switzerland. Family reductions also apply (see above). They are issued during the summer season within the following regions: Montreux/Vevey, Chablais, Bernese Oberland, Lake Lucerne, Churfirsten/Santis, Graubunden, Locarno/Ascona, and Lugano. Holders of Swiss Half-Fare Cards, Swiss Cards and Swiss Passes can obtain Regional Passes with a 20 per cent reduction. Further details are included in the brochure *Regional Passes* available from the SNTO.

Seat reservations

Generally it is not possible to reserve seats for internal train journeys except for groups of 10 or more. Reservations are obligatory for the Glacier, Bernina and William Tell expresses.

Luggage

A normal amount of luggage may be taken on trains without charge. Heavy baggage can be registered between any two railway stations and to destinations on the principal lakeboat services and postbus routes. There is a standard charge per piece of luggage up to 30kg. Special rates are applicable to sports equipment. On Alpine

postbuses, passengers are allowed 50kg of luggage free of charge.

By bus

Switzerland's Postal Motor Coach service not only covers the remotest and most thinly populated corners of the Swiss Alps, but also offers organised excursions with or without guides. Its buses are easily recognisable by their bright yellow coachwork and distinctive red stripes, and their unmistakable three-note horns (the opening bars from Rossini's *William Tell Overture*). Various bus passes such as special excursion and circular tour tickets, as well as weekly passes for certain regions, allow travel at advantageous fares on the postbus services. Further information is obtainable from the local tourist offices in the Swiss Alps.

By air

In addition to the domestic carrier, Crossair, there are a number of privately owned freight and passenger light aircraft services operating within the country. These include pleasure flights over parts of the Swiss Alps by helicopter or small aircraft. In general terms the cost of internal air travel is very high, and the size of the country and its excellent land-based transport system renders it somewhat unnecessary.

By boat

Lake and river travel is well catered for by a number of private companies, mostly affiliated with Swiss railways. Elegant pleasure cruisers operate on all the major lakes and some stretches of the Rhine, Rhône and Aare rivers.

RELIGION

Catholic and Protestant churches are found in most towns and resorts throughout the Swiss Alps. There are synagogues in Berne, Davos, Fribourg, Lucerne, Lugano, Montreux and St Gallen.

SENIOR CITIZENS

The Swiss Alps have long been a popular destination for the elderly, especially during the summer. Contrary to expectations many Alpine resorts offer superb panoramas from vantage points that require little physical effort to reach. This is especially true of lake resorts such as Interlaken, Lucerne, Locarno and Lugano which offer lovely lakeside strolls along flower-decked promenades.

Lake steamer

There is usually a surcharge on calls made from hotels.

TIME

Switzerland and Liechtenstein observe Central European Time; namely, one hour ahead of Greenwich Mean Time and six hours ahead of New York time. Swiss summer time is one hour ahead of Central European Time.

TIPPING

Tips are automatically included on all hotel and restaurant bills, as well as at hairdressers and on most taxi fares. It is neither expected nor necessary to leave an extra tip, except in the case of hotel porters and cloakroom attendants.

TOILETS

Even in the most remote areas, toilets in the Swiss Alps are usually modern and invariably clean. They are indicated by a variety of signs including WC, *Toiletten* (in German), *Toilettes* (in French) or *Gabinetti* (in Italian). Women's lavatories are described as *Damen* or *Frauen*, *Femmes* or *Dames*, *Signore* or *Donne*, and men's as *Herren* or *Männer*, *Hommes* or *Messieurs*, *Signori* or *Uomini*.

TOURIST OFFICES

Swiss National Tourist Offices (SNTO)

Switzerland (head office)
Bellariastrasse 38, CH-8027 Zürich
(tel: 01 288 11 11)

Britain
SNTO, Swiss Centre, New Coventry Street, London W1V 8EE
(tel: 071 734 1921)

USA
SNTO, Swiss Center, 608 Fifth Avenue, New York, NY 10020
(tel: 212 757 59 44)

Australia
SNTO, 203–233 New South Head Road, Ridgecliff, Sydney NSW 2027
(tel: 02 320 17 99)

Canada
SNTO, CS Tower, 154 University Avenue, Toronto, Ontario M5H 3Z4

Elsewhere, the Swiss mountainlift system is so sophisticated that even the highest Alpine belvederes need involve nothing more strenuous than a gentle walk from the top station to a viewing terrace. Altitude may, however, present some difficulties, and the elderly should take extra care to acclimatise themselves before ascending to heights exceeding 2,000m.

The Swiss Hotel Association (Monbijoustrasse 130, PO Box 2657, CH-3001 Berne, tel: 031 50 71 11) publishes a list of hotels offering special terms to senior citizens off season and frequently throughout the year. To benefit from the scheme women must be over 62 and men over 65 (proof of age is required). Holders of an official disability pension also qualify. In the case of married couples, only one spouse need fulfil the age requirements. The inclusive special price covers overnight stay, breakfast, service charges, heating and taxes. Bookings (specifically referring to the scheme) can be made direct with the hotels.

STUDENT AND YOUTH TRAVEL

Inter-Rail is a special travel facility available to young people under the age of 26. It involves the purchase of the Inter-Rail Travel Authority Card, which allows the holder to travel for one month at half-fare on the lines of the railway issuing the card and free of charge on the lines of other participating European railways. Young travellers are also entitled to

special discounts under the Family Card scheme (outlined above).

TELEPHONES

To operate a public telephone, insert coin (or phone card) after lifting the receiver. The dialling tone is a continuous sound. Use coins to the value of 40 centimes for local calls and Sfr1 or Sfr5 for national and international calls. The dialling code for the UK is 00 44; omit the initial digit 0 of the STD code. Otherwise dial 191 for details of dialling codes when calling abroad. Cheap rate is Mon-Fri 9pm to 8am, Saturday and Sunday all day. The following numbers may be dialled for information:
110 - Telegrams
111 - Directory enquiries within Switzerland
114 - International calls, when no direct dialling
117 - Police, emergency calls
118 - Fire brigade, emergency calls
120 - Tourist information bulletin (including snow
  report, avalanche bulletin etc in winter)
140 - Vehicle breakdown
144 - Ambulance
160 - Foreign exchange rates
161 - Time
162 - Weather report
163 - Traffic conditions, roads and passes
166 - Stock prices
167 - News in German
168 - News in French
169 - News in Italian
187 - Avalanche bulletin
191 - Information on dialling abroad

·GLOSSARY·

	French	German	Italian
Good day	Bonjour	Guten tag	Buon giorno
Good evening	Bonsoir	Guten Abend	Buona sera
Excuse me	Excusez-moi	Entschuldigen Sie	Mi sousi
Please	S'il vous plait	Bitte	Per favore
	('see-voo-play')	('beater')	('per-fav-oray')
Yes/no	Oui/non	Ja/nein	Si/no
Thank you	Merci	Danke	Grazie
	('mare-see')	('danker')	('gratzee')
Do you speak	Parlez-vous	Sprechen Sie	Parla inglese?
English?	anglais?	Englisch?	
Do you understand?	Comprenez-vous?	Verstehen Sie?	Capisce?
I don't understand	Je ne comprends pas	Ich verstehe nicht	Non capisco
Pardon	Pardon	Verzeihung	Mi scusi
Please speak slowly	Parles lentement	Bitte, sprechen	Parli adagio,
	s'il vous plaît	Sie langsam	per favore
Is there...?	Y-a-t'il...?	Gibt es...?	C'e...?
Where is/are...?	Où est/sont...?	Wo ist/sind...?	Dov'e/dove
			sono...?
...a garage	...un garage	...eine Garage	...un autorimessa
...a bank/exchange	...une banque/	...eine Bank/	... una banca/
	change	Wechselstube	agenza di cambio
...a pharmacy	...une pharmacie	...eine Apotheke	...una farmacia
...the police station	...le poste de police	...die Polizei	...la polizia
...the toilet	...les toilettes	...die Toilette	...i gabinetti
...the railway station	...la gare	...der Bahnhof	...la stazione
			ferroviaria
...the airport	...l'aeroport	...der Flugplatz	...l'aeroporto
...a bus for...	un autobus pour...	...einen Autobus	un autobus per...
How much?	Combien?	Wieviel?	Quant'e?
When?	Quand?	Wann?	Quando?
At what time?	A quelle heure?		A che ora?
What is this?	Qu'est-ce-que c'est?	Was ist das?	Cos'e questo?
Today	Aujourd'hui	Heute	Oggi
Yesterday	Hier	Gestern	Ieri
Tomorrow	Demain	Morgen	Domani
Sunday	Dimanche	Sonntag	Domenica
Monday	Lundi	Montag	Lunedi
Tuesday	Mardi	Dienstag	Martedi
Wednesday	Mercredi	Mittwoch	Mercoledi
Thursday	Jeudi	Donnerstag	Giovedi
Friday	Vendredi	Freitag	Venerdi
Saturday	Samedi	Samstag	Sabato
Open/closed	Ouvert/ferme	Offen/geschlossen	Aperto/abierto
Goodbye	Au revoir	Auf Wiedersehen	Arrivederci

·INDEX·

120

ACKNOWLEDGEMENTS

The Automobile Association wishes to thank the following photographers and libraries for their assistance in the preparation of this book.

ADRIAN BAKER was commissioned to take all the photographs for this book except those listed below.

INTERNATIONAL PHOTOBANK Cover Grindelwald

MARY EVANS PICTURE LIBRARY 84b Pilate washes his hands, 85b Mark Twain

RICHARD SALE 6 Sphinx/Mönch, 12 Matterhorn, 13 Upper Valais, 97 Piz Gloria, 102b Jungfraujoch, 118 Kleine Scheidegg

SPECTRUM COLOUR LIBRARY 22b Gsteig at night, 24b Rhône Glacier, 32 Zermatt, 75 Unteraar Glacier

SWISS NATIONAL TOURIST OFFICE 8 ballooning, 10 costumes, 11 Graubünden, 42b Mendrísio, 43a Monte Generoso, 44b Rossura, 45a Vogorno, 45b Vogorno, 52b Lenzerheide, 53 Pontresina, 56 Faido, 57 Pontresina, 60a Zernez, 62a Mimosas, 62b edelweiss, 63 pink camelias, 71 Wildhaus, 80 folklore dancing, 84a Mount Pilatus, 85a Mount Rigi, skiing, 86a Sarnen, 88a Seelisberg, 88b Weggis, 112 Klosters, 116 Swissair aeroplane, 117 lake steamer

ZEFA PICTURE LIBRARY 1 Appenzell detail